The Man Without A Memory

by

Arthur W. Marchmont

Double 9
BOOKS

The Man Without A Memory
by Arthur W. Marchmont

Copyright © 2023

All Rights reserved.

ISBN: 978-93-59952-88-8

Published by

DOUBLE 9 BOOKS
2/13-B, Ansari Road
Daryaganj, New Delhi – 110002
info@double9books.com
www.double9books.com
Tel. 011-40042856

This book is under public domain

ABOUT THE AUTHOR

Arthur W. Marchmont is an awesome but especially lesser-regarded writer who made valuable contributions to the world of literature, especially at some stage in the early twentieth century. He is recognized for his prolific output of thriller, adventure, and espionage novels, lots of that have garnered a dedicated following of readers who appreciate his storytelling talents. Marchmont's works frequently function gripping plots, complicated person improvement, and an aptitude for creating suspenseful narratives. His writing fashion displays the literary tastes and pursuits of his era, with a focus on intrigue, espionage, and romantic factors. While his name might not be as broadly recognized as a number of his contemporaries, his novels stay cherished via those who are seeking for out classic stories of journey and thriller. Marchmont's books offer a window into the early 20th-century literary panorama, imparting a glimpse of the topics and genres that were popular all through that point. His capacity to craft attractive memories with enduring enchantment underscores his contribution to the arena of fiction, in which he remains a respected discern amongst aficionados of conventional literature. Although Arthur W. Marchmont might not have completed the equal stage of repute as some of his friends, his legacy endures within the hearts of these who've found satisfaction in his charming memories, making him a noteworthy author in the annals of early twentieth-century literature.

CONTENTS

CHAPTER I
HOW I LOST MY MEMORY

It was a glorious scrap, and Dick Gunter and I had the best of it right up to the last moment.

We were about 6,000 feet up and a mile or so inside the German lines when their two machines came out to drive us away.

"We'll take 'em on, Jack," shouted Dick, chortling like the rare old sport he was, and we began our usual manœuvre for position. Our dodge was to let them believe we were novices at the game, and I messed about with the old bus as if we were undecided and in a deuce of a funk.

They fell in, all right, and at the proper moment I swung round and gave Dick a chance which he promptly took, pouring in a broadside which sent one of the machines hurtling nose first to earth. This put the fear of God into the others, who tried to bolt; but we were too fast for them and, after a short running fight, Dick got them. The pilot crumpled up and down went the machine like a stone to prevent the other from feeling lonely.

We were jubilating righteously over this, when the luck turned. A third machine, which, in the excitement of the scrap, we hadn't seen, swooped out of the clouds and gave us a broadside at close range, which messed us up pretty badly. We were both hit, the petrol poured out of the riddled tank, the engine stopped, and I realized that we could put up the shutters, as we were absolutely at the beggar's mercy.

I was wrong, however. Dick had managed to let the other chap have a dose of lead, and either because we had had enough of it or his bus was damaged, he didn't stop to finish us off but scuttled off home to mother.

I was hit somewhere in the shoulder, but it wasn't bad enough to prevent my working the controls, and I pointed for home on a long glissade. There was a "certain liveliness," as the communiqués say, during that joy ride. The Archies barked continuously as we crossed the lines, the shrapnel was all over us, Dick was hit again, and the poor old bus fairly riddled; but we got through it somehow, although my pal was nearly done in by the time we reached the ground.

Some pretty things were said about it and we each got the M.C. I was very little hurt, and came out of the base hospital a week or two later feeling as fit as a fiddle again, but as the chief decided I had earned a good spell of leave, I went off to old Blighty to convalesce.

Then it was that for the first time I heard of the trouble about Nessa Caldicott. Both my parents had died when I was a kid, and Mrs. Caldicott, the dearest and sweetest woman in the world, had been like a mother to me, had taken me into her home, and thus I had grown up with Nessa and her sister. Nessa and I had been to school in Germany; had travelled out and home together; I had spent my holidays in their home; and I can't remember the time when I wasn't in love with her.

Mrs. Caldicott was keen that we should marry, and a year or two after I came back to England for good from Göttingen University we had been engaged. But there was a "nigger in the fence." I had plenty of money and preferred being a sort of "nut" to working; and Nessa didn't like it. She urged me to "do something and make a career for myself"; but I was a swollen-headed young ass, and shied at it; so at last the engagement was broken off until, as she put it, I "had given up the idea of lounging and loafing through life."

She was right, of course; but like a fool I wouldn't see it; so we quarrelled, and she went off to Germany to stay with an old school friend. She was still there when the war broke out, and thus did not know that I had found my chance and had joined up. There was nothing "nutty" about the army training and work, and when I went home, of course, my first thoughts were of her and what she would say when she knew I had taken her advice.

But I found poor Mrs. Caldicott in the very depth of anxiety and despair. Nessa had never returned from Germany, and there was nothing but the most disconcerting and perplexing news of her. During the first few months she had been able to write home that all was well with her, although she could not get out of the country.

Then came a gap in the correspondence, followed by a short letter that her school friend was dead, and that she feared she would not be allowed to remain in the house. A month or so later another letter came, saying she had left Hanover to go to another friend in Berlin, and that her mother was not to worry, as she expected soon to be home.

"And that's the last letter I've had from her, Jack, and that's three months ago," said Mrs. Caldicott, the tears streaming down her cheeks. "The only news I've had is these two odd communications."

They were odd, in all truth. The first was a sentence which had evidently been cut out of a longer letter in Nessa's handwriting and pasted on a sheet of paper. "I am quite well, but cannot get away yet." That was all, and a very ugly-looking all too. The second was a postcard in a strange handwriting, like a man's fist. "Your daughter is well and is going to be married. She will communicate with you after the war."

I did not let the dear old lady see what I thought of the matter, nor did I tell her how my months at the front and what I had seen there led me to put the most sinister interpretation on the affair.

"I've tried every means in my power, Jack, to find Nessa," she declared; "but with no result at all; and it's killing me."

I did what I could to reassure her, and then a somewhat harum-scarum idea occurred to me—that I should use my leave to go to Berlin and make inquiries. She wouldn't hear of it at first, because of the danger to me; but I showed her that there would really be very little risk, as I had often passed for a German, and that the only real difficulty was getting permission from the authorities.

I set about that at once and succeeded—the result of having a friend at court in the War Office; but before that was settled Nessa's brother-in-law, Jimmy Lamb, an American manufacturer, came over on munitions business and wouldn't hear of my going.

"See here, Jack, this is my show, not yours. For one thing I can do it better than you, as I'm a bit of a hustler and have a good friend, Greg Watson, in our Berlin Embassy. More than that, I can go safely, while if you were found out, you'd be shot as a spy;" and he wouldn't listen to my protests.

But the scheme fell through at the last moment. On the very day he was to have started, he had a cable that his father was dying; and he had to catch the first boat home.

"I'm real sick about it, Jack, but there's nothing else for it. I've booked a berth in the *Slavonic* to-day."

"Then I shall go, Jimmy. I can't bear the thought of Nessa being in those beggars' hands. I'm certain there's some devilment at the bottom of it;" and I told him a few of the items I had seen with my own eyes.

"Well, what price your going in my name? Much better than the German stunt; and you can actually see about the business that I meant to do. Here are all the papers needed, my passport and ticket, a bunch of German notes I've picked up at a good discount, and you can see Greg Watson—I'll give you a letter to him—and you'll find him a white man right through, ready to do his durndest to help you."

A few minutes clinched the job; an hour or two sufficed for all the preparations I needed to make for the trip; and that night I left Harwich for Rotterdam in a little steamer called the *Burgen*, as Jas. R. Lamb, an American merchant, equipped with all the credentials necessary to keep up my end.

It was all plain sailing enough, but it didn't turn out so simple as it looked. There was another American on board and I kept out of his way at first, but when he had heard me talking to a waiter in German, he came sidling up and scraped acquaintance. He soon let out that he was as genuine an American as I was, and the best of it was that he took me for what he was in reality—a German.

"You speak German well for—an American," he said suggestively. "You know Germany, perhaps?"

"I was at school there and afterwards at Göttingen."

He was cautious enough to test this, and I let him have some choice specimens of student slang which strengthened his opinion.

"I was also at Göttingen. Need we pretend any longer?" and he held out his hand. He was very much my own build and colouring, but I hoped the resemblance stopped short there, for I didn't like his looks a bit.

"Pretend what?" I asked as if on my guard.

"That we are Americans."

"You needn't, but I didn't say I wasn't one."

He made a peculiar flourish with his left hand which was one of the membership signs of a secret society among the students, and I answered it. It was enough, and he let himself go then. He was a good swaggerer; told me that he had come from America to England, where he had been ferreting out every possible scrap of information, having represented himself as the agent of an American firm of munition makers; that he had sent his report to Berlin and had been summoned to go there at once on the strength of it; and that he was to join the Secret Service.

He was so full of his self-importance and seemingly so glad to have some one to listen to him, that, with a very little prompting, he told me a whole lot about himself, and the great things he had done. He only stopped when he got sea-sick, and before he went below he told me his real name was Johann Lassen, and scribbled his address in Berlin on his card, so that we might meet again there.

I was a little worried by the business. It might be awkward if we did run against one another in Berlin; but there was no need to look for trouble before it arrived, so I dismissed the thing and went on thinking out my own plan of campaign. But the affair had very unexpected results.

We were nearing the Dutch coast and I was considering how to avoid Lassen on landing, when there was the very dickens of an explosion. As if the lid of hell itself had lifted!

What happened I only learnt afterwards, for the next thing I knew was that I was lying in bed somewhere, with a grave-eyed nurse bending over me.

"Herr Lassen!" Just a whisper. After a pause the name was repeated with slightly more solicitous emphasis.

I was too weak and exhausted to reply or feel either surprise or curiosity at the mistake about my name; and with a sigh of utter weariness I closed my eyes and fell asleep. When I woke it was in the dead stillness of the night.

I was far less exhausted and my mind was beginning to work again. I was lying alone in a small bare-walled room, lighted by one carefully shaded electric light. There were two other beds in the room, both unoccupied; and I was not too dazed to understand that it was a hospital ward. Then I remembered the nurse had addressed me as "Herr Lassen"; and was puzzling over the mistake when the remembrance of Nessa and her peril flashed across my mind and stirred a confused jangle of disturbing thoughts.

I was still too weak to clear the tangle then, however, and fell asleep again, and did not wake until the morning.

I was much better and the nurse was very pleased at my improvement. "You will soon be yourself again," she said, speaking German with a quaint accent. "You were so exhausted that at one time we feared you would not recover from the shock."

"You are very good," I murmured, with a feeble smile.

"Do you think you could eat some solid food? The doctor said you could have some when you recovered consciousness."

"Where am I?" I asked after thanking her.

"This is the Nazareth Hospital in Rotterdam. You were brought in by the fishermen who found you in the sea when the *Burgen* went down."

I did not ask any more questions then, as I wanted to think matters over; and during the day I succeeded in getting it all clear. The only point that bothered me was why I should be mistaken for Lassen; but I got that at last. I remembered the card he had given me and how I had shoved it in my pocket.

But why hadn't my pocket-book with my passport and papers and all the rest of it been found? It had been in my jacket pocket. It looked as if it must have been lost. That set me thinking and no mistake. How was I to get on to Berlin without the passport? It looked as if I must either give up the search for Nessa, when every minute might be invaluable, or go back to England for fresh papers. That wouldn't do, as too much of my leave would be used up.

It was the dickens of a mess, and then an idea occurred to me. Lassen must have gone down with the steamer, for they wouldn't take me for him if he had been saved. And then I soon had a plan—to drop the Jimmy Lamb character and continue to be Lassen as long as necessary. I might get across the frontier in that way, and must trust to my wits for the rest. There might be a bit of risk in it, but that needn't stop me; and then a very pretty little development suggested itself which offered a promise of safety even if I was found out.

Why shouldn't the "shock" of which the nurse had spoken have destroyed my memory? The more I considered it the more promising it looked. It was the easiest of parts to play; I had done a lot of amateur theatricals; and any one could look a fool and act one.

I had a first rehearsal of this stunt—as Jimmy would have called it— with the nurse; and the result quite came up to expectations. I reckoned that she would tell the doctor, and it was clear she had done so when he came to me next morning.

He was tremendously interested in the case now, and, after telling me how much better I was, began to question me about the loss of the *Burgen*.

I looked as vacant and worried as I thought necessary.

"You remember being on her, don't you?"

"The nurse told me so. Was I?"

"Yes, of course. She struck a mine; you remember that?"

I affected to try to remember, stared round the room, and then helplessly at him and gestured feebly.

"You were picked up at sea. Does that help you?"

It wasn't likely to, and I shook my head.

"She came from Harwich—England, you know, and was blown up."

"Harwich, England," I murmured, as if the words had no meaning for me.

He muttered something in Dutch under his breath. "Does your head trouble you much?" and he smoothed my hair, feeling my head all over carefully.

I looked as stupid as a sheep. "It—it——" and I frowned and gestured to suggest what I could not express.

He looked rather grave for a second or two and then smiled reassuringly. "It will be all right in time, quite right. You are suffering from shock; but you needn't worry. No worry. That's the great thing. A day or so will put you all right, Herr—let's see, what's your name?"

But I didn't bite. "Is it Lassen? The nurse said so."

"Don't you know it yourself?" he asked very kindly.

"No." That was true at any rate. "How did you find it out?"

"From the card in your trousers' pocket. You are the only survivor from the *Burgen* and had a very narrow escape. Even most of your clothes were blown off you. Doesn't anything I say suggest anything to you?"

I lay as if pondering this solemnly. "It's all so—so strange," I muttered, putting my hand to my head. "So—so——" and I left it at that; and he went away, after giving me one more item of valuable information—that my belt which contained my money had also been saved.

I played that lost memory for all it was worth and with gorgeous success. I became a "case" for the doctors who trotted along to interview me as a sort of interesting freak and held learned discussions over me. All this gave me such ample practice that I became perfect in the part.

But there was a fly in the amber. As the only survivor from the *Burgen* the Dutch authorities regarded me as a person of quite considerable importance. Officials came to visit me, pouring in regular broadsides of questions; and as they got no satisfaction, and the doctors differed about my recovering my memory, the official verdict was that I should remain in Rotterdam until I did recover it.

This threatened complications; but I had no intention to remain, so I prepared to get away, sent out for a ready-made suit of clothes—ye gods, what a beautiful misfit!—and was going to leave the hospital to see what I could do at the German Embassy about a passport, when my luck propeller snapped and I saw myself nose-diving to the ground.

A nurse brought me a card and said some one was waiting to see me in the doctor's room. The card told me it was a certain Herr Heinrich Hoffnung, 480b, Ugenplatz, Berlin!

It was just rotten luck, for it meant the collapse of the Lassen show. The instant he clapped eyes on me he'd know I wasn't the real Simon Pure; and it might be the dickens of a job to get across the frontier.

As I thought of Nessa and what the delay might mean to her, I was mad. But I couldn't shirk the meeting; so after giving him time to learn all about my "case" from the doctor, I went down, wondering what ill wind had blown the fellow to Rotterdam at such a moment, and what the dickens would happen when I was no longer Lassen.

CHAPTER II
THE FIRST CRISIS

As I opened the door the doctor jumped up to help me to a chair, and the man from Berlin gave a start of surprise and then stared at me keenly; but whether he recognized me or not, I couldn't decide.

"You've picked up wonderfully, Herr Lassen, wonderfully!" said the doctor. "I declare no one would guess from your appearance what you have been through."

"And I feel as well as I look, doctor, thanks to you and the nurses," I replied. "I owe my life to the doctor here," I added, turning to the stranger.

"You are Johann Lassen?" he asked.

I shrugged my shoulders. "That's what they tell me."

"I told you how we know," put in the doctor, adding to me: "I have explained the nature of your case to Herr Hoffnung. He has come to take you to Berlin."

It was clearly time to bring matters to a head, so I turned to the man. "Have I ever had the pleasure of seeing you before?" I asked, with a perplexed and rather bewildered look.

He shook his head. "No, we have never met, but——" He paused and then added: "But of course it must be right."

I could have shouted for joy, but I put my hand before my eyes that he should not see the delight in them.

"You will wish to see Herr Lassen alone, of course," said the doctor. "You will bear in mind all that I have told you, I trust."

Hoffnung crossed to the door with him and the two stood speaking together in low tones for a minute, giving me an opportunity to observe my visitor. He was rather a good-looking man of about thirty, well-dressed and smart, and I placed him as somebody's secretary. Certainly a decent sort and not too quick-witted.

"First let me congratulate you on your marvellous escape, Herr Lassen," he said when the doctor had gone.

"It seems to have been touch and go; but— —" and I gestured to suggest that I knew nothing about it.

"The doctor tells me he quite despaired at one time of saving your life. But he says you are quite fit to travel. Do you agree with that?"

"It's all the same to me. I feel all right."

"It is rather urgent that I should return to Berlin as soon as possible. Do you think you could manage the journey to-day?"

"I don't see why not. But—er—it's a bit awkward, you know. Are you sure I'm your man?"

He glanced at his watch and started. "It's just possible that we could catch the express, and we can talk in the train; that is, if you haven't many preparations to make."

"I haven't any. I've nothing but what I stand up in, and one place is as good as another to me unti— —" and I sighed and gestured hopelessly.

"Then I should like to go."

"Can I go without any papers or anything?"

"With me, certainly. I have everything necessary, and will explain on the journey."

And go we did to my infinite satisfaction.

In the cab to the station he was silent and thoughtful, and as my one consuming desire was to get across the frontier before anything could happen, I didn't worry him with any questions. It was all clear sailing at the station. Whoever Hoffnung might be, there was no doubt about his having authority. He secured a special compartment, although the train was crowded, and did all possible for my comfort.

"That's the best of travelling officially," he said pleasantly as he settled himself in the seat opposite me, while the train ran out of the station. "Now, you asked me a question at the hospital which I did not answer—whether I'm sure you're Lassen. Frankly, I'm not; and the more I look at you the more I'm puzzled."

"It's a bit awkward. I don't wish to be somebody else."

"Do you feel fit to talk? The doctor warned me against worrying you; but there are things I should enormously like to know."

"You're not half so keen as I am," I told him truthfully. "If I am Lassen, what am I; where do I live; have I any friends anywhere; isn't there any one who knows me anywhere? It's such a devil of a mess."

"There's one thing certain, my friend, you're a German; and as for the rest you'll find plenty of people in Berlin who'll know you. The von Reblings, for instance. Which reminds me I have the Countess's letter;" he opened his despatch case and handed me a sealed envelope.

But I had already told the doctors that I could not write and could not read handwriting, although I had fumbled out some large print. That had been one of the specialities of my peculiar aphasia. So I just smiled vacantly and shook my head. "Will you read it to me?" I asked.

He agreed after some little demur, and a very charming letter it was. The Countess addressed me as "My dear Johann," wrote in the familiar thee and thou, said how anxious she and Rosa—especially Rosa, it seemed—had been about me; urged me to hurry to Berlin as soon as possible, where, of course, I should be the most welcome guest in the world, and signed herself "Your affectionate aunt, Olga von Rebling."

"Doesn't that remind you of anything?" asked Hoffnung.

"Not in the faintest. Who is Rosa?"

Instead of telling me, he smiled suggestively and I smiled back. "Did the Countess send you to fetch me?"

"Oh, no. I came officially. I'll tell you about that directly; but it is because of what she told us about you that I was sent. She received a letter from you from England saying that you were crossing in the *Burgen*, and when the newspapers reported the loss of the steamer and that you were the only survivor, she told me about it. I reported it at Headquarters, and—well, here I am in consequence."

"And you've never seen me, or Lassen, or whoever I am, before?"

"Never. I have seen a photograph of you, but it was taken some long time ago; and while you answer to the likeness in some respects, you certainly do not in others, although I can see that you may be Lassen, allowing for the difference of time."

"Well, anyway, these von Reblings will know, thank Heaven."

But he shook his head. "I'm not so sure. You see, it's a good many years since you were in Berlin. The family arrangement dates back many more years than that, moreover—since you were children."

"What family arrangement?"

"Your betrothal to Miss Rosa."

"The devil!" I exclaimed. "Do you mean to tell me I'm engaged to marry this Rosa von Rebling?"

"Certainly I do, and a very charming girl she is, and very rich too," he replied, smiling unrestrainedly.

But it cost me some effort to smile in return. It was the very deuce of a mix up; there were no end of bothering complications in it, and I leant back in my seat to try and think it out. It was quite on the cards, after what he had said about my photograph, that even these people themselves might mistake me for Lassen; and if they did, I should be hampered at every turn in my search for Nessa.

"Is it really possible that you don't remember anything about it?" he asked after a long pause.

"Not a thing."

"The doctor hoped that the mention of them would stir your memory."

I shook my head hopelessly. "It may when I see them—if I'm really Lassen, that is. Phew! What a kettle of fish!"

We reached the frontier soon afterwards, and I breathed more freely as soon as I was on the right side of it. Whatever happened now, I could play at being a German. I recalled with immense satisfaction his confident assertion that whoever I might be I was certainly one of his countrymen; and I could gamble on it that when the von Reblings met me, my "case" would still continue to be interesting enough to secure my safety.

Hoffnung had begun to study some papers from his grip and presently looked across at me and put a surprising question. "Do you speak English?" he asked in my own tongue.

I had presence of mind enough to be instantly very American. "Gee, don't I, some."

"Then you've been in America?"

"Have I?" My practice with the Rotterdam people was coming in well.

"Oh, yes. You went from there to England," he replied, going back to his own language. "Can't you remember that?"

I shook my head and frowned.

"Nor anything you did in England?" Another mystified shake of the head. "It's a pity. Don't you know that you sent a report from England of what you'd seen there?"

A little duet followed in which he asked me a series of questions, and I replied each time with a shake of the head. The subject matter of them all was the mention of persons, places, dockyards, ships and so on, which had obviously been embodied in the report Lassen had sent to Berlin. He referred to them in a casual tone and in a way which would not give anything away supposing I should turn out not to be Lassen.

"I'm inclined to be very sorry for all this, and fear it may affect you very seriously. You're not just playing at this, I hope?" he asked then very earnestly.

"Playing at what?"

"This loss of memory. I mean that you need not have the faintest hesitation about speaking to me; and it occurred to me that you might have put it all on just to avoid questions at Rotterdam."

"Are you serious?"

"Absolutely. It's a tremendously serious matter. It's this way. We've seen the *Burgen's* manifest, of course; we know there were only two male cabin passengers on board, both travelling as Americans; one as Jas. R. Lamb, the other as Joseph Lyman. If you are Lassen, that was you. The other man, Lamb, as he called himself, we have good reason to believe was an English spy. It follows, therefore, that if you are not Lassen, you are the Englishman; and I need scarcely tell you that at such a time as this, spies find Berlin a very unhealthy place."

He was a quicker-witted fellow than I had believed, but he made a mistake in not springing this beastly surprise on me more suddenly. His long preamble gave me time to get myself well in hand.

"It'll be a pretty climax for me if I am the Englishman," I answered, laughing, and without turning a hair.

"You're sure you're not?" he rapped.

I tried to appear amused. "I wish I could be sure of anything."

A pause followed, and then he tried another shot. "You may have noticed that I stared pretty hard at you this morning when you came into the doctor's room, and that afterwards I rather rushed you away from Rotterdam. I reached there yesterday morning and spent the day making such inquiries as I could about you. I was instructed to, of course; and I came to the conclusion that you were the Englishman, and I thought so when you came into that room. That was why I hurried you away; I wished to have you on this side of the frontier. It is also the reason why I am sorry you cannot recover your memory."

I declined the opening without thanks. "I'm just as sorry as you are; but I suppose we can clear up the tangle at Berlin."

"Oh, yes. I've wired to the von Reblings to meet our train. Of course you'll understand that I have some men at hand here. It is better you should know that," he added in an unpleasantly suggestive tone.

But I only laughed. "I wish you would send one of them to get me something to eat."

"I will, of course;" and he looked out into the corridor, beckoned some one and gave him the necessary order, returned to his seat and busied himself with the papers from his despatch case.

A substantial meal for us both was brought to the compartment, and although very little was said as we ate it, I was conscious that a considerable change had come over the relations between us. His manner had become distinctly official, and I understood that I was virtually under arrest until at least we reached Berlin.

Afterwards he went back to his papers, suggesting that I might like to sleep; so I leant back in my corner and gave myself up to my thoughts.

They were anything but pleasant. He had given me a shock that was almost as great as the explosion on the *Burgen*. I was in the very devil's own mess. I had no delusions about my fate if I was held to be an English spy; and that would almost certainly be the case if the von Reblings declared I was not Lassen. That that would be their decision was a million to one chance. It was a sheer impossibility that they would be unable to recognize a relation who was actually engaged to the daughter; and how to meet the difficulty baffled me.

I was right in the eye of the net. The fact that there had been only two men as cabin passengers on the *Burgen* was like a mine sprung under my feet. I had reckoned on being able to recover my memory at any necessary moment; but this cut the ground from under me. I couldn't become Jimmy. That was a cert. And I certainly couldn't become any one else, because every lie I might tell would most surely be scrupulously investigated.

Poor Nessa! I was a heap more troubled about her and her mother than about myself. Whether the von Reblings knew me or not, the result would be much the same to her. Tied up as the betrothed of another girl, it would be next to impossible in the short time at my command to do a thing to find Nessa. The only possibility that occurred to me was that if the million to one chance came off and the von Reblings didn't denounce me at once as a fraud, I might manage to lose myself in the city somehow and set to work on the search.

But even in that case I should be in hourly danger of discovery; a state of things which would make it virtually impossible to carry on the search with any hope of success.

How Hoffnung's people could have got on the track of my not being Jimmy, baffled me utterly. But they clearly had; so there was no use in wasting time worrying over it. I did worry over it, however, as well as over every other detail of the job, and continued to ask myself all sorts of unanswerable questions for the rest of the journey.

Hoffnung looked at his watch, shovelled his papers back into their case, and looked across at me. "About ten minutes now only," he said. "Have you slept?"

I all but gave myself away by blurting out the fact that I never slept in trains, but checked the words in time. "Dozed a bit," I said.

"You look fresh and fit enough," he replied, as if the fact rather justified his suspicions of me, "Wonderful after what you've gone through. You must be as hard as nails. Military training, I suppose."

Neat; but I didn't tumble in. "Have I had any?" I asked.

He shrugged his shoulders and squinted at me with a suggestive smile. Then he grew earnest. "We won't have a scene at the station. We'd better wait till most of the people have got away, and you'll give me your word of honour not to attempt to get away or anything of the sort?"

"What the deuce good would that be? Of course I shan't make a fool of myself in any such fashion. If I'm the man you call the Englishman, well, I am, that's all."

"You have all an Englishman's coolness."

"Then perhaps I am English," I said with a shrug.

"We'll hope not, at any rate;" but it was clear he was fast making up his mind that I was. After a pause he added: "When the crowd has cleared off, we'll walk together to the barrier, and my men will be behind us. We shall find the von Reblings there."

"And if we don't?"

"Oh, I'll see that you're taken care of for the night; but they'll be there to a certainty."

I don't deny that when the train stopped at the platform and we stayed in the carriage while the other travellers cleared away, I had more than a little trouble to maintain what he had termed an Englishman's coolness. But my anxiety didn't show in my face.

Nessa's fate as well as my own depended upon what occurred in the next few minutes at the barrier; and I think that if it had been practicable to have choked Hoffnung, and his men, into insensibility, I should have been sorely tempted to make the attempt.

But the thought of Nessa made me keep my end up; there was nothing for it but to face the music; and when at last he rose to leave the carriage, all I did was to yawn and stretch myself and say that I should be jolly glad to get to bed.

"What a magnificent station!" I exclaimed, stopping on the platform to look about me as if that was the one subject which interested me at the moment.

Then I went on with him, my eyes fixed on a little knot of people at the barrier on whose words and acts my life not improbably depended.

CHAPTER III
ROSA

I remember a little commonplace incident in Hyde Park one bank holiday which made me smile at the time. Three children were scuffling and squabbling over the division of some sweets when the mother, a kindly-looking soul, came promptly and settled the matter in a somewhat Spartan fashion. She scolded the kids, smacked them impartially, and then snatched the sweets and shied them away. Loud yells followed, of course, and repenting her haste, she kissed and hugged her little brood, immediately produced a bigger bag of sweets and in this way pacified them all.

This has nothing to do with my experience in Berlin, except to serve as a crude illustration of how the fates dealt with me. Just when Hoffnung's story had thoroughly shaken me up and prepared me to face the worst possible, the pendulum swung right over to my side and the fates handed out the bigger bag of sweets.

In other words I was at once recognized as Johann Lassen by the Countess von Rebling.

There were several circumstances to account for her mistake. For one, my bride that was to be was not present: I learnt the reason afterwards; and only her son Hans was with her, a lad who had never seen me. The old lady was, of course, prepared to meet me; she saw me in Hoffnung's company; then just as I reached the barrier the big arc lamps in the station almost went out for a few seconds, leaving the place in comparative gloom; and lastly, being a tender-hearted little woman, her eyes were full of tears and no doubt blurred her sight.

"My poor dear Johann!" she cried, throwing her arms round my neck and giving way to her mingled sympathy for my sufferings and joy at seeing me safe and sound. Then she called to her son, and after I had been kissed by him, she clung to me and could not make enough of me, so that even Hoffnung had to be satisfied.

"You are quite sure that this is your nephew, Countess?" he asked.

"Sure? Of course I am. Whatever do you mean, Heinrich?" she cried in amazement.

He explained my loss of memory; but the only effect was to increase her concern on my account and to make her hug me closer to her side, with many endearing expressions of affection and compassion.

I felt an abominable hypocrite at having to allow her to mislead herself, but the thought of Nessa's plight made it impossible for me to undeceive her; and we all went to the carriage which was in waiting, the Countess clinging to my arm and pressing close to me.

Hoffnung was very decent about it. As I was stepping into the carriage, he held out his hand. "I hope you will believe that I am sincere in saying how glad I am to find I was wrong, Herr Lassen," he said with what seemed like genuine cordiality; and of course I wrung his hand and said something appropriate.

Why my arrival should have affected the dear little lady so deeply I did not know; but during the drive to her house she could do nothing but press my hand in both of hers and murmur words of delight at seeing me again, mingled with sympathy with my misfortunes. Again the very dim light in the carriage stood my friend; and by the time she reached home she was thoroughly convinced that I was her nephew.

I had still to meet the daughter; but to my relief she was not at home. A meal was in readiness for me, and as I eat it, the Countess sat and feasted her eyes on me, noting the differences which, as she thought, time had effected in my looks. But these did not shake her conviction.

"You are very much changed, Johann; but of course, you would be in all these years. It must be ten quite since you were here. But you are just what I expected you would be, although not so much like your father as I looked for," she said, and then drew attention in some detail to the points of difference. I learnt then that the upper part of my face, shape of head, forehead and eyebrows, and nose had "changed less" than the lower part.

Then the son gave me a rather nasty jar. "You're not a bit like that photograph you sent over to Rosa, cousin, is he, mother? She'll jump a bit when she sees you."

"Photograph? Did I send one?" I asked.

"Don't worry Johann, Hans," said his mother, frowning at him, and he coloured and collapsed with a muttered "I forgot."

"You did send one, dear," she said to me. "It was when you had a beard and moustache, and of course that hid the lower part of your face."

I breathed a little more freely. "I think Rosa will be surprised when she sees you; you're so much better looking than you promised to be. I suppose you don't remember sending the photograph?" she asked with nervous wistfulness.

I could truthfully say I did not; and in this way the talk proceeded until I obtained a really good description of myself as well as many details about my past. Lassen's engagement to the daughter was, as Hoffnung had said, the result of a family arrangement; one of those silly wills which left a fortune to the two on condition that they married. They had not seen him since he left Göttingen ten years before; during the whole of that time he had been out of the country; and was now coming back to marry his bride-elect.

The kind-hearted old soul hadn't a word to say against him; but Hans let drop one or two remarks which led me to think I was not likely to receive a very cordial welcome from his sister. Anxious to know all I could, I pleaded great fatigue as soon as I had finished eating and asked to be allowed to go to bed. They both went up with me and I managed to keep the son while I undressed.

He was rather an awkward youth, about seventeen, totally unlike his mother who might have sat as model for a delicate Dresden china figure. On the other hand he was fleshy, dark, and rather pudgy-featured; but I praised his figure, belauded his apparent strength, and generally played on his obvious vanity and wish to be considered a grown man.

"We must be the best of friends, Hans," I declared heartily.

He blushed with pleasure. "I should like it. You look awfully strong, cousin," he replied, looking at my biceps.

"You'll make a far stronger man than I am." It was as welcome as jam on a trench crust ten days old; and I kept at it until I felt I could safely lead round to the subject of his sister and learn how the wind blew in that quarter.

"Of course Rosa's a good sort in lots of ways, but she's getting so bossy," he declared boyishly. "She's the eldest for one thing, and then, you know, she's come in for old Aunt Margarita's fortune, and—well, she likes to run things, and I don't like it."

"A man can't be expected to," I agreed with an encouraging smile.

"That's just it. She thinks a fellow's never grown up. I can stand it from mother; but Rosa won't understand that six years' difference is one thing when a fellow's a kid of ten and another when he's nearly eighteen. I shall get my commission in another month or two, you know."

I made a note of the fact that my "betrothed" was about four and twenty and inclined to be "bossy," and let him rattle on about the army, a subject of which he was very full.

"Are you going to join your regiment, cousin?" he asked presently.

I looked appropriately blank and gestured.

"Oh, I forgot," he exclaimed, blushing again. "But can't you remember anything?" he asked, gathering courage for the question.

I shook my head and looked worried and perplexed.

"You don't mind my asking that question?"

"Not a bit. Of course I want to hit on something that will wake up my memory."

"Herr Hoffnung said something about your not wanting to go to the war and that you were joining the Secret Service; and Rosa was just mad about it. She loathes the idea; but there, I don't suppose she'll care so much if——" He stopped short in some confusion.

"If what? Out with it, my dear fellow."

"I don't think I'd better tell you. For one reason because you're——" and he pulled up again.

"Because I've lost my memory, do you mean?"

"I don't know. She's awfully funny sometimes, but I did mean that. I was going to say—you won't give me away to her if I tell you?"

"Of course not. Aren't we two going to be the best of chums?"

"Well, it's a rotten arrangement to tie up two kids to marry, like you two, just because of some money."

I laughed. "I'm not exactly a kid now, Hans, at any rate."

"Rather not; and what she'll think when she sees you I don't know."

This let in a glimmer of the truth and I made a shot. "You mean she doesn't much fancy the family arrangement?" His face told me it was a bull's-eye, but he hesitated to own it. "When a man's in my state it's only decent for his real friends to tell him the hang of things, Hans," I said as a little touch of the spur.

"I daresay it's a lot of lies now that I've seen you."

I tumbled to that, of course. "You mean that your sister has heard things which have set her against me?"

He nodded. "That you have only pretended to be out of the country all the time and then had to run away—oh, I don't know exactly what it was, but it was enough for Rosa. She always takes a different view of everything from the rest of us."

Rather good hearing. It seemed to offer a way of breaking off the engagement. "She wants to end things between us, you mean?"

"I don't know for certain, but I know what I think. She wouldn't come to the station to-night for one thing, and then, well, if I was engaged to a girl I wouldn't have her so thick with a fellow as she is with Oscar Feldmann. He's always here. But don't you breathe a word that I've told you about this."

"Not I, my dear fellow; I'm only too grateful to you. Is he in the army then?"

"Not he, but he ought to be;" and as this turned him on to the army again, I listened for a minute or two and yawned, and he took the hint and went away, promising to see me the first thing in the morning.

Things were going all right so far, and as I was really very tired, I put off my thinking until the next day, and went to sleep. In the morning I turned over the whole position in my mind and came to the conclusion that, for the present at any rate, there was only one difficulty to negotiate—that the daughter might not recognize me.

Hans' description of her was anything but alluring. She was "bossy"; inclined to oppose the others and run things on her own; she was already prejudiced against me as Lassen, and was probably ready to grasp at any excuse to break off the engagement.

That suggested a very disquieting thought. If she had heard that Lassen and I were the only cabin passengers on the *Burgen*, that I was the only survivor, that there was some question about my identity and that I had lost my memory, it was clear that she had only to refuse to recognize me, to free herself from the matrimonial entanglement. Obviously that must be postponed if possible.

In view of what her mother had said about the upper part of my face being most like Lassen's, it seemed a good moment to invent a bad face-ache, so that I could swathe my mouth and chin at our first meeting; and the remembrance of Lassen's rather pinched shoulders and stooping figure suggested the advisability of being in bed when she had her first inspection.

Thus when Hans came to me in the morning, he found me suffering from a severe attack of toothache with a bandage wrapped round my face, and the windows carefully curtained. He was a good-natured fellow, was genuinely sorry and, after saying Rosa was really anxious to see me, although she pretended she wasn't, went off to report.

Hans' report brought up the mother, full of solicitous sympathy and inquiries about breakfast and a suggestion that I had better stop in bed. I agreed, and she said that probably Rosa would come and see me during the morning. About an hour later all three came up together, and I augured well from the fact that Rosa was carrying a cup of tea.

She was more like Hans than her mother; fleshy, dark, and round-faced, better-looking and sharper, with fine, almost black eyes, and a certain air of masterfulness, which showed in her brisk manner and carriage. She was evidently very curious to see me.

She bustled up to the bedside, her eyes fixed on me searchingly, and her dark brows, which were rather heavy, pent and drawn together.

"So you've come at last, Johann—if you are Johann, that is," she said, as she drew up a small table and put the tea on it.

I met her look with a wan smile, turned so that she should have a good view of so much of my face as was visible, and held out my hand. "Rosa," I murmured, and waited to observe the result of her scrutiny.

"Mother said you were too ill to have any breakfast, but I knew better, so I've brought you a cup of tea," she said, managing to suggest that she had brought it less because I might like it, than because the others had declared I shouldn't.

"Thank you, Rosa, I shall relish it."

"There. You see I was right, mother," she said, and I saw I had scored. "Are you really so bad, Johann? You always were a coward in bearing pain, you know."

"Rosa!" protested the mother.

"It's true, mother. If he knocked his little toe he always thought he'd have to have his whole foot cut off. And whoever heard of a man wanting to stay in bed for a toothache?"

Better and better, this. Unintentionally I had evidently forged an important link in the identification; and then came something better still, in response to another protest from the mother.

"Nonsense, mother, it's exactly what he would do," she exclaimed sharply, and then turned again to me. "Mother thinks you're awfully altered, but I don't see it. Of course I haven't seen much of your face yet; but she always does take these queer fancies. Can't you take that thing off your face?"

"I think I'll drink the cup of tea," I replied, and drew the bandage down a little and put the cup to my lips.

To my astonishment she burst out laughing and clapped her hands. "How silly you are, mother. Why the thing's as plain as plain. He's had his teeth taken out, and that accounts for the difference you made such a fuss about. They used to stick out like this;" and she put her fingers in front of her own mouth to illustrate. "Don't you remember how we noticed the same thing when Mrs. Hopping had it done? It's made you quite passable, Johann," she declared.

"Is that it, Johann?" asked the mother, smiling.

"Is it very noticeable?" I asked, just escaping the pitfall of admitting that I remembered something about it. Rosa laughed and nodded. The ordeal was over, and the danger point passed; and soon afterwards she said she wanted to speak to me alone, and asked me to make an effort to get up.

I made the effort, laughed to myself as I cleaned my teeth that they should have been mistaken for false ones, and went downstairs to find Rosa waiting impatiently for me.

"I should have thought you could put those awful clothes on in half the time you've taken, Johann, but you were always slow in dressing," she bantered; and I was quite content to be chipped for a time until she was ready to come to the discussion of our own affairs.

"Is it true you've quite lost your memory?" she asked as Hans had done.

"The Rotterdam doctors said I should recover it. But I'm afraid I shouldn't have known even you."

"Don't you remember anything about my letters?" I shook my head. "Nor your own either?" Another wag of the head. "Well, do you still want to make me marry you?"

"I don't know. You're very pretty, Rosa."

"For Heaven's sake don't begin to pay me stupid compliments. I hate them. Hans takes good care I shan't forget my face isn't my fortune; and the moment a man begins to talk about my looks, I know he's thinking about my money. At least most of them," she qualified after a pause.

I understood the qualification. "Then there's an exception?"

She flushed slightly and was a little confused. "Yes, there is," she replied after a pause. "You'll have to know it some time, so you may as well know it now;" and she tossed her head defiantly. "I believe in coming straight to the point, Johann; and the question is whether you are still in the same mind as when you sent me that idiotic photograph, three months ago—the silly thing isn't a bit like you—and if you are, we had better face things at once."

"What did I say?" I asked, frowning.

"That you meant to hold me to the stupid engagement. But you can't do that, however much you wish. It's true that under the silly will the engagement can't be broken off till I'm five and twenty, unless you do it, but don't forget that I get half the money even if I don't marry you."

"Is that the will? It does seem silly, as you say."

"Oh, I know you believe you have the whiphand."

"Indeed, I don't know anything about it." It was really delicious to be able to tell the simple truth.

She frowned impatiently. "It's what you're thinking then," she declared rather snappily. I shook my head. What I really was considering was whether, since Lassen was at the bottom of the North Sea, I should make a friend of her by doing what she wished. "Well, anyhow, I want you to make haste and think about it all and let me know the result as soon as possible. I hate suspense, and things can't go on as they are," she continued vehemently.

I had no answer ready, and with a shrug of the shoulders she turned to another subject. "Is it true that you've turned spy?"

"Hoffnung seemed to suggest something of the sort yesterday."

She tossed her head and her lip curled. "If I were a man I'd rather be a street sweeper; but I'm not surprised at *your* liking it. It's these things in you that are so natural. Your new teeth may have altered your looks, but of course they haven't changed your nature."

I couldn't restrain a smile; things were panning out so well: and before I replied the door was opened gently and the loveliest child I had ever seen came in. She was a delicate-featured, golden-haired youngster of about eleven—the replica in miniature of the Countess—with big sea-blue eyes which fastened on me shyly as she stood hesitating at the door.

"What is it, Lottchen?" cried Rosa sharply. "Come in and don't stand fiddling with the door handle in that stupid fashion. This is Cousin Johann, and you needn't stand staring at him as if he would eat you."

My heart went out to the kid instantly. "How do you do, Lottchen?" I said; and she came up, put her little hand into mine and left it there, as she held up her lovely face to be kissed, and then nestled close to me trustfully.

Rosa laughed. "That's a new thing for Lottchen, I can tell you; she hates men as a rule."

"You won't hate me, Lottchen, will you?" I said, smoothing her wondrous hair. She shook her head and smiled up at me and then laid her face against my shoulder.

"Don't worry Johann. He's got a bad face-ache."

"Oh, I'm sorry. Am I hurting you?" and the great blue eyes were full of sympathy, just as her mother's had been the previous night.

"Not a bit, my dear."

"Well, you must run away now, child, you'll see plenty of Johann. What is it you want?"

"Miss Caldicott sent me to see if you're coming out with us as usual."

The name seemed to strike me in the face, and a sharp cry of amazement was out before I could check it. It was lucky that Rosa had reminded me of my forgotten face-ache, and I invented a violent paroxysm of pain, whipped out my handkerchief and hid my face in it, to cover up my confusion.

Was it possible that Nessa and I were in the same house, or had I gone clean out of my senses?

CHAPTER IV
NESSA

It was some time before I allowed myself to recover from the little attack and felt equal to the task of resuming the conversation with Rosa. If the Miss Caldicott the child had mentioned was really Nessa—and it was difficult to think there would be two girls of that name shut up in Berlin at the same time—it was just the biggest stroke of luck I had ever had in my life.

Indeed, all the luck seemed to be coming my way; but I should have to be careful how I played the magnificent cards fate had placed in my hand. I must certainly have Rosa on my side; and that could probably be done by freeing her from the engagement. It couldn't be done at once, however; not until I had pretended to take time to consider.

I must also find out the relations between Rosa and Nessa; and must, if possible, manage not to have any one present when Nessa and I met for the first time. Not the easiest of jobs, probably; although my peculiar footing in the house might enable me to find a means. The risk was, of course, that in her amazement Nessa might give everything away.

"That was a sharp spasm and no mistake," I said when I lowered the handkerchief at last.

"Was it real, or just shamming to make us pity you?" asked Rosa suspiciously. "You were always good at shamming, you know."

"Was I? Oh well, I'm better, so it doesn't much matter."

"Did Lottchen hurt you, then? She's apt to be clumsy."

"She's rather a pretty child and doesn't look clumsy."

"She's the dearest little thing in the world, but it doesn't do to make too much of her. Every one spoils her because she's so pretty and looks so fragile. She isn't really delicate and can be no end of a romp, and is quite able to take her own part. She wants to go to school, and she'd have gone before if it hadn't been for the war and Nessa being here as her governess. You never saw anything like the way she loves Nessa."

I wasn't caught napping this time. "Nessa? And who's Nessa?" I asked with a frown of perplexity.

"Nessa Caldicott, an English girl who——"

"An English girl here, in this house, at such a time!" I exclaimed, lost in amazement.

"Yes, of course; in this house; and at such a time," she repeated, imitating my manner. "Have you any objection?"

"Of course not; but——" and I gestured to suggest anything.

"I wanted to talk to you about her. That's the one reason why I wasn't altogether sorry to hear you were in the Secret Service;" and then she told me that she and Nessa had been at school together, and how, when she found Nessa had had to leave her friends and could not get permission to go back to England, she had brought her home as Lottchen's governess. "She was in awful trouble, of course, and mother hated the idea of her coming to us; but I got my own way. That's about two months ago, and ever since we've been doing all we can to get her sent home."

This sent Rosa up many hundreds per cent. in my estimation. "I think it was awfully good of you; but why can't she go home?"

The question seemed to trouble her considerably. "If I tell you all about it, will you help us?"

"I don't suppose I can do anything, but I'll try."

"You may be able to find out the truth; and that will help, for we should know how to get to work. I think I know it, though, and I believe it's all the fault of a man who pesters her incessantly. He's a horrid beast, named Count von Erstein;" and she told me he was a wealthy Jew who had great influence with the Government; had tried and was still trying to get Nessa denounced as a spy and sent to one of the concentration camps; dogged her everywhere and set spies to watch her; had spread all manner of lying reports about her; and was intriguing in every possible way against her for his own infamous ends.

My blood boiled as I listened to all this, but I had to smother my rage sufficiently to assume just a conventional amount of indignation in keeping with Lassen's character. "An ugly story," I muttered.

"It doesn't seem to have roused you very much," she replied, her eyes flashing indignantly. "I should have thought it would have fired the blood of any ordinary man. It makes me feel that I could kill him; but then I'm only a woman."

It was clear that my manner was Lassenly enough, so I let it pass. "I'm curious to see the man."

"If he had his deserts, you'd see him in prison; but he's probably with Nessa and Lottchen now. He always hangs about near the house at this time, when they go for their walk. That was the meaning of the child's coming in just now. I generally go with them. Do you feel well enough to come out and see?"

After a little sham hesitation I agreed, and she went off to get ready, leaving me able to work off some of my rage alone. It was in all truth an ugly story, and, what was worse, threatened to make it very difficult to get Nessa away. No doubt it was abominably stupid of me, but until that moment I had never considered the practical means of getting her out of Berlin.

I had rushed off with the idea of finding out the truth about her in order to relieve her mother's anxiety, and somewhere at the back of my head was the idea that Jimmy's friend at the American Embassy would help me to do the rest.

But that was knocked on the head if this beast of a Jew had sufficient influence with his Government to block the way. And that he had considerable influence, Rosa's story left no doubt. She certainly could not get away openly, without permission from the authorities and a passport and all the rest of it; and it looked like a thousand to one chance against any such things being forthcoming.

That did not exhaust the resources of civilization, however, as the politicians are fond of saying; and at the worst we could try and make a bolt of it together, without any papers if necessary, but preferably with some in false names. So far as I was concerned I was ready to tramp it to the frontier on foot; but that wouldn't do for Nessa.

At any rate we must get her out of Berlin and away from this von Erstein's persecution. Nessa could gabble German quite as freely as I could; and once away from the capital, supplied with plenty of money as I was fortunately, we could try our luck and trust to fate.

"You've made me feel awfully strange about that fellow," I said to Rosa as we started from the house. "I suppose it means I'm angry. I feel I should like to kick the brute."

"I'm glad to hear it; but kicking won't be enough. What you've got to do is to find means to get Nessa away."

I shook my head doubtfully. "How are these things managed?"

"She must have a permit to travel; that will be difficult enough: and to cross the frontier there must be a passport, of course. That's where the Count stops everything. He has dinned it into the powers that be that she's a spy and wants to get away to carry her information to England. We nearly got one; but at the last moment the whole plan failed."

"Did Aunt Olga help, then?" I asked, hesitating how to speak of the Countess.

"No, mother wouldn't. It was—was a friend of mine, Herr Feldmann, if you wish to know," she said, with a slight tinge of colour, hesitating over the name and laughing self-consciously as I looked down at her and our eyes met.

"It appears to me that your English girl is lucky to have found such staunch friends, Rosa," I said as earnestly as I felt. "And between us we ought to be able to outwit this von Erstein."

"I wonder if you mean that," she replied, with a searching look.

"I think you'll find I do. They told me at Rotterdam that I had had a very near squeak of death; and whether it's that or something else, I don't seem to have any of the meannesses you associate with me. I am perfectly in earnest. Perhaps I've dropped the rest with my memory."

"I hope you have, Johann, and there's certainly a sincere look in your eyes there never used to be. Ah! There they are," she broke off, pointing a little distance ahead; and I saw Nessa and the child coming toward us, with the man in attendance.

We had turned into the Thiergarten and were in one of the larger side walks at the moment; the part where Nessa usually brought Lottchen, Rosa told me: and I had a good view of them before they saw us. Nessa had the child between her and von Erstein, and I was deeply concerned to notice how worn and troubled and harried she looked.

The man was talking to her over Lottchen's head and appeared to have no eyes for anybody or anything except her. He was about forty, I thought; the ruddy-faced type of Jew, clean-shaven, square of face, rather high cheekbones, a very un-Jewish nose, small eyes, with bags of sensuality under them, a somewhat heavy jowl, with little rolls of flesh under his chin and on his thick neck. Not by any means a bad-looking man and very smartly dressed in faultlessly cut clothes which, however, did not hide his tendency to paunchiness. An ugly customer to get across with, was my verdict.

I was more than a little bothered about Nessa meeting me for the first time in his presence, as it was extremely probable that she would give vent to her astonishment in a way that might start his suspicions, so I stepped out into full view while they were still a little distance away, hoping to prepare her.

But there was no trouble of the sort. Lottchen caught sight of us first and, breaking away, rushed up to me. I stopped with her, therefore, and Rosa went on to the other two; and to my intense satisfaction, she held von Erstein in talk while Nessa, glad no doubt of the relief, came to us.

It could not have happened more fortunately. Just before she reached us I managed to place the child so that she could not see Nessa, and then turned and raised my hat, giving her a clear view of my features.

"You!" she exclaimed, starting and turning as white as death and trembling so violently that for an instant I thought she was going to faint. But I did what a look would do to caution her and turned to the child.

"You must introduce me, Lottchen."

"This is my new Cousin Johann," she said a little shyly. And the slight interlude gave Nessa time to pull herself together sufficiently to return my bow.

It was a very formal bow, and the look in her eyes and the instinctive droop of the expressive mouth was much more suggestive of indignation than pleasure at seeing me. It was a great deal more like contempt or disgust; but by the time the others reached us she had entirely recovered her self-possession.

My introduction to von Erstein followed, and he displayed an amount of cordiality at making my acquaintance, which puzzled me at the moment. But I was not long left in doubt. My first uneasy impression was that he suspected the impersonation, gathered from the smiling slyness with which he looked at me.

As we were to cross swords it was necessary for me to probe this at once; and when Nessa entrenched herself securely between the two sisters and he showed a disposition to drop behind with me, I was glad of the chance.

He opened the ball by speaking of my loss of memory, and I soon found that I was wrong about his suspecting my imposture. He professed great sympathy with my misfortune, throwing in a hint that it might after all have its compensations. "A good many of us have memories we might be glad to lose, Herr Lassen," he added with a laugh, but in a tone which reminded me of what Hans had said about my past.

"I should be glad to have mine back, good or bad," I replied with a laugh as easy as his.

"Perhaps. One never knows," he retorted meaningly. Then he switched off to the von Rebling family. "Most charming people; delightful; but unfortunately there's one little fly in the amber. You know it, of course?" and he nodded toward Nessa.

"I only arrived late last night. What is it?"

"It is a thousand pities; but these are times in which no one can afford to run risks, even with the highest motives. I know, of course, that Miss von Rebling's motives are of the highest; but we have to think imperially; especially in regard to this plague of spies. You agree with that, of course?"

"Naturally; but how does that apply here?"

He paused, rolling his eyes round at me with a significant shake of the head. "Why do you suppose that English girl there, Miss Caldicott, finds it so desirable to be an inmate of their house?"

"Rosa told me she was Lottchen's governess."

He put his forefinger to the side of his nose and winked and nodded. "Ostensibly—yes; but in reality—eh?"

"Do you mean she's a spy?" I cried, appropriately shocked.

He nodded emphatically. "I do; and I'm relying on your help in the matter. They may have told you that I have a great deal of interest in circles that would enable me to be of considerable help to you; and I have every wish that we two should be great friends. My influence is such that you may depend upon getting high in the service you wish to join. Very high."

"I'm not likely to quarrel with any one who can help-me in that way, of course; but you see there's a bit of a stumbling-block at present until I can get over this infernal loss of memory."

"Oh, that'll soon come right."

"So all the doctors at Rotterdam told me; but so far——" and I broke off with a flourish of the hands.

"I think I can help you about that, too. Of course when you were known to be coming here I made such inquiries about you as were open to me, and the result made me feel sure that you would wish to be friendly with me;" and he leered at me in a way that left me in no doubt as to his sinister meaning. He thought he had me in his power.

"I shall be tremendously interested to learn what you heard. So far as I know, I might have been born about a week ago, and it's a devilish unpleasant feeling."

He favoured me with another leer. "Ah, you're a good deal older than that," he said meaningly. "I fancy I can convince you if you'll come and have a chat with me. Here's my address," giving me his card.

"Certainly I'll come," said I readily. "You've roused my curiosity tremendously. What time and day?"

"Come and lunch with me to-morrow. In the morning you'll be wanted in the Amtstrasse; Baron von Gratzen, you know. Come on to me from him. I can open your eyes to a thing or two; and I'm altogether mistaken if we can't come to understand one another thoroughly. I'll manage to refresh that lapsed memory of yours, Lassen, and perhaps find the real reason for it."

"The Rotterdam people put it down to shock," I replied, as if I had not understood him.

"Ah, the doctors don't know everything, my friend," he returned drily. "But I must get off. Till tomorrow, then. Don't forget;" and he quickened after the others, shook hands, patted Lottchen on the cheek, much to her disgust, and went off.

A pleasant fellow, very. Evidently a strong believer in the knuckle-duster methods; meant to use them to force me to help him in his infamous scheme against Nessa, and had discovered something about my past which would bring me to heel. That was his ideal of friendship. Certainly a very pleasant fellow!

That was a generous offer of his influence, too. Thinking me to be as big a scoundrel as himself, he was ready to betray his country by pushing me up the ladder of promotion if I would only help him in his blackguardism. A staunch patriot, too. Deutschland über alles! but von Erstein first!

I was certainly curious to know what it was he had discovered; but my speculations were interrupted by Lottchen, who came back to me and took my hand and made me chatter to her until we reached the house.

This was all right, as it saved Nessa from having to talk trivialities with me in Rosa's presence, gave her an opportunity of accustoming herself to my presence in Berlin and nerving herself for the inevitable deception it involved.

How she would treat me I could not guess; but I was utterly unprepared for the attitude she did assume. She hurried into the house the instant we reached it and disappeared. We met at the midday dinner; but she steadfastly refused even to cast so much as a glance in my direction.

Rosa made more than one attempt to draw her into conversation with me; but every effort was foiled by Nessa pretending to have to pay some attention to Lottchen, who sat by her. In fact, she ignored me as completely as if I had not been present and seized the first opportunity to leave the room.

I had looked for any treatment rather than that; and felt more than a little riled and aggrieved. It was no harmless picnic, this jaunt of mine to Berlin; and I thought she might have taken that into consideration.

But there was more than mere pique involved. If she meant to keep up this attitude, how was I to come to any understanding with her?

I might as well go back to my flying—if that were possible. Itself a pretty stiff proposition, as Jimmy would have said.

CHAPTER V
ABOUT SPIES

Nessa's treatment of me both offended and distressed the Countess, and Rosa tried to draw her attention away from it by engaging her in a discussion about the afternoon's arrangements. It appeared that the Countess always spent an hour or two on that particular day with a very old friend, an invalid; Rosa herself had an engagement; Hans had to attend some lecture or other in connection with his military studies; and Nessa generally took Lottchen for a drive.

I would not hear of the arrangements being altered on my account, declaring that I should be glad of the opportunity to get some decent clothes.

"Then there will be an empty house," declared Rosa as we rose from the table.

There were two servants—an elderly woman, named Gretchen, and Marie, a younger one—in the room during the discussion; an important fact in the light of after events.

Some letters arrived for the Countess and Rosa; and when the former took hers away to the drawing-room, Rosa detained me in the library to speak about Nessa's conduct. "I can't understand it, Johann," she said irritably.

"Does it matter much?" I asked with a shrug.

"Of course it does. How are you going to help her if she keeps up this ridiculous attitude? I've no patience with her."

"Oh, I have. She knows about our engagement, of course, and being staunch to you looks on me as an enemy."

"But she knew you were coming and was most anxious to see you, and even promised to try and bring you to reason."

"Have you told her that I'm willing to help her; if I can, that is?"

"No, but I'll go and tell her now, and tell her also that if she doesn't wish to make mother furious, she'd better take things differently."

"Perhaps if I could have a quiet chat with her, it might do the trick," I suggested casually.

"Then you mustn't lose any time about it. Why not this afternoon? I can take Lottchen with me, and if you stop in, it could be managed easily. And when I come back the three of us can talk the thing over together."

I agreed to this like a shot, and we went into the drawing-room, where her mother was still reading her letters. Rosa glanced hurriedly at hers, locked them in a little bureau, and hurried off to tackle Nessa.

The Countess was standing by a very handsome cabinet, a drawer of which she had opened, and called me up to her. "Come here, Johann, I want you to see me put these letters away," she said to my astonishment, and, drawing my attention to the neatness with which her letters and papers were arranged, asked me to remember precisely where she put those which had just arrived, and to make sure that the drawer was locked. "I want to have a witness," she added.

Then she spoke of Nessa's behaviour to me, saying how it had grieved and surprised her.

"It is really not of the least consequence," I assured her.

"But I'm sorely afraid it is, Johann, and I'm very troubled. That's one reason why I wished you to do that just now. I was always against her coming to the house, but Rosa would have her;" and then by degrees the reason came out.

She was afraid that von Erstein's story was true, that Nessa was really a spy. Some one had a key to her drawer in the cabinet; she had found her papers disturbed more than once; she kept money in the same place, but none of it had ever been taken, so that it could not be the work of a thief; she believed that Rosa's bureau had also been tampered with; and as the servants were above suspicion, there seemed to be only one conclusion.

The dear little lady was more grieved than angry about it. "I'm very sorry for Nessa really, Johann, but we can't have a spy in the house; yet I don't know how to get rid of her. But I won't open that drawer again until you are with me, and then we shall both know that I'm not making a mistake. Meanwhile, don't say anything to Rosa or any one."

We went upstairs together, and she was telling me the address of Hans' tailor and how I was to find it, when the old servant, Gretchen, passed us. Rosa was waiting dressed to go out, and told me she had spoken to Nessa, who would come down to me in the drawing-room after the rest had left the house.

"She baffles me, Johann. She just jumped at your offer to help her get away—after her conduct just now, too! But she seems to have taken a violent dislike to you, and even declared she wouldn't stop in the same house with you," she said in a tone of consternation.

I passed it off with a smile and some banal remark about feminine inconsistency, and went downstairs to wait for Nessa. There was a lounge at the end of the drawing-room, a big comfortable sort of winter garden, with lots of big plants, and rugs and easy chairs and so on, and I sat down there to think over the position. I didn't smoke; a lucky fact in view of things.

It worried me excessively that Nessa should be regarded as a spy, and I was puzzling over the explanation of what the Countess had told me when I heard the front door shut. That meant they had left the house and that Nessa would soon be down.

But she did not come for some time, and presently I heard a movement in the big room, the faint click of a key being turned and then of a drawer being cautiously opened.

The conclusion was obvious. The spy was at work, believing that I had gone to the tailor's and meaning to fix the thing on Nessa, should her little operation be discovered. So I got up noiselessly and, from the safe shelter of some plants, did a little spy work on my own account.

It was one of the servants, of course; but I could not at first catch sight of her face. She was at Rosa's bureau, reading a letter, probably one of those which had come just before. That did not occupy more than a minute, and she next opened the Countess's cabinet drawer, picked out a couple of letters, glanced at them rapidly, just tossed them back carelessly, relocked the drawer, and turned to leave the room.

I saw her clearly then, for she went out by a door which stood at my end of the room, near the big stove in the corner. It was Gretchen.

It would never do to have a possible eavesdropper when Nessa and I were together, and, being unwilling to let the woman know she had been seen, I crept over to the door we all used, opened it noisily, shut it with a bang, and began to whistle.

This had immediate results. I heard the door of the stove opened at the back, some logs were thrown in, and directly afterwards Gretchen came out, with an apology for disturbing me.

"It's my work to see to the stoves, sir," she explained with a smirk. "And the door to our quarters is locked."

"All right, Gretchen. It's getting chilly, isn't it?"

"It gets cold in the evenings, sir, and my orders are to see that the stoves are kept going well." She was a little uneasy; and after she had been gone a while, I had a look at the hiding-place.

It was a passage with cupboards on each side, and as the door at the other end was fastened, she had been compelled to return through the room when she had heard me. There was a bolt on my side of that door, and I shot it to prevent her coming back to listen while Nessa and I were together.

I was only a minute or two in the place, but when I left it I found Nessa already in the drawing-room. She had caught me apparently in the act of playing the spy, and her look left no doubt about her opinion.

I laughed. I really could not help it. It was such a preposterous misreading of the situation that the ludicrous absurdity of it appealed to me. Of course my laughter added to her indignation and also to the awkwardness of the meeting.

"You are practising your new profession, I see. It appears to rouse your sense of humour," she said icily.

"It would probably rouse yours also if you understood everything," I retorted, not at all relishing her prompt condemnation.

"I don't see anything particularly humorous in your sneaking into the house of my friends and spying in its holes and corners."

"Perhaps not, but I had a good reason," I said shortly, a bit rattled by her sneer.

"No doubt; but I have no curiosity on such a subject. Rosa has induced me to see you, so I——" She got so far in the same level, cutting tone, evidently putting a great restraint upon herself; but she could not keep it up. Her eyes blazed suddenly, her cheeks flushed, and raising her voice in her indignation she exclaimed: "How dare you come——"

I had to stop that, however, as the old eavesdropper might have followed her to the room and be on keyhole drill. "I am very glad to meet you, Miss Caldicott," I broke in in German loudly enough to be heard outside, and added in a low tone in English: "It is not safe to speak so loudly as you did. Come away from the door;" and I led the way into the conservatory.

She stared at me as if I were a dangerous lunatic, but after a moment's pause followed me. "Say what you like now, but lower your voice," I said, lowering my own tone.

She hesitated, but acted on the warning and returned to her former icy tone. "What I want to know is why you dare to come here in a false name, as the sham lover of my friend, and humiliate me in this way. If you must be a spy, haven't you enough decency to avoid blackening me by making me a partner in such treacherous baseness?"

I met her angry look for a second, realizing that this was the reason for her conduct to me; and it was all I could do to prevent myself smiling at her injustice, although it riled me considerably.

"Rather a rough judgment," I replied with a shrug, "and your manner doesn't smooth it out much; but as no one else can hear you now, I don't mind so much. I can explain— —"

"Explain!" she broke in scornfully.

"Yes, explain. That's what I said. If you understood— —"

"I do understand as it is—too well," she fired in again.

I really could not help smiling again, both at her words and flashing anger. "I must either smile or lose my temper as you have done; and it's better to smile."

This was like petrol on the fire. "Just what I should expect of you—to see nothing but a joke in my indignation."

"I'm not laughing at your indignation, but at your mistake. You always have been ready to make the worst of anything I do."

"What have you ever done that was worth doing?"

"Nothing much, I admit."

"If you were like other men you'd be doing what they are doing—fighting."

"Perhaps I should; but we can't all be soldiers."

Her lip curled. "Men can; but even you needn't have sunk so low as to be a spy!"

"Go on. I'm not ashamed of what I'm doing; and if you'll let me explain— —"

She stopped me again with an impatient gesture. "I need no explanation, thank you. Aren't you here as Johann Lassen?"

"Yes."

"Pretending to be engaged to Rosa von Rebling?"

"Yes."

"And pretending to have lost your memory?"

"Yes."

"Haven't you both spoken and acted lies to gain admission to this house?"

"I had to, of course."

"You convict yourself out of your own mouth, then?"

"Apparently."

"Aren't you trying to get employed in the Secret Service here?"

"Looks black, doesn't it?"

"Looks!" and she drew a long deep breath and repeated the word. "But you don't imagine for one instant that I will be a party to it!"

"You are already, for that matter."

"You shall leave this house at once and never set foot in it again, and I shall find the means to let Rosa know the disgraceful trick you have played."

"And if I refuse?"

"I'll expose you as surely as my name is Nessa Caldicott."

"You know what the result would be to me?"

"I neither know nor care."

"Then I'll tell you. I should certainly be imprisoned and most probably shot."

She wavered somewhat at that. "It is easy for you to avoid it by doing what I say—leave the house."

"That's out of the question."

"Do you expect me to allow you to go on imposing on the girl who has been my friend at a time when I was absolutely helpless? Wouldn't you be ashamed of me if I were to consent to such treachery? Can't you see what a vile degradation it would be, and that I should hate myself as well as you if I consented?"

"No. Yes. Yes. I wish you'd ask one question at a time."

"Do you expect me to smile at such insufferable flippancy as that?"

"No. But it wasn't flippancy at all. I was answering your questions in order. You appear to think that I like being compelled to deceive Miss von Rebling."

"How can you talk about having been compelled to do it?"

"Because it happens to be the truth."

"Your version of the truth, you mean?"

"Exactly. My version of the truth, although you won't believe it. I was forced into the thing against my will by a series of coincidences which I found it impossible to avoid; and, as a matter of fact, I am not harming Miss von Rebling in the least."

"Haven't you led her to believe you may break off the engagement?"

"I've been considering it."

"Don't you call that harming her?"

"No."

"How can you say that? What will happen when the real man arrives?"

"Not even then."

She gestured incredulously. "It's impossible," she cried. "In any case I insist upon her being told."

I stopped to think a bit. I knew Nessa so well that I could quite understand her mood. Her first fierce rush of anger had spent itself, checked, I was sure, by my statement of the consequences to me if the truth were told. She had not a suspicion of the reason for my being in Berlin, evidently believing that I had come as a spy, and knew even better than I what my end would be if I were denounced; and her words had cut me too deeply to let me tell her the truth then—that I had only come on her account.

At the same time I could quite appreciate how she would shrink from being made a partner, as she had said, and her impatience for me to leave the house. It was an awkward corner, but I thought I could see a way round it.

"I'll do what you suggest," I said at length.

"Go away?"

"No. Tell Miss von Rebling."

This alarmed her at once. "But you? What you said about the risk?" she protested.

"Oh, never mind about me. You said you couldn't endure it; and, of course, nothing matters compared with that. I should have taken care to let her know everything as soon as I'd done what I came to do."

"What is that?"

"Your mother is very anxious about you, and when she knew I was coming here, naturally wanted me to find out things."

"But they've had my letters, surely?"

"Not a line since some time after Christmas."

"Do you mean that, Jack? Oh, poor mother! I've written regularly every week. When Julia Wassermann died, her father, who hates the English and hated me because I'm English, turned me out of the house. I should have gone to one of these dreadful concentration camps, if it hadn't been for Rosa. That's why I can't bear the thought of deceiving her; but—I—I don't want to get you into any trouble. We—we can't tell her. We—we mustn't. You can go away, can't you?" and she bit her lip in desperate perplexity and distress.

"I'm going to tell her, Nessa," I said.

"But I don't wish it, Jack. I really don't. I didn't mean all the horrid things I said just now; I—I'm sorry. I've been just distracted."

"Don't worry. Nothing very terrible is likely to come to me; and I quite agree that she ought to know the truth."

She looked at me wonderingly. "How different you are, Jack. What has changed you so? You're so quiet and so—so firm. You don't look the same. Not a bit like you used to be in any way, manner, bearing, everything. I saw it the moment I came into the room."

"You didn't show it. You went for me in much the same old style, you know," I said with a smile. "You always did think me a rotter."

"Do you mean that you've risked coming here merely because of—of what mother told you about me."

"Not very likely, is it?"

"It wouldn't have been at one time, but— — You mustn't say anything to Rosa. You mustn't, really. You won't, Jack, will you?" and she laid her hand on my arm appealingly.

"I must, Nessa."

"No, no. I won't be the cause— —"

And then, just as she was clinging to my arm and urging me, she broke away with a sudden cry of consternation.

I turned to find Rosa standing in the doorway, staring at us wide-eyed in amazement.

CHAPTER VI
ROSA IS TOLD

Whether I should have yielded to Nessa and allowed myself to be persuaded not to tell Rosa the truth, I can't say—she always had great influence with me—but after we had been surprised in this fashion it was no longer possible to hesitate. Nessa would have been compromised and I suspected.

I acted promptly, therefore. I crossed the room, and shut the door carefully, both girls watching me with expectant curiosity.

"Please come into the conservatory, Miss von Rebling," I said quietly in English, which she spoke quite fluently. "I have something of the utmost importance to say to you. And we had better speak in English and not too loudly, please."

She stared at me, desperately perplexed by my words and manner; but after a moment's hesitation went into the conservatory, to where Nessa stood in trembling agitation by the plants, and linked her arm in hers and kissed her.

"I am going to put my life in your hands. I am not Johann Lassen. I am an Englishman and my name is Jack Lancaster. Nessa and I are old friends, and we were discussing the question of telling you when you came in," I said in a slow deliberate tone.

She was literally astounded and could not at once grasp all that my words meant. She turned to Nessa as if appealing for confirmation. "Nessa!" she exclaimed, much too loudly to be safe.

"Let me tell you why it is necessary not to speak loudly. You have a spy in the house: the servant I have heard you call Gretchen;" and I described what I had witnessed. "It will no doubt explain why Nessa's letters have never reached England and other things probably."

Rosa's face being incapable of expressing more astonishment than she had already shown, she just tossed up her hands feebly, suggesting that the whole affair was beyond her understanding. But she was a practical, level-headed girl, and soon recovered her self-control.

"Do you mean that you have recovered your memory?" she asked.

I shook my head. "I have never lost it."

She frowned ominously at this and her expression signalled suspicion. "Then why are you in Berlin?"

Clearly she regarded me as an English spy, and there was nothing for it but to tell her the full reason for my presence, although I had not wished to let Nessa know it. "I will tell you everything, but you'd better sit down as it will take some time."

She sat down and drew Nessa to her side, taking her hand and holding it all the time I spoke. "I am an officer in the English army, and was home on leave when I heard for the first time about Nessa;" and I told them all that Mrs. Caldicott said, and described the two peculiar communications which had reached England. Then the whole story: My first plan; Jimmy's intervention; how I had taken his place at the last moment; the blowing up of the *Burgen*; my being mistaken for Lassen; my feigned loss of memory; how I had been unable to get away from Hoffnung, and how his suspicions had forced me to continue the impersonation.

Nessa was terribly distressed to hear of her mother's anxiety and grief; Rosa wept in sympathy, and they both listened to the whole story with rapt attention.

"You will see now," I concluded, "what I meant by saying I am putting my life in your hands. If I am known to be an English officer, there will be only one construction put upon my presence here—that I am a spy, and I shall of course be shot. We should do the same on our side if one of your officers was found in England in similar circumstances. I give you my word, however, that my sole object is to get Nessa away home."

Rosa looked very grave and rather frightened. "You know the consequences to me if I attempt to shield you?"

I nodded. "I can understand they would be very serious, if it was discovered."

Then we all sat silent for a long time, several minutes, and Nessa was trembling like an aspen leaf. Rosa broke the silence at last.

"Where is my cousin?"

"He went down in the *Burgen*. There is no doubt that I am the only survivor. He was below at the time of the explosion, and not even any of the men on deck were saved."

"But if he should not have been drowned and should come here?"

"Your mother and Hans, every one believes I am your cousin, and not so much as a breath of suspicion that you know the truth could ever be roused, unless of course you admitted it."

This had all the effect I had hoped, and she nodded understandingly. "And what do you wish me to do?" she asked after another pause.

"To allow matters to remain as they are until we can get Nessa away; but it is entirely for you to decide."

She shook her head. "I—I can't decide now. I must have time to think. I was never so perplexed or astounded in my life."

"Rosa dear!" appealed Nessa.

"It is not for us to settle, Nessa," I put in; and then another long silence followed.

"If I wait till to-morrow, say, will you use the time to escape, Mr. Lancaster?" asked Rosa then.

"That is impossible, Miss von Rebling," I replied uncompromisingly. "I have come to get Nessa away, and that cannot be done in the time."

That drew a smile: the first since she had arrived. She guessed how the land lay with me, and glanced round at Nessa, who coloured slightly. I believe that that little blush had more effect than anything else. She had the usual streak of German romance in her disposition, and the situation appealed to it strongly.

"I wish I dared," she murmured; and I began to hope.

I gave the new idea a minute to germinate, and then began to nurture it by suggesting how her risk would be minimized. "Let me tell you just what is in my mind. I will not remain in the house, and the first thing to-morrow will go to rooms or an hotel."

"But mother?" she protested nervously.

"I shall tell her of my discovery about Gretchen, and that in view of my connection with the Secret Service, it is essential for me to be absolutely secure against anything of the sort." She nodded approval.

"I shall then be too busy officially to come here much, and this will relieve you from all the unpleasantness of open deception with her and others." Again she nodded.

"The next thing will be to obtain the necessary papers for Nessa and me to leave. Have you any friends in Holland?"

She started rather nervously. "Yes, several old school friends; but——" She paused and gestured.

"My idea is that you should invent a sudden desire to go to them; say that one of them is dying or very ill, or something. You could not very well travel alone at such a time, and thus Hans would naturally go with you. It would be simple enough for you two to obtain permits to travel and passports and so on, and——"

"But I should be instantly questioned and—— Oh, that would never do," she interrupted, with a vigorous shake of the head.

I smiled reassuringly. "I have thought of that, believe me. On the morning you were to start, after you had obtained your tickets, something would occur to make it impossible for you to go. Nessa or I would then get the tickets and things, and she and I would use them. You would not discover the loss until we had had time to cross the frontier, and could then give information of their loss; and as soon as we were safely in Holland, I would write to you a letter explaining everything."

This lessened her uneasiness considerably. "It is possible," she admitted.

"Such a letter from me, confessing my imposture and everything, would free you from the slightest taint of suspicion that you had been in any way a party to the scheme, and, of course, as Nessa and I should be in safety, I could make the confession with absolute impunity."

She sat with her dark brows drawn together, considering the scheme very carefully, and after a long silence asked: "How long do you think it would take?"

"Only so long as is needed to get the passports, etc."

But she shook her head. "There is a difficulty—Hans. He could not possibly get away, even if he were willing to go; which I doubt."

"Can you think of any one else?"

She hesitated, glancing first at me and then at Nessa. "Do you remember the two Apeldoorn sisters, Nessa?"

"Yes, quite well, dear."

"They are Herr Feldmann's cousins," said Rosa: and then I knew what was coming. "One of them is going to be married and wants me to go to the wedding. I should have gone if it hadn't been that we heard just then about my Cousin Johann. Herr Feldmann and his sister are going, and I should have gone with them; but his sister is ill," she added, looking to see how I took this.

"It would certainly open the way to the necessary credentials, but how could I get hold of his permit?"

"I can't think of anything else," said Rosa as I did not answer. "But I think Herr Feldmann would help if I asked him," she added.

"Do you mean you would tell him everything?" I asked, not at all relishing the suggestion.

"It would be necessary, wouldn't it?"

"I'd rather try to think of some other plan," I replied, and sat racking my wits for some alternative; without avail, however, and presently she got up and walked about the drawing-room.

When she had left us, Nessa stirred uneasily, glanced once or twice at me, and then held out her hand. "I'm—I'm sorry, Jack," she whispered.

"All right; don't worry;" and I just pressed her trembling fingers.

"But to talk to you as I did—all the brutal things I said. I'm so—so ashamed."

"No need. Not the faintest. You couldn't know; and you caught me in the very act of prying into that place there. If you hadn't fired up a bit, it wouldn't have been natural."

"But after you'd run all this risk simply for me, you must have thought me a regular beast, Jack."

"The fact is your mother's worry got on my nerves, and as I knew I could come into this beastly country without any risk to speak of, of course I came. That's all about it."

She didn't quite like this, but I meant her to believe it had been more for her mother's sake than hers.

"Poor mother!" she murmured, and was silent for a while. "You've joined the army then?" was her next question.

"I'm in the Flying Corps, and your mater didn't tell me anything about you for fear it would get on my nerves."

"Then I had something to do with your coming?" she asked, with a flicker of a flash in her bonny eyes.

"I couldn't very well ease your mother's mind in London, could I? She was against the thing, but I explained there was really no risk. Of course there would not have been any if the steamer hadn't blown up and this Lassen business turned out as it has."

"But it was I who made you tell Rosa?"

"And probably the best thing we could have done if——" and I gestured toward Rosa, who was still pacing the room in troubled perplexity.

I did my utmost to lead Nessa to think I took the position lightly; but I was in reality almost desperately anxious, and every moment of Rosa's indecision added to the disquieting tension of suspense. If she went against us, I could see nothing but a mess of trouble ahead; and I was only too conscious of how big the danger to her would loom in her German-disciplined mind. They all go in deadly fear of the authorities; and it was impossible to deny that, if she were discovered, it might mean the prospect of a spell in prison.

"You haven't said yet that you forgive me, Jack," said Nessa presently.

"Simply because there's nothing to forgive. I should probably have done just what you did," I replied with a smile.

"Do you mean that anything I could have done would have made you take me for a spy, then? I took you for one," she said ruefully.

"The only difference is that I might not have been quite so impatient, and have been ready to listen to your explanation. But don't let us worry over that. Let us think how we're going to get out of it all."

"I think Rosa will help us."

"But this fellow, Feldmann?"

"You needn't trouble about him. He worships her, and the instant he knows her cousin is drowned and the way is clear for him, he'll be ready to—well, to do anything she wishes."

"That's good hearing, anyhow, but I wish she'd look sharp and make her mind up."

Nessa laughed gently. "You don't understand girls, Jack. Her mind was made up before she left us two together. She's one of the kindest-hearted souls in the world."

But Rosa seemed in no hurry to come back to us, and before she could tell us her decision, the opportunity passed, for Hans came in with a man whom Nessa whispered to me was Feldmann himself.

Rosa introduced me to him as her cousin. This set me speculating whether it was an indication of her intention or merely a sign that she had not yet decided what to do, and I was worrying over it as I returned his stiff and rather discourteous greeting, when Hoffnung followed.

After a few words of general conversation Hoffnung drew me aside, and I had a significant proof of von Erstein's intimate acquaintance with official matters. He had puzzled me earlier in the day by saying that I had to interview a Baron von Gratzen the next morning, and Hoffnung now brought me the note making the appointment for eleven o'clock.

"How's the memory, Lassen?"

"Pretty much the same," said I, shrugging. He had evidently abandoned all his former suspicions, I was glad to see.

"You'll find old Gratz, as we call him, a decent sort; but I'm afraid he may have to tell you what you won't like much."

"Meaning?"

"Well, a man without a memory isn't much use to the Secret Service, although he may be in other ways."

I didn't like his tone. "But I can remember all that's passed since the *Burgen*."

It did not draw him, however. He just laughed. "I mustn't anticipate him, of course; but I'll give you a tip. Be at his office on the stroke; he hates nothing so much as unpunctuality."

With that we rejoined the rest, and again the conversation was about matters in which I had no interest. I studied Feldmann carefully. He was a handsome fellow; fair, blue-eyed, rather round-faced and weak; but he had a very pleasant smile which I saw often, for he smiled every time he looked at Rosa. But not once did he address me; and his dislike and hostility were plain each time he glanced in my direction.

He certainly wasn't the man I would have chosen to trust; but beggars can't be choosers, and I had to be satisfied with the fact that both Rosa and Nessa herself were ready to vouch for him.

Hoffnung did not stay long, and when he had gone Rosa reminded me about going to the tailor's, and as I was leaving the room, she said to Nessa: "You might show it to Johann now, dear."

"Rosa has asked me to show you the portrait of your mother, Herr Lassen, as she hopes it may perhaps help you to remember things."

"Please do," I answered eagerly, her look telling me this was merely an excuse; and we went to the library together.

"It's all right with Rosa," she whispered then; "but only if Herr Feldmann is told and agrees. I am to go back and tell her what you say."

"Are you quite sure of him?"

"Yes, quite, in the altered circumstances. So is Rosa."

"Carry on, then; and if there's anything wrong, let me know the moment I get back;" and off I went, not letting Nessa see how it worried me to have this infernal suspense kept hanging round my neck like a millstone.

CHAPTER VII
BARON VON GRATZEN

I was very curious to have a look at Berlin in war time; but as I am not writing a chronicle of the struggle, my impressions need not be laboured, except as they touched me personally.

The struggle had been going on for about eighteen months when I reached the capital, and, except in one respect, matters were pretty much as I had known them. There were more soldiers about, perhaps; there seemed to be as much bustling activity as usual, and certainly there was universal confidence that the result would be a glorious victory.

The one genuine surprise I had was when I came upon an unwontedly demonstrative crowd shouting that they were short of food. They were chiefly women, and a boisterous, vociferating lot they were. It was not so much the crowd that impressed me, however, or the row they kicked up, as the fact that the police didn't interfere. In my experience, a crowd might look for a very short shrift at the hands of the police of Berlin.

I referred to the matter when I was at the tailor's—where, by the by, I succeeded in getting a very passably fitting suit and other things I needed— and he explained the reason. There was no real scarcity of food, he declared, but much grumbling at the distribution; and the police had had orders not to resort to drastic measures.

"It will have to be stopped, however, or the trouble will grow. There has already been some window smashing. Imagine it, window smashing in our beautiful, well-organized city!" he cried, as if it were akin to impiety and sacrilege.

"Very shocking," I agreed gravely.

"If it is not put down with an iron hand, it will not be safe for a well-dressed person to be in the streets. My own wife and daughter, only yesterday, were all but mauled in the Untergasse. But the English will pay for it!"

I cut short that subject by speaking about the business in hand; it wasn't prudent to talk about the war, and I took care not to give him an opportunity of returning to it before I left the shop.

On my way back to the von Reblings' house in the Karlstrasse, I could think of nothing except the news I was to hear and what I should do if the scheme I had suggested was turned down. I could see nothing for it but to make a bolt almost at once, take Nessa with me, and trust to our wits and luck to get away.

Not a hopeful job at the best, and at the worst involving no end of risk and danger for us both. I knew my Germany too well not to be painfully conscious of all that; and the knowledge made me profoundly uncomfortable. But I've a sanguine streak in me and am generally lucky, so I put off the consideration of the disagreeables until they had to be faced in earnest.

I need not have worried, however, for I found everything running as sweetly as a well-oiled engine when I reached the house. I knew it instantly by the manner in which Feldmann greeted me.

Instead of the previous sullen angry looks, he was all smiles, gripped my hand cordially, nearly fell on my neck, and I rather dreaded that he would wind up by kissing me. Rosa and Nessa were in much the same hilarious mood, and might have been arranging the details of a wedding rather than a little conspiracy against the Government.

They had it all cut and dried, and my crude plan was hailed as if it had been a piece of the most wonderful strategy in the world.

"Oscar will help us all he can," said Rosa, blushing a bit as she used his christian name; "and he can get the passports and everything without any trouble. He has his already, and suggests that we shall have one for Hans as well. I've seen Hans, and he has consented to go if he can get leave. He doesn't think he can, but agrees we had better get one in case. That will be for you."

"Won't there be some sort of description of him on it?" I asked.

"I can arrange that," declared Feldmann. "Luckily it is in my department. It will do for you, and, of course, he'll never see it."

"I shall take charge of everything," said Rosa. "And Oscar says he can get everything through in three days at the latest, perhaps in two."

There was a great deal of Oscar would do this and Oscar could do that, in it all; but everything seemed as good as the best, and I was soon in as high spirits as the others. It was settled that we should travel by the morning express, which would get us across the frontier in time for me to let Rosa have my confession the following day.

"Oscar" wrung my hand again at parting, as if I was his dearest friend; declared he was not among the English haters; that he thought I had acted splendidly in risking so much to rescue Nessa; and that he hoped we should be great friends after this abominable war.

My next move was to prepare for leaving the house the next day, and at supper I announced my determination. The Countess was very much against it, but afterwards I went with her alone into the drawing-room and gave her my "official" reasons.

"I want you to open your cabinet drawer, aunt; but before you do it, I'll tell you that you will find some one has been to it— —"

"Nessa?" she broke in excitedly.

"I'll tell you in a moment. You are quite right that there is some one in the house who is playing the spy, and, of course, you'll understand that if I am to join the Secret Service, it is a sheer impossibility for me to remain here with any one like that about the house."

"They shall leave it at once, Johann."

"We'll discuss that directly. You will find that the letters you so neatly put away here are just flung in anyhow in order to suggest that whoever did it was surprised and had to act in a hurry."

She unlocked the drawer then with shaky fingers and there lay the letters as I had told her. "Nessa shall leave the house to-morrow, Johann," she cried immediately.

"But it wasn't Miss Caldicott at all, aunt; it was Gretchen;" and I described what I had witnessed and went on to advise her not to take any open notice of the matter at all. "You know now who it is and can be on your guard, keeping such papers as are of no account here and putting others in a safer place."

"But to have such a person in the house, Johann!"

"She can't do any harm now; and you must remember this. You don't know who has put her here nor the reason. It might do much more harm than good if you were to make any disturbance about it. These are curious times, and the fact that you have an English girl in the house may be the reason. By sending Gretchen about her business you may only have some one else put here, or one of the other servants bribed or forced to take her place;" and I hammered away at this until I persuaded her to adopt the suggestion.

I had a strong object in taking this line. I was sure that Gretchen was von Erstein's creature, and that if she remained in the house, we might find her very useful in putting him off the scent by letting her find out some false facts in case of trouble.

During the night I thought carefully over our conspiracy scheme. It looked good; very good indeed; perhaps too good, and in the end I decided to prepare for a possible hitch in case the unexpected happened.

I couldn't see one anywhere; but you can never be prepared for an air pocket, as I knew well enough; so I resolved not to be caught unawares. If anything went wrong on the journey, it was on the cards that we might be able to dodge the trouble and get away, if we were provided with good disguises. I worked on that idea and thought of several other items which would probably come in handy.

I adopted the notion of turning myself into an aero mechanic and changing Nessa into my young assistant. There wasn't much about any sort of flying machine I didn't know—except Zeppelins, of course; so I could keep my end up all right, and could easily coach "my assistant" well enough to pass muster.

We should have to dodge the beastly German system which makes every workman carry his record card about with him; but if we couldn't get things of the sort, we must put up a bluff—have lost them or something—and trust to my skill with the tools to see us through.

I was off pretty early in the morning on the hunt for rooms, and almost immediately found a place which fitted my needs like a glove. It was a little furnished flat in the Falkenplatz; just a couple of rooms with a bathroom at the rear, the window of which opened on to the fire escape; an emergency exit which might be invaluable in case of need.

But there was a hitch when I said I would take the place. I was asked for the inevitable papers to satisfy the police; and of course I had none. My explanation was listened to politely, but without effect; so I said I would obtain them, paid a deposit, and went off to buy some of the little items I had thought of during the night.

Then I had a bit of a jar. I was coming out of a shop just as a tall, grey-haired, soldierly man in uniform was passing who glanced casually at me.

The glance was followed by a start of surprise, his look became intent and interested, and he stopped as if to speak. Naturally I took no notice and walked on; but a few seconds afterwards he passed me, stopped a few yards ahead to look in a shop window, and as I overtook him, he turned to give me a very keen, penetrating stare.

Of course there were heaps of people in Germany who had known me well, and I had discounted the risk of running against some of them. But I could not place him, and I was not a little relieved when he appeared uncertain and went off without addressing me.

It was a disturbing incident and brought home to me the advisability of keeping indoors as much as possible during the days I was to remain in Berlin. The matter didn't end there, however.

Remembering Hoffnung's hint about keeping my appointment with Baron von Gratzen punctually, I turned up a little before time, and exactly on the stroke of eleven was shown into his office. My astonishment may be guessed when he proved to be the stranger I had just met.

I think that his amazement was even greater than mine, as he stared at the slip on which his subordinate had written my name and from it to me.

"Then you are Herr Lassen?" he asked in frowning perplexity.

I bowed and held out the letter he had sent me. "You sent for me, sir."

He waved me to a chair and sat back lost in thought for so long that I began to wonder what the dickens was coming.

"You came from England, didn't you?"

"I believe so, sir."

"And you're the man without a memory, eh? Very extraordinary; very extraordinary indeed. Most remarkable case. And why have you come to Berlin?"

"Herr Hoffnung brought me. I understood he had instructions to do so."

"Tell me about your experiences there."

I looked as blank as a wall and shook my head.

"Surely you can remember something. Let me jog your memory. I know the country well, you understand. Were you in London?" After another blank look from me, he took out a paper, glanced over it, and questioned me about a number of places and matters contained in it; to all of which I replied with either a vacant look or shake of the head.

The examination lasted for some considerable time, and presently he pushed a sheet of paper and a pen to me, telling me to write my name. I had expected some such test and took hold of the pen clumsily and, with infinite apparent trouble, wrote the name "Johann Lassen" in big sprawling printed capitals.

He watched me like a lynx at the job, took the paper, scanned it closely, and asked: "That the best you can do?"

"I can read the big letters of type, sir," I replied, and I fancied that he had to restrain a smile.

Next he folded down the paper he had been reading from and showed me a sentence in it. A very non-committal sentence I noticed. "You recognize the writing?" More head wagging from me. "You should, you know; it's your own handwriting;" and he put the document away, and sat thinking again.

I'd have given something to be able to read his thoughts at that moment, especially when he roused himself sufficiently to favour me with some keen stares. I couldn't resist the unpleasant thought that he suspected something; but he gave no overt sign of suspicion, and his manner was less official than friendly. After a time something in his mind brought a heavy frown to his face.

"Let me get the matter quite clear. You were blown up in the *Burgen*, found yourself in a hospital in Rotterdam with no papers of identification on you except a card, you remembered nothing at all of what had occurred, and came to Berlin with Herr Hoffnung. You know that there was only one other male passenger on the steamer, a Mr. Lamb, about whom we have some reason to be curious. Now, are you sure you are not that man?"

"I don't know, sir. I am not sure about anything except what has occurred since I was at Rotterdam."

"Well, when you arrived here the Countess von Rebling recognized you as her nephew.—Were you at Göttingen?" he asked so suddenly that I only escaped the trap by the skin of my teeth.

"I believe so, sir."

"Then, of course, there will be plenty of people there to identify you."

"Naturally, sir," I managed to reply, although a chill of dismay made my spine tingle at the meaning smile accompanying the words.

"We know, of course, that no one of the name of Lamb was ever there," he said and paused again, as if to give me time to absorb all that this might be intended to suggest.

"Do you speak English?" was the next question, put with a perfect accent in my own language.

"Sure," I replied, with what I meant to be a very correct twang. But it didn't appear to impress him as much as I could have wished; and after regarding me curiously for a moment or two he rose, got a volume of Mark Twain's *Innocents Abroad*, and laid it open before me, asking me to try and read a passage.

I looked at it earnestly and gave it up as hopeless.

But he was too many for me. "Well, I'll read it to you and get you to repeat it after me." And he did read it and I had to repeat the words in such American as I could manage. "Thank you," he said as he closed the book and put it away again. And then another long pause followed.

I recalled Hoffnung's disturbing words—that the Baron would have something to tell me I might not like. He had certainly made that good, and I was beginning to be abominably troubled about the run of things when he started in again.

"And so you wish to join our Secret Service?" he asked with the abrupt shift of subject which worried me.

"Herr Hoffnung told me so, but——" and I smiled vacantly.

"Do you imagine that a man without a memory would be of much use to us?"

"I'm afraid not, sir; but to tell the truth, I have no sort of desire to do it. The doctors at Rotterdam told me I should recover my memory in time, and if I could have a good rest and just be absolutely quiet for a time it is all I wish."

He nodded, not unkindly, and then suddenly bent on me the keenest look I have ever seen in any man's eyes and asked: "Are you sure you mean that?"

"Absolutely, sir, on my honour," meeting his eyes steadily.

He held them for a moment with the same intentness, as if he would read my inmost thoughts, and then nodded and leant back in his seat. "I can understand that and believe you. I'm glad to hear it."

What he meant I couldn't tell, but I felt relieved because I appeared to have risen in his opinion, for some reason it was impossible even to guess. Some minutes passed before any more was said, the longest silence yet. That he had evidently been running over all that had passed his next move showed.

"I am intensely interested in your case, and quite as intensely puzzled about it all. Personally, I take your view—that the best thing would be to give you time to see if the memory comes back. But that's rather a point for the doctors than for me. You have done very valuable work for us in England and, other things turning out all right, there is no doubt you could do more of the same sort. But these are times when we can't do all we might; matters are too strenuous. Except for this loss of memory, you seem to be absolutely normal—doctors again; and you'd better see them at once;" and he rang his table bell. "If you pass them and, from your appearance I have no doubt you will, you will, of course, go to the Front."

I caught my breath at this, but he did not see my consternation, as he had risen while speaking and went out, leaving his secretary, named von Welten, to remain with me.

CHAPTER VIII
VON ERSTEIN

Baron von Gratzen was away some minutes; and exceedingly unpleasant minutes they were for me. At first I could see nothing but checkmate to all my plans. That the doctors would pass me as fit for service in the field was beyond question; and, as Germany wanted as many men as possible in the fighting line, I was certain to be packed off without any delay.

But then I needed only a delay of a couple of days—the papers would be ready by then—and it was still possible that something might happen which would give me just enough time to get away. It was a devil of a mess, however; and it cost me no end of an effort to pull myself together by the time the Baron came back and himself took me to the doctors.

They had been primed about the case, and all three of them were as deeply interested in me as the others had been in Rotterdam. One of them was a specialist in such cases, and he conducted the first part of the examination—that in regard to my memory. He put numberless questions on all sorts of subjects, endeavouring in every conceivable way to get me to admit that I could remember something; but I had no great difficulty in answering him. He appeared to lay most stress on everything that had occurred immediately before the explosion on the *Burgen*; and was still on that when the Baron came back to us, listened to his concluding questions and suggestions, and then took him out of the room.

The physical examination followed. I stripped to the buff, and a very few minutes sufficed to satisfy them about my fitness. I was, of course, in the pink of condition and as hard as nails.

"You must have had military training," said one of them.

"That can't be so, so far as I know. I understand I've been travelling about the world for a long time."

"I'm sure of it," was the positive verdict. "Every muscle tells the tale too plainly for any one to be mistaken. Just stand over there; I want to look at your back;" and he placed me close to the wall, and stepped back some distance himself.

"No, perhaps not," he murmured, and just as I was chuckling at his blunder, he suddenly yelled at me in English, "'Shun!" with military abruptness. Instinctively, being for the instant quite off my guard, I brought my heels together and straightened up. He chuckled, and I could have cursed myself for an idiot in having given the show away.

The doctor who had trapped me couldn't contain his delight. "I knew I couldn't be mistaken. You can put your clothes on," he told me, rubbing his hands gleefully, and after another chortle to his colleague, he hurried off to report the result of his experiment.

I was mad at having made such a blithering ass of myself just when things had been going so well. The game was up, of course, and there was nothing for it but to face the music. It was now a toss up whether I should be packed off to the front or popped into prison, and it didn't need a Solomon to see that the odds strongly favoured the latter.

The Baron and the two doctors came back in about five minutes, and the man who had bowled me out was laughingly rubbing it in to the specialist.

"I can't imagine how it escaped you, Gorlitz," he said as they entered; and the specialist looked about as pleased as I felt.

"Try it again," he growled in a half-whisper.

"He may be prepared this time," was the reply in an undertone, but not low enough to prevent my hearing it. I couldn't get the hang of things for the moment; but when, after a few desultory questions, the doctor pretended to take some measurements and then turned me with my back to him again, I knew what was coming, and I thought I would do a little bit of pantomime of my own.

They spoke together in low tones, and in the middle of it the doctor yelled "'Shun!" at me once more. I started, hesitated and then came to attention, but not nearly so smartly as before.

"Just turn round," called the specialist. "Now, march across the room." I obeyed, and was halfway across when the doctor shouted "Halt!" I stopped instantly.

"There you are," exclaimed the doctor. The specialist nodded, told me to sit down, and plied me with all sorts of questions about the army, appearing rather pleased than otherwise when I failed to answer them.

A long pow-wow followed between the three doctors and was developing into a pretty hot wrangle whether my having obeyed the word of command was really a recurrence of memory or not, when the Baron intervened and I was sent back to his room with his subordinate.

"You have set them a difficult problem, Herr Lassen," he said to me when he joined me after some ten minutes; "and given me one also. But it will do no harm to postpone the decision about you for a few days, at any rate. You have no idea how you come to know the English words of command?"

I affected to think deeply. "Can I have been in the army there?" I asked, looking blankly at him.

He smiled and then nodded. "Yes, you are a deserter. Your report says that you joined it to obtain certain information."

"It's very odd, sir."

"Very," he replied a little drily. "It makes it a little difficult in regard to a suggestion Dr. Gorlitz threw out; he's the mental specialist, you know. He thinks it not improbable that if you were placed again in the surroundings immediately preceding the shock which deprived you of your memory, it would greatly facilitate its recovery. Perhaps your only chance of doing so. But you might not care to run such a risk. You should understand that I wish to help you in any way I can," he added kindly.

"I am very much obliged to you, sir. Of course it would be a risk, but my great wish is to get my memory back."

"Does that mean you would like to go back to England?"

I could scarcely believe my ears and tried to conceal my overwhelming delight under the cover of frowning consideration. "The risk wouldn't frighten me, sir."

"Very well. I'll see about it. That's about as far as we can get to-day; but there's one thing I should tell you. There is some one in Berlin who knows you and declares that your loss of memory is a mere pretence, and that you have assumed it because of some exceedingly sinister business in which you were involved a year or two ago."

I could smile at that sincerely. "Can you tell me his name?"

He paused a moment. "There will be no harm, if you keep it to yourself; I don't believe the story, but then I know the man too well. It is Count von Erstein."

"He's a scoundrel, I know that; but it may be the truth, of course."

"We won't discuss him," said the Baron, rising. "I only told you to put you on your guard because of the genuine interest I take in you;" and with that he shook hands and was sending me away, when I remembered my difficulty that morning about papers of identification. I explained it to him and he sent for von Welten and instructed him to do what was necessary.

I left the place feeling pretty much as any one would feel who had rubbed his back against a prison door and by the merest squeak escaped finding himself on the wrong side of the bars. The whole business baffled me. Knowing as I did so well the usual methods of German officialism, the Baron's treatment was incomprehensible; and rack my wits as I would, I could not hit on a clue to explain it.

And then the luck of it! Actually to be sent back to England with official credentials! I could have whooped for joy! But as it was already passed the time I was to lunch with von Erstein, I rushed back to the Falkenplatz, made sure of the little flat, and then cabbed it to von Erstein's address.

What a rotter the brute was, I reflected as I thought of the story he had already spread about me. He meant to make things hot for me and no mistake, and had lost no time in setting to work. And what a brick the old Count, to have given me that warning. If I had been going to stop in Berlin, I might have taken von Erstein's enmity seriously; but as it was I could afford to laugh at him, for a few days at the most would see both Nessa and me out of the country, if the luck only held.

I was so late in reaching the Gallenstrasse, where von Erstein had his sumptuous flat, that he had already begun lunch. "I'd given you up, Lassen," he said as I entered. "Thought something might have happened with old Gratz to detain you. He's a downy old bird. Sit there, will you. Everything all right?"

"Why shouldn't it be?" I knew what he meant.

He turned the question off and we talked about nothing in particular until lunch was over, except that every now and then he shot in a question which might have committed me if I had not been on my guard. But I had been through the mill so thoroughly that morning that the part I was playing had grown into my bones, so to speak.

"Now we can chat at our ease," he said as we settled into easy chairs. "Is it still your habit to smoke a cigarette before a cigar?" he asked, grinning, as he held the box toward me.

"Was that one of my habits, then?" I countered, declining the little trap.

"All right, you do it very well. Ought to be on the stage, on my word you ought," he said with a broader leer. "But now, let's get to grips. How do we two stand?"

"About what?"

"Don't fool about in that way. You know what I mean."

"I shall when you tell me."

"Do you want to have me for a friend or the other thing?"

"I told you yesterday I wasn't likely to quarrel with any one who has such influence as you have."

"And I told you that it would be a bad day's work for you if we did quarrel; and quarrel we shall if you try to beat about the bush, as you're doing now. I believe in plain talk; and you'd better bear that in mind, not only now but always."

"Then let me have some plain talk now."

"You shall," taking his cigar out and flicking off the ash. "I've only to utter a word or two and I can flick you out of my way as easily as I flicked that ash off. Mind that, too."

I laughed. "You have a pleasant way with you, von Erstein."

"I don't care a curse about pleasantness or unpleasantness. When I want a thing, I have it. And what I want now is that English girl at the von Reblings', and you'd better be careful not to get in my way about it."

"How am I likely to be in your way?"

"Because you're a relative of the von Reblings, my friend, and you're going to marry the fair Rosa, whom, by the way, I can tell you as an old hand you'll find a handful. But she likes the English girl and will try to influence you, and if I know her, as I certainly do, she'll succeed, if I don't stop it."

"Stop it? How?"

"By showing you on which side your bread has the butter. Now look here. I know a heap about you; quite enough to queer your pitch with the von Reblings and put an end to your engagement and lose you the coin on which you're counting. All this rot about a loss of memory is just— —" and he waved his cigar in the air to emphasize his meaning.

"What do you know about me?"

"Oh, don't try that fool's game on me."

"But I should be intensely interested in the story. I'm itching to know all about myself," I persisted, seeing how this line provoked him.

"Where did you go from Göttingen, my young friend?" he asked with a meaning nod, as if the question would confound me.

"How the devil do I know?"

"You went to Hanover. You know that perfectly well."

"Did I? And do I? You're getting me regularly mixed, you know." I was delighted to see that he was fast losing his temper.

"You did. And when you were there you had a friend, who called himself Gossen; but was in reality a Frenchman, named Gaudet. Don't say you don't remember, because it will be a lie," he snarled.

"That's an ugly word, von Erstein."

"And the whole thing was an ugly business. He was a spy and wanted some secrets; you were able to find them out; and you were suddenly found to be in possession of a big sum of money. How did you get it?"

"Honestly, I hope," I answered with intentional flippancy.

"How did you get it? And how did you get the information, too? That's the question; and if you won't answer it, I can. But you'd better not force me to open my lips."

"I'm beginning to get awfully interested. Like a story, isn't it?" and I laughed.

"You'd better laugh while you can," he rapped, swearing viciously.

"Of course you mean I sold the information to the Frenchman and that that accounts for my having that sudden money."

"I not only mean it, I can prove it. Prove it, do you understand that?"

I gave him another grin and shook my head. "Some one's been pulling your leg, von Erstein. The whole thing's just bosh."

"It's no good, Lassen. I've got you here;" and he held out his hand and clenched it. "Here! And no wriggling humbug about loss of memory will help you to get out."

"I must be an infernal blackguard, then."

"That's the truest thing you've said since you came. It's just what you are; and the von Reblings ought to know it."

"You haven't told me how I got that valuable information yet. I should like to know that."

"If you'll let that lost memory of yours wake up for a second, just long enough to remember the name of Anna Hilden, you'll know all about it without a word from me." His sneering suggestive tone clearly showed that this was one of his trump cards, and he fixed his eyes on me, keenly watching for the effect.

"But my memory won't oblige me by waking up, you see. Had she anything to do with it?"

"To the devil with all your pretended innocence! You know she had, and that you induced her to worm it out of the man she was to have married, if you hadn't come in the road; just as you're trying now with me," he cried, scowling at me threateningly. "But you've got a man to deal with this time, not a woman, and the wrong sort of man too."

I dropped the bantering tone and answered seriously. "Of course all you say may be the gospel truth, but I give you my word that I haven't the faintest recollection of anything you've mentioned."

He laughed scornfully. "That's a lie," he growled with an oath.

I had had more than enough and I got up. "If this weren't your own place, I'd cram that word down your throat; and the next time we meet, wherever it is, I'll do it," I told him.

He seemed to understand that I meant it, and a change came over his face. "I'll take that back," he muttered. "Sit down again."

I didn't sit down, but I stopped. Either he was as arrant a coward as such a brute was likely to be and I had scared him, or some thought had struck him which accounted for the change.

He let his cigar drop; made a to-do in finding it, pitching it away, and lighting another; and it was an easy guess that all this was to gain time. Then he sat thinking, fiddling nervously with a very singular ring he wore on his middle finger. He saw me looking at it and, no doubt to get a little more time to think, he spoke of it.

"You're looking at this," he said, holding up the hand. I nodded, and he drew it off and handed it me. "It's a puzzle ring I picked up in China," he explained, showing how it was really a little chain of rings which fitted very ingeniously to form a single ring.

I examined it and, still to gain time, he told me to try and put it together. I did try and failed, and when he had thought out his problem, he took it back and showed me the fitting.

"I'm sorry I lost my temper just now, Lassen," he said in a very different tone from his former angry one. "It's always a fool's game. But I did really believe you were shamming about your memory. What I told you about the Hanover business is quite true, however, and the fact that you don't remember it, wouldn't make an atom of difference with our people. But now, what about the English girl?"

I hesitated a second and then resumed my seat. "I'm willing to listen to you," I said; and he couldn't keep the satisfaction out of his fat, tell-tale face. He reckoned that he had frightened me, of course.

"What are you going to do about her?" was his next question.

"What *you* want to do is the point, man."

"She's a spy and ought to be interned."

"And why are you so keen about that? You said a little while back that you wanted her; how's the internment going to help you there?"

"She'd be sent to Krustadt and the Commandant— — Never mind; you can leave the rest to me. You won't know anything."

I couldn't trust myself to speak for a time, I was so furious at the suggestiveness of the leering brute's words and manner. But there was probably more to learn yet, so I choked down my rage and at last even forced myself to nod and smile meaningly. "And my part?" I asked.

"Two things; both easy enough. Old Gratz has shoved a spoke in the wheel so far, curse him, and as you're in the house you can tell him you know I'm right that she is a spy and you can give him proofs."

"Proofs?" I echoed, with a start.

"I said proofs, didn't I? I'll give you some papers and you can plant one or two on her and give the rest to him saying you've found them in her room or somewhere. He'll be obliged to order a search then, and that'll do the trick."

"Confound the thing!" I exclaimed, jumping up and wringing my fingers as if I'd burnt them with my cigar.

"Here, take another," he said, and by the time I had lit it, I had myself in hand again.

"But if she was caught red-handed like that, she might be shot, and that wouldn't help you much."

"You leave that to me," he replied with a leer and a wink. "The question is, are you going to help me?"

"I don't like it, von Erstein, and that's the truth," I said.

"I didn't ask you that."

"And if I do help you?"

He put his fat finger to his lips. "Mum about that Hanover business."

"And if I don't?"

He paused, squinting hard at me. "I think you will."

I affected to consider the proposal. "But why take this roundabout trouble to get her? If you want to marry her, why not ask her?"

That touched his Teutonic sense of humour and he burst into loud and evidently genuine laughter. "Why didn't you marry Anna Hilden? Because you could get her without, wasn't it? Same here, of course."

"It comes to this, then," I said after a pause. "You think you know that I played the traitor in that Hanover business in a way that renders me liable to be shot; but that you're willing to hush it up if I'll help to put Miss Caldicott into your power. That about it?"

"Put it how you like," he growled, not relishing the bald statement. "But you'd better toe the line, my friend, and at once. Now, what are you going to do?"

"I'll toe the line, von Erstein."

He chuckled. "I thought you'd see wisdom," he sneered.

"Not quite as you think, however. What I'm going to do is"—and I paused—"to give you forty-eight hours to clear out of Berlin; and if I find you here then, I'll not only tell the von Reblings the whole of your confounded scheme, but I'll tell Baron von Gratz as well. And I'm thundering glad you've put that card in my hands."

CHAPTER IX
A BREAD RIOT

It would be difficult for any one to appear more absolutely dumbfounded than von Erstein when I delivered my ultimatum and got up.

That I had scared him, his chalk-white cheeks showed unmistakably, while the quiver of his lips, clenched hands, and the fierce light in his piggish little eyes testified to his rage. He jumped up instantly to stop my going.

"Don't go, Lassen, at all events in that way. Let's talk it over," he clamoured. "The thing can be explained and we can come to an understanding."

"You swine!" I growled. "Get out of the way or I shall forget I'm in your room and lay my hands on you."

He tried not to wince, but was too much of a cur. "Look here, I'm not going to utter a word about that Hanover business. I swear that," he said as I went to the door.

"You've done it already, you lying hypocrite. You know that; and so do I. I've heard of it, and I shall hear if you say any more. And by Heaven, if you dare to say another syllable about it, I'll—well, keep out of my way afterwards, that's all"; and I left him to judge for himself what I would do.

I had to go. I should have mauled the brute if I'd stopped. I was mad with fury; and I walked off, unable for the time to think of anything but his disgusting cowardice and bestiality. I'm no saint, and don't pretend to be one; but this brute's infernal plan to get Nessa into his power was more than flesh and blood could stand. I believe, anyway I hope, I should have felt just as hot if any other girl had been concerned.

I ramped about the streets, taking little notice where I went, and it was not until some of my fury had cooled that I began to consider what steps I ought to take. I was glad I had lost my temper and gone for him; but after a while it began to dawn on me that I had blundered badly. All I needed was to gain a few days' delay; and it would have been far more diplomatic if I had seemed to fall in with his plans and just made a few excuses to account for any inaction.

But one can't always be worrying about diplomacy; and anyhow the beggar was thoroughly scared. Probably he'd be just as much put to it to hit on a new offensive as I was to decide what to do next; and whatever happened I wasn't going to be sorry I'd let myself go. What I was sorry for was that I hadn't been able to "go" with my hands instead of only words.

It wouldn't do merely to twiddle my thumbs, however; and after a while it struck me that the best thing would be to get another interview with old Gratz and just tell him the whole pretty story. If it did no good, it would do no harm, and certainly it would prepare him for any other scheme by von Erstein to prove Nessa to be a spy.

At this point some one clapped me on the shoulder. "Hallo, Cousin Johann, whatever are you doing in this out-of-the-way place?"

It was Hans. "If it comes to that, what are you doing, young man?"

"There's a shindy on in the Untergasse, and I've been watching it. A lot of women kicking up a row about food, or something. It looked like getting warm, so I thought it time to go home."

"Let's go and look at it," I said directly. I had heard rumours in England about bread riots and rather liked the idea of seeing one for myself, and I recalled what the tailor had said about it.

The place was close at hand; and sure enough there was a big crowd and a noisy one, too. Quite a couple of hundred women with a sprinkling of men, and as much noise as at an Irish faction fight. We stood a minute or two at the corner of the street when Hans caught sight of a friend, and asking me to wait for him, ran off.

I observed that although there were police about, the tailor was right in saying they were not taking the usual steps to stop the row; and I noticed also that the crowd was growing in numbers and moving in my direction.

Then came the sound of smashing glass, with loud shouts from the women who clustered round the spot where the smash had been, and I went down the street far enough to see that a baker's shop had been forced.

The police interfered then; but it was too late, and there were too few of them. Moreover, the mob had tasted blood, or rather smelt food; and soon afterwards there was another smash; this time a provision shop. The crowd had been allowed to get out of hand; and I saw some of the police rush away, presumably to telephone for more men.

I was standing in the road at that moment and had to skip aside to avoid an open car which came rattling down the street toward the mob. An old lady and a girl were in the car, and as they passed me, the latter stood up and called excitedly to the chauffeur to stop.

If it hadn't been a German he would never have been fool enough to have attempted to enter the street at all; but I suppose he had been told to take that route, and his instinct of slavish obedience to orders did the rest. The result was what any one might have foreseen.

He was too late to turn back, and his one chance to get through was to have driven bang into the crowd and trusted to luck to clear a way. As it was, he came to a halt on the very verge of the crowd; and in less time than it takes to tell it, the car was the centre of a yelping, hungry mob of viragos to whom the sight of rich people in a costly car was like a good meal spread before a lot of famished wild beasts.

Worse than this, moreover, was the fact that some ruffians who had been hanging back began to push their way toward the car, whose occupants were calling for the police. They might as well have cried for the moon; and every cry was greeted with jeers and yells of anger from the women around. The trouble soon thickened.

One woman more reckless than the rest started a shout to have the two out of the car, and herself jumped on the step, grabbed the chauffeur, who seemed about paralyzed with fright, lugged him off his seat, and the crowd hustled and jabbed and cuffed him, till he was lost in the throng. Then some one opened the door of the car, and made a snatch at the dress of the girl, who set up screaming.

This was too much; so I shoved and shouldered my way through, pushed aside the woman who had tried to grab the girl, and urged the two panic-stricken ladies to come out. They hesitated, however, and a filthy hooligan with a long iron-shod bludgeon barked curses at me for a Junker and aimed a vicious blow at my head. I managed to dodge it, and jabbed him one in return on the mouth which sent him staggering back and enabled me to snatch his stick away.

Armed with this, I soon cleared a space about the car and again urged the two frightened occupants to leave it. The girl jumped out at once and had to help her mother, while I kept the mob at bay, and then fought a sort of rearguard action in miniature.

But we hadn't a dog's chance of escape. The mother was half an invalid, and could only move very slowly, while the women round, furious at being baulked of their prey and led by the brute I had hit and a couple of his cronies who had come up meanwhile, surged round us like a lot of devils gone mad.

We reached the pavement, however, and as I spied a deepish doorway, I changed my tactics and made for it, treating some of those who stood in the way pretty roughly. We were able to gain the doorway all right, and I hustled my two charges into momentary safety behind me and told the girl to keep hammering at the door till some one opened it, while I tried to keep the crowd back.

It was no picnic; but I reckoned on being able to stem the rush for the minute or so until some one came in reply to the girl's knocking. It was in our favour that the fight we had already put up had rendered some of those in the front of the crowd a little chary about coming too close; and as the doorway was very narrow and the stick I had captured a long one, I put it across the outside, thus forming a useful barrier, and was able to hold it in position by standing back at arm's length, and thus almost out of reach of both the hands and feet of those in front.

To my dismay, however, no attempt was made to let us enter the house, although the girl had kept up an incessant knocking. The mob soon tumbled to this and things began to look ugly. The old lady, scared to death and ill, was on the verge of collapse; the daughter, almost equally panicky and alarmed by her mother's condition, stopped hammering at the door and bent over her; the crowd was getting more furious every moment; those at the back began to push those in front forward, the brute I had struck first came on with the rest, and I came in for some pretty hot smacks and kicks.

But the little barrier of the stick kept off the worst, and, as every second was of vital importance, since help might come from a reinforcement of the police, I took the gruelling and just held on.

A couple more invaluable minutes were gained in this way when another of the men, a dirty little red-haired beggar, more wary than the others, tumbled to the weak spot in my defence—my hold on the stick. He tried his fists on my hands first, and finding that was no good he whipped out a pocket knife and jabbed me with it.

I loosed the right hand and dropped him with a tap on the nose which brought the blood in a stream and gave him something else to think about. But his two companions had seen his little dodge and made ready to flatter it with imitation, so I had to adopt other tactics.

I was pretty reckless by that time, and in no mood to be man-handled by a set of German roughs; so I changed the barrier into a weapon of offence; it made a fine sort of pike with its ironshod end; and I used it without scruple or mercy. I drove it slap into the face of the man who had struck me first, then into the chest of the fellow next him, and lastly downed a third with a crack on the skull.

That accounted for all the men and took off a lot of the edge of the crowd's appetite for more. They fell back a pace or two and I stepped in front of the archway, swung the bludgeon over my head and swore that I'd brain the first person, man or woman, who moved a single foot forward.

Nobody in the front ranks seemed in any hurry to accept the invitation; but again those at the back, who had no knowledge of the happenings, began to shove forward, and slowly the people in front were pushed forward against their will and despite their efforts to resist the pressure.

The result was plain. I couldn't break every head in sight, of course, and I was at my wit's end what to do, when a really happy thought occurred to me. I had a lot of small money in my pocket, whipped it out, and sent it scattering into the street.

"If it's money you want, there it is," I shouted at the top of my lung power, and sent a second lot after the first.

It was a truly gorgeous scheme. I yelled loud enough for nearly all to hear, and the flash of the coins did the rest; the pressure round the mouth of our shelter was relieved instantly, and both back and front rows joined in a fearsome scramble in the middle of the road, where I had been careful to shy the money. I never saw a finer scrimmage in my life.

"We can go," I called to the couple behind me, seeing that the pavement was clear enough for us to get away. But the elder woman had fallen and was incapable of any effort whatever.

"Have you any small money?" I asked the girl. "My own's all gone."

She felt her own pockets and in the handbag on her mother's arm and gave all she could find.

It was enough to keep the crowd busy for another minute or two, and I stepped out, and just as the people were easing off from the first diversion of the scramble, I yelled out that there was more to come, and flung the whole lot broadcast among the tossing heads, taking care to shy it as far down the street as possible. There was an instant rush for it.

I slipped back into the doorway, picked up the old lady and made a dash for it, telling the girl to bring the stick with her and keep close to the houses, which by that time were all shut and barred.

We managed to get some yards toward the street corner when two of the men who had given us trouble spied us, and, thinking that I was now unarmed, came rushing in pursuit, calling to a lot of the others to follow.

They soon overtook us, and there was nothing for it but to put up another fight, this time without the friendly help of a doorway. I laid my burden on the pavement, took the stick from the girl, and turned to face the oncomers. The instant they saw I was still armed, they pulled up in surprise and hesitated. I promptly seized the moment of their consternation and went straight at them, clubbed the nearest and was making for the next when I heard a whoop behind me, suggesting an attack from the rear.

I turned to meet it, and to my intense relief saw Hans standing by the two ladies. "Come on, Hans," I called, and he was by my side in a jiffy. We had a rough and tumble for a few seconds in which he joined like a brick, and then relief arrived. We heard the sound of horses, with the jingle of accoutrements, and the next moment a small troop of cavalry turned the corner of the street, and we left the rest of the proceedings to them. They soon scattered the mob, who fled in all directions except ours, and the street was quickly cleared, leaving the car the one conspicuous feature in the foreground.

As the chauffeur was nowhere to be seen and the old lady couldn't walk, I sent Hans back to her and went to see if the car had been much damaged. It had certainly been in the wars; stripped of everything, even to the cushions, but the engine was all right, so I started it, climbed in, and backed to the spot where the ladies were.

Then it flashed suddenly on me what an ass I was making of myself to let any one see that I knew anything about cars; but it was too late to make a pretence now, and I consoled myself with the reflection that there was no need to let the people know who I was.

But there I reckoned without Hans. The mother had sufficiently recovered to get up, and was speaking to him when I reached them, while Hans and the daughter were casting sheep's eyes at each other in a fashion which told tales. They were evidently old friends, and a little bit more; and I wasn't, therefore, surprised when the mother knew me as Lassen, Hans' cousin.

She was awfully sweet and grateful and the tears trembled in her eyes as she thanked me, holding my hand in both of hers, declaring that both she and her daughter owed me their lives, and making so much of the matter, that I had to chip in with a suggestion that she had better get home as soon as possible.

"But how?" she exclaimed hopelessly. "Where's Wilhelm?"

But Wilhelm, evidently the chauffeur, was nowhere to be seen; and there was nothing for it but to volunteer to drive the car myself.

All this time friend Hans had been making the best of his opportunity with the daughter, who also thanked me profusely when I had helped her mother into the car.

"Where am I to drive?" I asked as I took the wheel.

"Hans knows the way," suggested the daughter, with the faintest little flush of confusion as she hazarded the suggestion. He grinned.

"Come along then, Hans," I said; and he nipped in and told me where to go and which way to take.

"Rather a nice little child," I said presently, chipping him; the girl was about sixteen, I guessed, as her hair was still down. But he resented the speech.

"Child! She's only a year younger than I am," he exclaimed quite indignantly.

"So that's how the wind blows, eh?"

"I wish to Heaven I'd come up sooner; but I say, you did make a fight of it, cousin. Nita's been telling me all about it. She says they'd have been torn to pieces if it hadn't been for you. You're a lucky beggar!"

"I don't take too kindly to that sort of luck, Hans, I can tell you."

"I only wish it had been mine," he declared regretfully.

"You did all right as it was when you came; and of course she saw you. Rather a pretty name—Nita."

He smiled self-consciously and coloured. "But her mother didn't; if she had it might change her opinion and——" He didn't finish the sentence and exclaimed: "But I say, you do know how to handle a car!"

This didn't suit me, however, so I went back to the pretty Nita. "The mother's against it all, eh?"

"Only for the silly reason that we're too young. And I shall be an officer in a month or two; but the Baroness is like Rosa in that, she can't understand when a fellow's grown up."

"It'll come all right when you've been in the army a year or two," I said consolingly.

"A year or two," he exclaimed in some dismay.

"Well, if she won't wait for you as long as that, she isn't worth bothering about, Hans."

But he wasn't in a mood for any philosophic consolation. "But she will; she's said so a hundred times. There's no doubt about her; but there's something else; somebody else, rather."

"And which are you? Number one or number two?"

"Oh, I don't mean with her; but old Gratz has some one else."

"And what's he got to do with it?"

"Johann! Seeing that he's her father, he's got everything to do with it, of course."

This was something like a jar in all truth. He was about the last soul in Berlin who ought to know that I had so far recovered my memory as to be able to handle the car. "Do you mean that this old lady is Baron von Gratzen's wife?"

"Of course she is. I thought you knew it."

CHAPTER X
COMPLICATIONS

The fact that it was Baron von Gratzen's wife and daughter whom I had managed to snatch from the clutches of the mob was startling, and might have vital consequences. But whether it would help or harm me, it was difficult to decide.

The first impression was that it was rotten luck. By all accounts Lassen was far too great a coward to have faced the mob; and that fact alone was dangerous since it tended to emphasize the difference between us. More than enough had transpired in the interview with the Baron to show that he already suspected I was not Lassen; and this business might put the finishing touch to his suspicions. My handling of the car, moreover, might be accepted as an additional proof of the impersonation.

There was of course another side. It was his wife and child who had been rescued; and if he hadn't a stone in place of a heart, he was bound to feel some amount of gratitude. But would that be sufficient to cause him to smother his suspicions?

The German official is commonly a two-natured individual; showing one side in his private life and the other in his office. His manner to me that morning had been friendly enough; but that was after his suspicions had been quieted and he had regarded me as Lassen. What the effect would be when his suspicions were again roused, it was impossible to say.

If he was like many of those I had known in the old days, he would be quite capable of professing and even feeling the deepest gratitude privately and at home, and the next minute at his office regretting, with tears in his eyes, that his duty compelled him to pack me off to gaol. That's the worst of Teutonic sentimentality. It's pretty much like a compass needle in an electric storm; you never know where it will point next.

When we reached the house nothing would satisfy the Baroness but that I should go in so that her husband should have an opportunity of thanking me; and in we went. It was a relief to find that he wasn't home; but she would not hear of my leaving until she was satisfied that I was not seriously hurt, and wished to send straight off for a doctor to examine me.

Discussion resulted as usual in a compromise, and Hans carried me off to the bathroom. There was nothing the matter that soap and water and a clothes-brush couldn't put right. I was very dirty; had a bruise or two, a couple of scratches on my face, and a cut on my hand where one of the men had jabbed at it to make me release my hold of the stick.

The last looked the worst, because of the drop or two of blood smeared about; but it didn't amount to anything, and I was really lucky to have got off so lightly.

While I was removing the traces of the scrap, Hans told me a good deal more about Nita and the position of affairs in the von Gratzen household, together with his impressions of Nita's father.

"I think he's a regular bear, you know. He is to me; but then he doesn't like me any more than I do him, worse luck," he said dolefully.

"Do you think the best way to get any one to like you is to begin by disliking him?"

"I didn't begin it; but he always scowls when he finds me here, talks to me as if I was a kid of ten, and calls me 'Hansikin.' It makes me regularly sick, I can tell you. Of course he's awfully decent to his wife and Nita, and they both worship him; and so does he them. But he's always trying to make fun of me; and he's such an artful old beggar that I never get a chance of scoring off him. I believe he's as big a humbug as any in Berlin. And I'm not the only one who thinks so, too."

"What you've done to-day ought to change his opinion, Hans."

"That's just my rotten luck. I came up too late to do anything, and even the little I did do, the Baroness couldn't see."

"But Nita saw it."

"And a lot he'll care for what she says. He'll just grin and say I was a good boy, or some such rot as that, and forget it."

"We'll see about that. He'll know that no boy could send a grown man headlong into the gutter as you did."

"Did I?" he cried excitedly.

The truth was that he did not; but there seemed a chance of doing him a good turn, so I described a little fictional incident of the sort, telling him that he was too excited at the moment to remember anything. "It was the turning point of the whole show, Hans, for if the beggar hadn't been downed at that very moment, they'd have got us to a cert."

"Do you think Nita saw it?" he cried boyishly.

"How could she, when her mother was lying all but fainting on the pavement? She wanted all her eyes for her."

"Just my luck!" he exclaimed with a disconsolate toss of the head, as we went downstairs.

Nita and her mother had also been using the time to repair, and both of them appeared to have rallied from the shock. I had to go through more of the thanksgiving ceremonial. Only the plea of an urgent engagement got me out of a most pressing invitation to remain to supper in order to be thanked over again by the Baron; and I had to stem the torrent of gratitude by bringing Hans' part into action.

"It's awfully sweet of you to give me all the credit, my dear madam, but you're overlooking my cousin's part; and you owe quite as much to him. I'm afraid there would have been a very different tale to tell, if he had not come up when he did."

"I didn't know that," she exclaimed in great surprise; and I saw Hans and Nita, who were snugging it together in a corner, prick up their ears.

"I don't want to make him blush," I replied, lowering my voice, and repeated the fable I had told him in the bathroom, garnishing it with one or two more or less artistic touches.

"I didn't see all that."

"Unfortunately at the moment you were not able to take notice of anything, I'm afraid."

"Nita hasn't told me about it either."

"She could not have had eyes or thoughts for any one but you just then. It's only natural, of course."

"Then I've done the boy an injustice, Herr Lassen."

"Boy!" I echoed with a start. "No boy could have done what he did, and no man could have behaved more bravely;" with special emphasis on the "man."

It worked all right. After a moment she called him up, repeated the pith of the story, and showed her gratitude in a way that made him blush like a girl. Then she kissed him and declared, to the profound delight and astonishment of them both: "That's a good-bye kiss to the boy, Hans. I shall never think of you as one again after this; neither will the Baron, I am sure. You must stop to supper and hear what he thinks of it."

He was so overwhelmed by all this that he could scarcely stammer out his acceptance of the invitation, and when I was leaving he came to the door and couldn't say enough to thank me. He had a very hazy idea of all that he had really done, and it wasn't surprising that, being a German, he was ready to accept the story as gospel and rather to preen his feathers over his own prowess.

Still he was a decent youngster, and his little harmless swagger was very intelligible. "I say, cousin," he added as he opened the door, "I wish you'd do me a favour and tell Rosa. She'll believe it, if you say it."

"Of course I will. I'm taking the Karlstrasse on my way," I promised readily. I wanted to hear if there was any news about the progress of our "conspiracy." The afternoon's affair wasn't all honey, for there was the question of its effect on the Baron; and the sooner my back was turned on Berlin the better.

It was old Gretchen's job to attend to the front door, and when she answered my ring, she told me no one was at home, and that Rosa had left a parcel for me. A glance showed that the paper wrapper was torn and that the packet had been put up clumsily as if in a great hurry by unskilled fingers. Gretchen had evidently been curious about the contents.

I opened it in her presence, therefore, as there could be no harm in her having a second look at it, and found a quaint card-case inside, with some cards printed, "Johann Lassen," and a line saying she thought I should understand and find them useful. It was rather neat of her, and clearly was intended as an assurance that she meant to keep our secret.

She came in soon afterwards and I thanked her for it. She was pleased that she had succeeded in making her intention clear; but she wasn't so pleased when she heard that old Gretchen had had a peep at the card-case. Nor was she at all overjoyed at the story of the afternoon's doings in the Untergasse. She looked mighty grave about it, indeed.

"I'm not going to say I'm pleased about it, Johann," she declared. We had agreed that it would be better practice for us to use the Christian names even when alone. "It wants thinking over."

"Your reason?"

"Von Gratzen. You saw him this morning, didn't you?"

I nodded and gave her a very brief report of what had occurred and that he had been quite friendly.

She shook her head. "You'll have to be awfully careful with him. He knows, as well as I do, that my cousin is an arrant coward, and that no man in all Berlin would be less likely to do what you did this afternoon; or could have done it, in fact. The Baron's a man I could never understand. No one can. He does the most extraordinary things; he's horribly keen and shrewd; quixotic at one time and abominably harsh at another; although from his manner you'd think he wouldn't hurt a fly."

"Well, let's hope he'll show his quixotic side over this, for it's too late to alter things;" and we were still discussing it when Feldmann arrived, and she asked him eagerly for news.

"There's a hitch, I'm sorry to say. About Hans," he reported with a worried look. "His permit to travel has been refused. They won't release him from his training even for twenty-four hours. I did all I could, I assure you, Rosa."

"And about the other?"

"Oh, that's all right, of course. A mere matter of form; and it will be ready to-morrow, I expect. But one's not much use without the other."

"Johann could use yours, Oscar," suggested Rosa.

"Not on any account," I protested. "Herr Feldmann might get into no end of a mess."

"It isn't that, Lassen. I'm so well known all along the line that it would be hopeless. You'd be spotted in a moment. I'd run the risk like a shot otherwise; I know how Rosa feels about it."

"What can we do?" she exclaimed, turning to me.

"Make the best of it. Nessa must go without me, if I can't get off; and there's no chance of that tomorrow. Will the papers have a definite date for the journey?"

"I gave the date we agreed, but I dare say I could get that altered to allow us a margin of a day or two, perhaps a week; but then this wedding is the excuse; and of course that date can't be altered. But I could see Miss Caldicott into Holland all right."

"What, with a false passport! It's awfully good of you to offer, but I'm sure she wouldn't hear of it for a second. No; we must try the other way."

"What's that?" he asked.

He shook his head ominously at the mention of von Gratzen. "I know a lot about him, and I wouldn't put a pfennig's reliance on any hope from that quarter," he said emphatically. "I don't say he won't do anything, mind you, because one never knows what he will do next. He's one of the sharpest and ablest men in the country; we all admit that; but— —" and he gestured and shrugged his shoulders.

"Unreliable?" He nodded. "In a shifty unscrupulous way, you mean?"

"Oh dear, no; not that at all," he said vigorously. "Individual. That is the best word. If he thinks a thing should be done, he does it whether it is according to official rules or not. That is not German. He is not thorough, as we understand the word."

There remained only the other plan—that Nessa and I should get away in some disguise, and at a tentative suggestion about false papers, Feldmann laughed.

"You will easily understand that when a people are subject to so many rules and regulations as we are, plenty of men set their wits to work to break them. False identification cards are as common as false coins, and if you knew where to go, a few marks would buy one, or a genuine one either, for that matter," he declared; but he made no offer to get them, and it was better not to press the thing farther then.

I left soon afterwards. The failure to get Hans' permit and all that had passed about von Gratzen served to make the position more and more difficult and complicated. The man seemed to be an enigma even to those who were in constant touch with him, and it was ridiculous to imagine, therefore, that any one who had only seen him once should understand him. A close and careful review of the interview with him threw no light on the matter. He had been exceedingly kind and friendly; but there had been a moment of startling contrast. That one keen look of his; so sharp, intent and piercing that it had seemed almost to change him into a different man; and it might well be accepted as the one instant in which the mask had been allowed to drop.

In the morning there was another incident. A curt formal summons arrived summoning me to his office at noon. This, after the previous day's job in the Untergasse! He might at least have had the decency to write a private note; and naturally enough the thing increased my uneasiness.

And then, if you please, it turned out that he had named that time as it was the hour when he went home to lunch and wished to take me with him! How could one judge such a man?

I put the note before him, with a word to the effect that I had thought it was on official business, and he laughed it away, saying he had told his secretary just to ask me to call.

He couldn't make enough of me; kept speaking to me as "My boy," and "My dear boy"; smothered me with protestations of gratitude; and capped it all by asking me to make his house my home while I was in Berlin.

That didn't appeal to me in the least. "Wouldn't it be very invidious, sir, if I was to go to you when I've only just left my aunt's?"

"I've a good mind to use my official power to compel you, my boy," he returned laughingly; "but the wife shall talk to you about it. In any case you must promise to let us see as much of you as possible."

That was easy to promise; and after a few moments we went out together.

If he wasn't sincere, then he was one of the best actors in the world either on or off the stage.

Which was he?

I could find no answer to the question. Yet everything probably depended upon it—Nessa's fate and my freedom, and possibly even my life.

CHAPTER XI
THE PROBLEM OF VON GRATZEN

As soon as we were in the street von Gratzen linked his arm in mine. "It won't do you any harm to be seen in public with me," he said jestingly; and even in that half-bantering remark he managed to convey a subtle meaning.

"I can understand that, sir."

"And now I want to hear all about that affair yesterday."

"I expect you've already heard what there is to tell."

"Of course I've had my wife's and Nita's story, but I want yours. I may need your statement for official purposes, you see."

"I would rather not have to do anything official," I replied. An appearance as witness in any police proceedings was unthinkable.

"Don't let that worry you; I'll make it all right. But the affair was by far the most serious of the sort we've had, and I want all the facts available. That's all."

He listened to my description of the scene; questioned me about the men in it particularly, asking if I could recognize them; and laughed outright at the story of the scramble for the money.

"It was a stroke of genius, boy; positive genius," he declared, and asked me how much I had thrown away. A very German touch. I expected him to offer to repay me; but he spared me that and let me continue the story. When I came to the closing part, I made the most of Hans' share, declaring that if it had not been for him the result would have been very serious, and that he had acted like the brave man he was.

It made an impression; but he did not evince anything like as much interest as in the other parts.

"You've left out one thing, haven't you, my boy? Something that pleased me exceedingly and set me thinking. I mean about your being able to drive the car. Nita says you not only drove like an expert, but were able to put the engine right."

Nita had much better have held her tongue, was my thought. "I was awfully perplexed about it myself afterwards," I replied, feeling deucedly uncomfortable.

"You haven't had anything to do with cars since you came, have you?"

"Not a thing, of course. That's what worried me. I just went up to it as if it was the most natural thing in the world—I didn't have to touch the engine, though—and got in and drove it."

"You see what it means, of course. Why, that it was an instinctive recurrence of memory. It was most fortunate."

That was a matter of opinion, however; but as we reached the house then no more was said about it.

At lunch all the talk was on the subject of the scrap. They were full of it, and went over the ground again and again until one might have thought I had won the Iron Cross by some conspicuous act of most gallant bravery and resource.

That was the sentimental side, and, at first, when the Baron and I were alone afterwards smoking in his sanctum, he grew even more embarrassingly flattering. "It's no good your trying to belittle the affair, my dear boy. If it hadn't been for you, Heaven alone knows what would have happened to my wife and Nita. I haven't a doubt that it would have killed the wife. She is not strong; she has been very ill; and is only just pulling round. The marvel is that she hasn't collapsed, as it is."

I tried to protest, but he wouldn't listen to me.

"I tell you my blood runs cold when I think what those devils would have done if they had got hold of her. I know that sort of Berliners; they'd have torn the clothes off her back and mauled and beaten her without mercy. And it was only the fortunate fact that you were present and acted so bravely that saved her. I shall never forget it; never; and if there's anything I can ever do to prove that I mean what I say, I shall grip the chance with both hands."

"You are very kind, sir."

"Don't talk in that way about kindness. I should be an ungrateful brute if I did not mean it. You can judge how I feel when I tell you that if my son had lived I would have him just like you;" and there was moisture in his eyes as he stretched out his hand and wrung mine impulsively.

That he was in earnest it seemed impossible to doubt. He sat looking at me steadily for a while and then surprised me. He leant forward and fixed his eyes on mine. "I want to ask you a question. Are you sure you have never seen me before?"

Rosa's warning flashed across my thoughts. This might be a trap; so I returned his look with equal steadiness and shook my head. "I don't recollect it, sir."

"Try to think. Try hard. Look back over the years to when you were a boy."

Of course I "tried," and equally of course failed.

He dropped back in his chair with a sigh which seemed to breathe the essence of sincere regret, and after a moment said with almost equal earnestness:

"You know all I have said to you; you believe it, believe that I am really a friend to you?"

"Of course, sir. No one could speak as you have otherwise," I replied, smiling. It was a queer question.

"Then, believing it, is there anything you would care to tell me?"

What the dickens did this mean? I smothered my doubts under another smile and then nodded. "There is one thing, sir." His face lighted and he was all expectation and interest on the instant.

"It's about the man you mentioned yesterday—Count von Erstein."

His look changed directly. All the light and eagerness died away and he put his cigar back in his lips. "Oh, about him, is it? Well?" he asked, as if the subject didn't interest him in the slightest.

But he listened carefully to the account of the interview with von Erstein, squinting at me curiously whenever Nessa's name was mentioned, and seemed sufficiently interested to put some questions about her.

"An ugly story, my boy, very ugly; although I'm not much surprised, knowing the man. But why have you told me?"

"Because I wish you to be prepared if he still tries to carry out his infernal scheme."

He smiled. "And because you're naturally indignant, eh?"

"I am. For my cousin's sake. The two are very old friends."

"I see. Then it's not for the girl's own sake?"

What the deuce was he driving at? His manner kept me guessing all the time. "Partly for her sake, of course. That sort of beastliness always makes me wild."

"I can understand that, my boy, and am glad to hear it. Just what I should expect of you. Is she pretty?"

"I suppose she is in an English way," I replied, shrugging.

"It's not because she *is* English that you feel like this?"

"I hope I should feel much the same if she was a Hottentot, sir."

"I wish all our young fellows were the same. Well, for your sake, I'll see that she comes to no harm. I presume, however, that you are quite sure she is not really a spy? Very serious, just now, you know."

"My cousin is, and she has known her many years."

"Then why doesn't the girl go home?"

"It's her one absorbing wish, sir. She has been trying for months to get permission, but von Erstein has managed to stop it."

He nodded once or twice and leant back in his chair thinking until he glanced at the clock and rose. "Time's up. I must get back. I make a point of being back always to the tick. It's a hobby of mine. I'll think over all you've told me, for I'm interested in it; far more so than you may imagine. I'll make an inquiry or two about this Miss Caldicott, and if it's all right, she shall go home. You can tell your cousin so. But it's a long way and a bad time for her to travel alone."

"I don't think she would mind that a bit, sir."

"You make a very earnest champion, my boy; but let me give you a hint. Don't let any one else get the same idea. I mustn't take you away with me now, unless you wish to make an enemy of my wife. You must stay and be heroized for a while. Now mind, don't fail to come to me, if you're in any sort of difficulty," he said.

"I certainly will come, sir."

As we went out into the hall and were shaking hands, he said, "By the way, I've had the doctor's report about you; and Gorlitz is very strong about our sending you to England to see if the environment would bring your memory back. What think you?"

It was all I could manage to prevent him seeing what I did think of it in reality, but I stammered, "I'm quite in your hands, sir."

He laughed softly and with such meaning. "Perhaps we could kill two birds with one stone, then. How would it do for you to take this Miss Caldicott there with you?" And without waiting to hear my reply he went, leaving me in such amazement that I could have almost shouted for joy.

But did he mean it? Or was it just a subtle test? A trap? I was worrying over this when his daughter came out to fetch me in for the "heroizing" business.

Nita was quite a pretty girl, and now that she had recovered from the previous day's shock and had a rich colour in her cheeks and brightly shining eyes, I wasn't surprised at Hans' infatuation.

"I do so want to speak to you alone," she said. "I want to thank——"

"My dear young lady, no one has been doing anything else since I entered the house. Do give me a breathing space."

She laughed; and a particularly sweet merry laugh it was. "I understand; but this is something special; something else, I mean."

"Oh! Shall I guess?"

With a start and a vivid blush she dropped her eyes, fiddled nervously with her blouse for a moment, and then looked up and laughed again. "I don't mind your guessing," she challenged.

"Something to do with——"

She interrupted with some vigorous nods. "You did tell some taradiddles though. Hans didn't really do anything. I saw it all."

"If he had not rushed up to me just when I called him, my dear young lady, none of us would have got out of the scrape as easily as we did," I said seriously. It would never do for her to think small beer of her lover. "It was that and the way he went for the brutes that decided everything and sent them scuttling off."

"But he didn't do anything, Herr Lassen!"

"Do you mean to tell me you didn't see him knock that dark brute, the biggest of them I mean, head foremost into the gutter?"

"Did he really?" she cried, open-eyed.

"If you didn't see that, you can't have seen everything as you said."

"But he told me he hadn't a chance to do a thing."

"Bravo, Hans!" I exclaimed. "Just like him. You wouldn't expect him to spread himself and swagger about his own pluck, would you?"

But all roads lead to Rome and so did this one. "He declared it was all your own doing, and after the way you fought before, I——"

"Come along, let's go to your mother," I broke in, and linking my arm in hers I moved toward the drawing-room door. "Hans is one of the best;

if he weren't, he wouldn't be so ready to give me the credit for what he himself did. But we can't have that, you know."

She held me back a moment. "What you said about him has done wonders with mother; changed her right round; and we're going together to the von Reblings. Oh, I *do* thank you so!" and being only a kid she squeezed my arm ecstatically.

I had to endure a bout of "heroizing," but something came out in the course of it that made me put my thinking cap on afterwards. Nita playing chorus to her mother's praise as she repeated some of the pretty things von Gratzen had said to her about me.

"I've never heard him speak in such a way of any one in my life before," she declared; "and he is so grieved about your extraordinary loss of memory. I think he is even rather provoked about it. He was in England as a young man, you know, and has made several visits there in later years."

"I did not know that," I said, pricking up my ears.

"He loves to talk of the country and the people, and, as you have just come from there, I am sure he is bitterly disappointed because you can't tell him about the things you saw and the people you met and all the rest of it."

"It would have been very interesting to me too," I said.

"You don't know how long you were there, I suppose?"

I shook my head. It seemed less mean somehow to do that than to lie outright in words; and it answered all the purpose quite as well.

"It must be a dreadful thing to lose one's memory," put in Nita.

"It makes everything very difficult," I said with a shrug. It did.

"And yet you can remember everything that's happened since, can't you?" she persisted.

"Perfectly. As perfectly as if I had never had that shock."

"It *is* odd."

Her mother took up the running again then. "My husband thinks you must have been a very long time in England," she said.

"That's very interesting. Why does he?"

"I don't know exactly. Of course it can only be a guess. But he declares you are much more like an Englishman than one of us. I fancy it's your reserved manner; the way he said you pronounced English to him; and then your knowing something of the English words of command. In fact he took you for an Englishman at first; and he questioned me ever so closely, almost cross-examined me indeed, as I told him, about your fighting yesterday, the way you used your fists, and so on. I was quite amused."

My feeling was anything but amusement, however. "It's a thousand pities I can't tell him anything."

To my surprise this seemed to make her laugh, and I thought it prudent to join in the laugh. But it was something else which had tickled her. "There was one thing he insisted upon worrying us both about. You remember, Nita?"

"Do you mean the kicking, mother?" The latter nodded and Nita continued. "I thought it awfully funny, Herr Lassen, to tell the truth; at least I should have done if it had been any one else; but father always has a strong motive in such things. If he asked me one question he must have asked fifty, I'm sure, taking me right over every incident of yesterday, to find out whether in beating off those awful men you had ever once used your feet. I told him I was sure you hadn't; and he seemed to think it was a most extraordinary thing for a German to have used only his fists. Don't you think it silly?"

"I don't know quite what to think of it," I replied truthfully.

"For shame, Nita, your father is never silly," said her mother severely; but Nita had her own opinion about that, judging by the pout and shrug which the rebuke called forth.

There was a moment's pause, and this offered me a chance to change the subject by putting a question about the war work which both were doing; and soon afterwards I left the house.

It was clear as mud in a wineglass that von Gratzen was still undecided about me. That close questioning about my method of fighting was disquieting; so was the reference to my reserved English manner; and the reference to my pronunciation, especially as I had rather plumed myself on my American accent. It all pointed to the conclusion that my nationality was suspect in his opinion.

He had been in England, too, and I myself knew how well he spoke the language. Altogether he was probably as well able to spot an Englishman as any one in the whole of Berlin. And yet all the while I had been flattering myself that he had been completely hoodwinked.

At the same time no one could have shown me greater kindness. That he was really grateful for the previous day's affair was beyond doubt; it had appeared so to me anyhow; and his implied offer of help—that I should go to him in any trouble—made with such earnestness as to amount almost to insistence, all suggested an intention to be a friend.

There was the reference to Nessa, again; his ready promise that she should be sent home "for my sake," and the startling proposal at the very last moment, that she should go in my charge, which had literally taken my breath away.

What was one to think? It was a very puzzle of puzzles, especially in view of the unreliable vagaries of German officials in general and of what Rosa and the rest had said about von Gratzen in particular.

What a lovely mix up it would be if his suggestion materialized and Nessa and I were packed off together under official protection! It seemed a million times too good to be even thinkable. Compared with such a gloriously gorgeous plan, our little conspiracy scheme seemed almost contemptibly mean and commonplace; scarcely worth bothering about for a moment. But it was best to have as many strings to the bow as possible, so I went to the von Reblings' to hear if Rosa had anything to tell me about it.

Ought the others to be told of the fresh development? It seemed better not for the present. It was hard luck to have to keep such stunning news secret, but there was nothing to be gained by raising Nessa's hopes until they were virtually certain to be fulfilled. What would she think of the notion? I hoped I could guess. Being a bit of a sanguine ass, I started castle-building on the foundation, and by the time the Karlstrasse was reached, I had planned, built, and furnished a very noble edifice indeed.

Old Gretchen opened the door as usual, and her look and start of surprise and general manner, suggesting something uncommonly like consternation, brought me down to earth and shattered my castle effectively.

"They are not at home, sir," she declared hurriedly; and instead of opening the door wide, she held it so as really to block my entrance. Her obvious nervousness probably accounted for a step which at once roused suspicions.

"No one at all?"

"No, sir. They will not be home until late."

"That's a nuisance; but I'd better speak to Miss Caldicott."

"She's not in either, sir." The reply was given hesitatingly, and she made as if to shut the door.

A smile and a casual, "Oh well, it doesn't matter," put her off her guard and her relief was shown in her change of look. "Can I give them any message, sir?" she asked. But her relief vanished and gave place to greater concern than ever when I pushed the door open and stepped inside.

"That's a good idea, Gretchen; I'll write them a little note," I said, as I passed her in the direction of the drawing-room.

She slipped before me and stood by the library. "You'll find paper and everything here, sir," she smirked.

It looked as if she wanted to keep me from the drawing-room; and it was not difficult to guess that she had been disturbed at her spy work there. It was a bad shot, however; for during the pause there came the murmur of voices in the drawing-room itself.

"You must be wrong, Gretchen. They must have come in without your knowing. I can hear them."

"Oh, no, sir. The door's locked. I have orders always to keep it locked when the Countess is not at home;" and she held up the key in proof and slipped between me and the door.

I started with a great appearance of alarm and pushed past her. "Then there's a thief in the house," I exclaimed.

At that instant there was the sound of some sort of commotion in the drawing-room; a cry of "How dare you?" in Nessa's voice, followed by a sneering laugh, uncommonly like von Erstein's.

CHAPTER XII
"LIKE OLD TIMES"

I snatched the key from Gretchen, who was now very white and shaky, opened the drawing-room door and was going to rush in, when it occurred to me that if Nessa was caught off her guard, she might let out something.

"All right, Gretchen, thank you," I said, loudly enough for Nessa to hear.

The woman flung up her hands and bolted, and I went in as if making an ordinary call.

Nessa had rushed into the conservatory to escape from von Erstein and came back as I entered, her face flushed and her eyes ablaze with furious indignation, while he, dumbfounded and looking as black as thunder, scowled at me viciously.

"This man has grossly insulted me, Herr Lassen!" she cried. "Taking advantage of the Countess's absence, he got me here on the pretence of a message to be given to her, and then— — Ugh! I can't speak it;" and she dropped into a chair and hid her face in her hands.

"I only took your advice, Lassen, and asked Miss Caldicott to marry me," he said sullenly. "And then she— —"

"Did you advise that?" broke in Nessa, starting up excitedly.

That wasn't the moment to explain things, of course. Something had to be attended to first. I walked up to von Erstein with intentional deliberation, feeling a little thrill of joy at the fright in his eyes, put my hand on the collar of his coat, and led him towards the door. He was too abjectly scared to make more than the merest show of resistance.

"Have you anything more to say to him?" I asked Nessa, halting when we reached the door.

"No, no. Only send him away. Send him away," she exclaimed.

I took him out into the hall and then released him. "I'm going to thrash you, von Erstein. Two reasons. You made your spy here lock this door so that you could have that girl to yourself; and yesterday you said things which made me itch to thrash you then."

"I didn't mean——"

"That'll do. Don't tell any more lies."

He tried to bluster. "You'd better not strike me, Lassen; I can——"

A smack on the face, given with all my strength, caused the threat to die stillborn and also showed the stuff he was made of. He pretended that the force of it knocked him down and nothing would induce him to get up again. So the fight ended where it began, as I couldn't hit him while he lay on the ground. Regretting that the one smack had been such a poor one, I dragged him into the hall, plopped him on to the doormat, and chucked him his hat, swearing that if he stopped in Berlin, the job would be finished in workmanlike fashion. He squirmed there long enough to see that no more was coming, then opened the door, paused to curse and threaten me, and bolted.

Nessa was furious, and her first question showed that some of her anger was for me. Von Erstein's little shaft about my "advice" had gone home. "Is what that man said true? Did you advise him to ask me to marry him?" the emphasis strongly on the "advise."

I nodded; and very naturally her lip curled.

"I wouldn't have believed it possible," she exclaimed.

"He told me yesterday about things and I asked him if he had asked you. If that's advising, I advised."

"And yet you know the kind of man he is and that he has been persecuting me in this fashion?"

"But anyhow I didn't advise you to accept him."

"Jack!" she cried indignantly.

"Herr Lassen's safer, and in German too."

"It's almost enough to make me say I'll never speak to you again."

"Worse than he is, eh?" It was really a curious thing, but we never seemed able to resist a chance of misunderstanding one another; and when she took this line, it was impossible for me to resist chipping her.

"Did you thrash him?" she asked after a pause.

"No; not an easy job in the circs."

"You've developed a wise discretion," she said with a smile which wasn't exactly soothing.

"He's a fellow with a lot of influence, you see."

There was one feature about our tiffs; they generally ended all right; and this time she seemed to realize that we were off the lines. She thought a while and her manner changed. "Do you want me to believe that after what happened here and what I said, you just thanked him and shook hands? Because I don't believe it. I heard you hit him. That's why I asked if you'd thrashed him."

"I smacked his face, as a sort of preface, but he lay down and wouldn't get up, so I had to cart him out to the front door. A poor show; but I fancy he'll give me a wide berth in the future. Would you care to tell me what passed?"

"He sent up that woman, Gretchen, to say that he was leaving Berlin and that the Countess had given him a message for me about something she had of his. I was only too thankful to hear he was going away, and when I got down, she locked the door. It was all planned, of course; and he asked me to marry him, and when I gave him his answer, he grabbed hold of me and kissed me. I broke from him and rushed into the conservatory, intending to get out that way into the garden; but he had fastened the window, and when I was trying to get it open, you came, thank Heaven."

"I guessed that was about the size of it."

"I was never more relieved in my life."

"Even though it was only me."

"Yes, even though it was only you." This with a smile, however, which quite belied her indifferent tone.

"Well, it's all right now. As a matter of fact he has found it wise to leave in consequence of a hint I gave him yesterday."

"Tell me."

"Better let it wait a while." There was nothing to be gained by telling her the truth. "I came to see if there is any news."

"There is, unfortunately. I've received an order from the police to report myself to-morrow."

"The deuce you have! I wonder what that means. Who signed it?"

"Baron von Gratzen."

I stared at her in amazement. Confound the man. Here he was cropping up again in this mysteriously unexpected fashion. "When did you get it?"

"Only a minute or two before that man called."

What on earth could it mean? It looked as if he had gone straight from his promise to help her to leave and then sent this. "Where have you to report?"

"The Amtstrasse," and she handed me the paper. It came from his offices and was signed in his own handwriting.

"I give it up. These beggars beat me every time. Only an hour or two back he told me that you should be sent back home," and I told her about that part of the interview and that he had said I could tell Rosa. "It's true he said something about making some inquiries about you, so as to be satisfied you're not a spy."

"Then of course he's going to begin by questioning me himself."

"Possibly, but—I get such different reports about him. You'll have to look out, too. He's sure to cross-examine you about me. I can't get it out of my head that he suspects I'm flying under the wrong flag. You'd better never have seen me before, mind; and whatever you do, look out for traps and things; and he's as artful as a cartload of monkeys at the game."

She was tremendously excited by the news about going home. I had to repeat every word he had said about it, and of course she got out of me that he had spoken about our going home together.

"Oh, wouldn't that be lovely!" she exclaimed.

"To go with me?"

"To go with any one, of course," she said with sudden indifference. "If you'd been through half that I have and had a quarter of the suspense I've had to endure, you'd be glad too."

"I'm glad enough, as it is. I think this beastly climate is anything but healthy for either of us just now."

"Oh, to be free once more!" she cried with a deep, deep sigh of longing. "Do you know that more than once I've been on the point of risking everything and just bolting and chancing my luck."

"Which reminds me that I'd better tell you the spare wheels I've been thinking about, if these other tyres burst. I haven't had much chance of talking to you yet, you know."

"We had one interview," she reminded me, her eye dancing.

"We'll try to do a bit better this time. The best thing will be old von Gratzen's scheme, if it comes off."

"We should have to be together a long time, if it does."

"Rather rotten, eh? But I could bear it, I think, if you could."

"I should have to, naturally."

"We could discuss our old grievances, at the worst."

"And at the best?" she said demurely, trying not to laugh.

"Find fresh ones to jingle-jangle about. But you'll have to behave yourself; for I shall be a German for the first part of the trip, remember."

"And if you don't behave yourself, I can tell people you're not one. You'll have to remember that, mind."

"Behave myself? Meaning?"

"That you're not to talk nonsense then or now; so go on to the spare wheels, please."

"All right. The next best will be for you to use Rosa's ticket and so on, and travel with her Oscar."

"But Rosa said you wouldn't hear of that, and you don't imagine I'm going to let the man run that risk for me. Any more wheels?"

"One. That if the worst comes to the worst, we just disappear and chance the weather;" and I described my idea—to go in disguise as a couple of mechanics.

"They're using a lot of women, but not as mechanics yet," she said.

I laughed. "But you'd go as a boy, Nessa."

"As a what?" she cried in amazement.

"I said boy. B-o-y. Easy word."

She stared at me for a moment or two as if I was mad, and then her eyes lit up and she burst out laughing. "Do you know why I'm laughing?"

"At me, probably."

"Not a bit of it. Because it's exactly the idea I had. I have the clothes ready for it and a set of overalls; and often and often I've locked myself in my room, dressed up, and rehearsed everything. You know how I've played a boy's part in the theatricals at home; I can shove my hands in my pockets and swagger along just like one. I make rather a good boy."

"Good?"

"Good enough for a boy, anyhow," she replied, laughing again.

"Show me."

She rose, pushed hands down as if into her trouser pockets, and walked up and down the room with a free stride. "Give us a fag, mate," she said when she reached me. "That all right?" she asked, relapsing into herself and sitting down again.

"Rather! Ripping! Why, you managed somehow to alter the very expression." She had. The change was wonderful. "With a touch or two of make-up not a soul would spot you. But you were always a bit of a boy, you know. Perhaps that accounts for it."

"That meant for a compliment?"

"Just as you take it. You were a self-willed little beggar, anyhow. Do you remember how shocked your mother was that night at the Grahams, when you came on their little stage as a boy?"

"I do, indeed. Poor mother! She must have been awfully worried by all this; and is still, of course. But Rosa has written to a friend in Switzerland and asked her to wire that I'm all right; and perhaps by this time she's had the message. It's horribly wicked, I suppose, but I declare I feel so vindictive that I could almost kill that woman Gretchen and von Erstein too, when I think of what they've made poor mother suffer by stopping my letters."

"He's a low-down swine; and if I get half a chance, I'll even things up with him before we leave. But we don't want to talk about him now. If your mother's got that wire, she'll feel heaps better. Now, tell me what you think of my third wheel?"

"Shall I tell you the truth?"

"Of course."

She paused and the colour crept slowly into her face, robbing it of the worried anxiety which had so distressed me and making her as bewitchingly pretty as ever in my eyes. "If you will have the truth I'd—I'd like the third wheel better than either of the others."

"Same here; but it wouldn't be so safe. We'll have the props with us, however, in case of mishaps. What say you?"

"Carried unanimously," she cried enthusiastically. "It would be lovely!"

"You haven't changed much, then, even with all this."

"Do you mean in looks?"

"Not much there, even; but I meant in the tomboy business."

"Ah, you don't know. I have changed. I've grown up, suddenly. It couldn't be otherwise," she answered very seriously. "At one time it looked a certainty that I should be sent to gaol, and the suspense was—well, almost unbearable. No one can tell what it meant to have to appear indifferent and confident, when I knew that any moment might be my last in freedom. That danger seemed to pass away, but only to give way to worse."

"You mean this——"

"Yes," she broke in with a quick nod. "I can't bear even to hear his name mentioned. I soon knew what his real object was; he has a friend, a man like himself, who is in command of one of the concentration camps: the one at Krustadt: and—but you can guess. There was only one thing for me to do, and I prepared for it. I have the poison upstairs."

"Nessa!"

"No woman can go through such an ordeal and come out unchanged. I should have made a fight for it, of course. I told Rosa, and, although she was horrified at first, she saw it afterwards, and then she got Herr Feldmann to get me an identification card as Hans Bulich, and helped me get the disguise. I should have gone by now, if you hadn't come. Oh yes, I'm changed; no one knows how much except myself."

The drawn intentness of her expression at the moment showed this so plainly that I was too much moved to find any words to reply. But she rallied quickly and laughed.

"And then when you came I was mad enough to believe you were a spy! I can't think why I was such a fool. There was no excuse; not the slightest; and I don't expect you ever to forgive me really."

"I don't blame you. I don't, on my honour."

"Well, I shall never forgive myself then. But—even now I can't help staring at you."

"Stare away. I like it. But why?"

"You're so—so utterly different."

"How?"

"In every way possible."

"Think so. Every way?" Our eyes met and she looked down.

"I wonder," she murmured under her breath; and then quickly in a louder tone: "Of course it's your new life. Tell me about it."

We both understood; but that wasn't the time to tell her she need not "wonder"; so I spoke about things at the Front.

"But I want your own experiences, Jack," she protested.

"I'm Herr Lassen, the man without a memory."

"You're just as provoking as ever. You know that I'm dying to hear everything, and you won't utter a word."

"Well, I'll tell you one thing. It was all your doing."

She crinkled her forehead in a way I knew so well. "How?"

"Do you remember one day at Hendon—we were engaged then, by the by—how you ragged me about not having the pluck to go up and about cricket being so much safer a sport, and how I flung away in a huff and marched off and got a ticket at once and went up. That was the start."

"And I remember, too, what a fright it gave me when I saw you go. I watched the aeroplane with my heart in my mouth all the time in a sort of fascinated panic lest something should go wrong."

"And when I came to look for you I found you'd gone up too."

"You don't suppose I meant you to crow over me, do you? And was that really the beginning?"

"Of course. I went up lots of times afterwards and got to like it; and when the trouble came, naturally I saw it was my job."

"Be a pal, and tell me all about what you did," she coaxed.

"All in good time, but not now. We've been alone together quite long enough to set tongues wagging as it is. I'd better be off;" and I rose.

"I suppose you're right; but it's been lovely. Like old times."

"Which old times?"

"Never mind. Don't be inquisitive."

"All right. Well, look here. Go on with that boy part of yours. Get into the skin of it, and have the names of things pat on your tongue. One never knows what may happen. And if you could persuade Rosa to persuade Feldmann to do for me what he did for you, do so."

"Sounds a bit mixed, doesn't it?" and she laughed with such genuine merriment that it did one good to hear her.

"You must sort it out. So long. We'll pull it off somehow or other."

"I think that's the oddest thing about you. You manage somehow to make me feel absolutely confident that you'll manage it. It's like a miracle. Only a day or two ago I was right down in the depths, and here I am laughing as if it were just one of our old kiddish pranks."

CHAPTER XIII
IN THE THIERGARTEN

The confidence of success which Nessa had so frankly expressed, she had certainly imparted to me. The fact that she had already hit on the idea of playing a boy's part in the attempt to escape, had obtained everything necessary for it, and had actually spent some time in rehearsing it, was a stroke of such luck, that I was more than half inclined to throw the other plans over and adopt that one at once.

If by any means the necessary identification card could be got, the hope of success was strong and full of promise. Nessa could speak German quite as well as I could, and her accent, when she had put that question to me about the fag and her wonderful change of expression, had been done to the life.

She had always been a clever character actress, and there was no doubt that she could keep it up in any sort of emergency. That she liked the idea, there was no question; and as for myself—the thought of such a companionship with her in such a venture pulled like a 200 h.p. engine.

Her instinct was right, too, in chiming with her inclination. It was our best chance—failing old von Gratzen's, of course. Ever so much better than risking any trouble for Rosa by using her passport. Feldmann must be made to see that, for it might induce him to get the card for me.

That night I went most carefully into all the details of the plan, trying to foresee all that might happen; and then I remembered the story which Gunter, my pal in the flying corps, had told me of his escape when engine trouble had brought him down inside the German lines.

"It's only a matter of bluff, Jack," he said, "when one can jabber the lingo as we can, and a few simple precautions. Here's one of 'em. I never go up without it."

"What the dickens is it?" I asked as he handed me what looked like a red flannel pad for his tummy.

"Looks innocent, doesn't it? My 'tummy pad,' I call it. Just a protection against chills, eh? That's what they thought when they searched me. But inside the flannel there's a coil of silk cord long enough and strong enough to tie up a man's arms, and his legs too at need. It's my own notion; and since my little trip, I've added something more. Sewn up in the flannel there's enough put-you-to-by-by stuff to keep a man or two quiet for as long as necessary. If I'd had that, I shouldn't have had to risk knocking my guard on the head and choking the breath out of him."

"Tell me, Dick."

"Well, my chance came almost as soon as they'd got me. Of course I burnt the old bus and shoved my hands up, and after they'd made sure I wasn't armed, they just put one chap in charge of me with orders to take me somewhere. It was quite dark then and, pretending that I was beastly uncomfortable after the search, I fiddled about with my clothes and managed to get my cord handy. Then I picked a suitable spot, asked him some fool question or other, and went for him. He was only a fat Landsturmer and hadn't more than a few wriggles in him; but I had to bash him over the head to make sure—that's where I wanted the dope, of course. Then I changed togs with him, trussed him up with my cord and started off on my own. Bluff did the rest, all right."

"But what did you do, old dear?"

He laughed and lit another cigarette. "I marched into the first cottage I came to, scared the folk out of their lives, and in the name of Kaiser Bill commandeered clothes for a wounded prisoner. They parted like a lamb, and five minutes afterwards I was transformed into a workman."

"But you'd no identification card?"

This brought another quiet laugh. "I worked that all right. There are no asses in the world too bad to bluff if you go the right way about it. My way was to go to the police. I pitched a yarn that I was an aero mechanic and had been sent for to go hotfoot to Ellendorff, a little place close to the Dutch frontier where I knew there was a factory, and that I'd been waylaid and robbed on the road. It sounds thin as I tell it; but I had mucked myself up to look the part, and, above all, I had gone to the police, mind you; itself the best proof that I wasn't a wrong 'un: and I chose the middle of the night, when only one sleepy owl was on duty. He swallowed it all right, except that he thought I was drunk and at first wanted to keep me till the morning; but when I kicked up a fuss, told him he'd get into a devil of a row, and said he'd better call his boss, he thought better of it, gave me what I wanted and was thankful to see my back and go to sleep again. I had no more trouble; was stopped once or twice, but the card got me through; and I reached the frontier easily enough. Luck favoured me there. I ran across a couple of deserters, palled up with them, and—well, that's all."

Gunter's story had made a big impression on me at the time, and in my old student days at Göttingen I had had quite enough experiences of the power of a good bluff on the average German official to know that it was quite feasible, so I resolved to profit by it now.

I had plenty of time the next day to complete all the necessary preparations and added a few of my own devising. These were some "iron rations," in case of difficulties about our food supply; two or three tools, including a heavy spanner which would serve as a weapon at need; and a shabby suit case to hold everything.

I packed everything into this, lifted a board under the lino in my bathroom, and hid it there, lest any one in my absence might take a fancy to go through my luggage.

With a road map and a railway guide the route to be taken was soon decided. The Dutch frontier was to be the goal. It was much nearer than the Swiss; and as Westphalia was the region of factories, it was much more plausible that a couple of mechanics would travel that way, than in any other direction.

Gunter's mention of the one at Ellendorff, a village near Lingen, and close to the frontier, suggested a good objective; and the rough idea was to make the journey in stages, so as to put people off the scent should suspicion be roused. It was safer than risking a trip in one of the through expresses, and also much easier to book from small towns than right through from Berlin.

All this took up a lot of time, especially as it was interrupted by several spells of speculation about the result of Nessa's interview with von Gratzen. This was very important, as it would probably determine the method of our departure; and when my preparations were completed and I was carefully reconsidering them over a cigarette, some one knocked at the door of my flat.

It was a stranger; a well-dressed, sharp-featured man and unmistakably a Jew. "Herr Lassen?" he asked. I nodded. "My name is Rudolff."

"What is it?"

"It would be better for me to tell you my business privately," he replied, with a gesture toward a couple of people passing on the stairs.

I took him into my sitting-room with an extremely uncomfortable notion that he was from the police.

"I am in a position to do you a considerable service, Herr Lassen," he said, squinting curiously round the room.

"Who sent you to me and how did you know where to find me?"

"Your arrival in the city is scarcely a secret, and I obtained your address from your friends in the Karlstrasse. No one sent me to you, sir."

He wasn't from the police. That was a relief, and nothing else mattered. "And the service you spoke of?"

"You will not be surprised to hear that a number of people wish to find you?"

"As it's been easy for you, would it be difficult for them?"

"Not so difficult as you might desire, perhaps. I say that because you appear somewhat to resent my visit. If that is really the case, of course I will go."

"I don't care whether you go or stop; but if you've anything that you think worth telling, tell it. I'll listen. I presume you haven't come out of mere philanthropy, by the way."

"I have not. I make no pretence of the sort. If the warning I can give you is worth anything, I am not so rich as to throw money away."

"Out with it then." It was not only curiosity which prompted me to listen. It was probable that he was going to tell me some lurid incident of Lassen's past, and it was just as well to hear it. It was also quite possible that after all he might come from von Gratzen with the object of catching me tripping. His question suggested that.

"It was at Göttingen, I believe, that you made the acquaintance of Adolf Gossen?"

"I dare say, but I don't remember anything about it,"

"Ah, of course. You are the man without a memory. I have heard of your misfortune," he said, with a sly suggestive glance.

"And doubt it, eh? Well, suppose you get on with the story?"

He took the hint, and it turned out to be about the same pretty affair von Erstein had made so much of. It seemed, according to my visitor, that some one was in prison because of it; that his friends, whose names he gave, were furious; that they were looking high and low for me; and that if I remained in Berlin they would find me and wreak their vengeance in any way that came handy. He declared he knew where to find them and they were prepared to pay for the information of my whereabouts.

The thing was either a palpable plant or this fellow had come from von Erstein to try and frighten me out of the city.

"Of course you mean that if I don't pay you, you will go to them?"

"Not at all, sir," he cried, with a fine show of indignation. "I know these people to be scoundrels; they have treated me villainously; I have merely come to warn you. You can act upon it or not, of course. That is entirely a matter for you;" and to my surprise he got up without asking a mark for his news. "I have done all that I can do by coming."

"I don't know anything about the affair, as I told you, but I'm very much obliged to you;" and I took out my pocket-book as a hint.

"Pardon me, sir," he exclaimed, flourishing his hands as if the sight of banknotes was an abomination, and shaking his head vigorously. "I could not think of accepting any money after what you have said. Good afternoon;" and he was still gesturing at the shock of the idea when he left the flat.

This was so extremely unnatural for a German Jew that it prompted suspicion. He had probably meant this pecuniary shyness as a startling proof of his honesty of purpose and general integrity.

That wasn't the effect it produced, however. It rather served to confirm the previous thought that von Erstein had sent him to scare me. That the brute would do almost anything to see my back was a certainty, of course; and then an odd notion flitted across my thoughts.

Whether it would be worth while to appear to tumble into the trap; go to him in the very dickens of a funk; make him believe my one object was to fly the country, in disguise, to Holland preferably; and get him to procure the necessary permit, etc. The possibility of hoisting him with his own petard looked good; and the thought of his chagrin when he discovered that he had helped me to take Nessa out of his clutches made the scheme positively alluring.

That it could be done, there was little doubt, and equally none that he could get the necessary papers; but the price to pay for them was too stiff. To have anything to do with such a mongrel was unthinkable so long as any other course was open; so I abandoned it until every other means had been tried.

The pressing question now was the result of Nessa's interview with von Gratzen, and I set off for the Karlstrasse to hear about it. This time the door was opened by the girl Marie; so I concluded that Gretchen had either bolted or been sent about her business as the result of the previous day's affair. Marie told me no one was at home and that Rosa had gone with Nessa and Lottchen to the Thiergarten.

I soon found them; and Rosa played the part of the good fairy and kept the child with her while Nessa told me the news.

"First let me tell you the good news," she said.

"Do you mean that the other's bad then?"

"Do have a little patience. The main thing is that Rosa has induced Herr Feldmann to say where we can get the things you want. Isn't that splendid?"

"Yes, if you are able to get away with me; and that may depend on what passed to-day. Is it all right?"

"You might as well ask me a riddle in Russian. Frankly I don't know what to make of it. Of course it was to see Baron von Gratzen that I had to go to the Amtstrasse. He seemed all right, but— —" and she shrugged her shoulders and frowned.

"That's just the impression he always leaves on me."

"He was awfully kind in his manner; but it was lucky you warned me to be careful, for he kept popping in some question about you just when I wasn't expecting it, and whether I gave you away I can't say. I don't think I did; but then I'm not at all sure he didn't see that I was fencing."

"What did he talk about?"

"Oh, he told me first that some one had declared I was really a spy; asked why I had stopped so long here? Didn't I want to go home? and so on. Of course that was all easy enough; but I think he was only trying to let me get over my nervousness; for, of course, I was awfully nervous; and at last he said he believed my story entirely, in fact that he knew it was the truth; that I wasn't to worry; that I need only report myself once a week;

that it was the merest formality; and that probably I should never have to do it all, as he was pretty sure I should be sent home before the first day for reporting arrived."

"And was that all?"

"Rather not; only the preface; and, mind you, he hadn't said a word about you up to then, not even mentioned your name."

"What came next then?"

"He asked me to talk about England and the English, saying that he had been there a lot and knew heaps of people; and then you came into the picture."

"Did he ask about me, do you mean?"

"Are you telling the story or am I?" and she rallied me with a smile which was good to see. She was much more like the Nessa of old times, was in good spirits, and had thrown off much of the worrying load of depression. "I don't know whether you've done it, but to-day somehow I can't take things seriously."

"That's as it should be; but how did he bring me in?"

"Well, he was either acting better than I could or he was perfectly sincere. What he did was to talk about people, mentioning a lot of names and asking me whether I knew any of them, and in the most casual tone in the world out popped yours."

"Lassen?"

"Of course not; your own, Lancaster."

"Phew! That's a caution, if you like. What did you say?"

She laughed softly. "I think I was one too many for him then. You see he'd prepared the ground in a way by mentioning people I'd never heard of, so I just shook my head, then pretended to think and said I wasn't sure that my mother had not known some Lancasters. He'd been so decent, that that seemed easier than just lying outright. He was eager for more and asked me to try and remember, as he had a very particular reason for being interested in them; but that looked dangerous, so I thought it best not to remember anything else Lancastrian."

"Well?"

"Don't rush me. I could tell that I was over that bridge all right; but it was only the first. After a bit he brought up Jimmy Lamb's name, and I laughed and clapped my hands and said he was my brother-in-law. Why, what's the matter? Was that wrong?" she cried, noticing my frown.

"Perhaps not, but it was Jimmy's passport I was to use, and he's supposed to have gone down in the *Burgen*. It won't matter, probably."

"I'd forgotten all about that. No wonder he was interested and poured a volley of questions into me about him. But that was all safe enough, because I haven't heard a word about Jimmy since I've been here, and naturally couldn't tell him anything. One of them was whether Jimmy knew the Lancasters, by the by. And I can see why he asked it."

Unpleasantly ominous, this; since it was clear he was trying to establish the connection between me and Jimmy. "And after that?"

"Butter wouldn't have melted in his mouth. He asked me about you as Lassen; safe ground again: and wound up by thanking me for having answered his questions so frankly; declared he was quite satisfied, and then, as I told you, said he would use his influence to see that I went home."

"Anything about our going together?"

"Yes. He said it might not be well for me to travel alone and asked if there was any one who could see me to the frontier."

"You didn't suggest me?" I broke in.

"Really, Herr Lassen! Do you think every English girl is a fool? I suggested Herr Feldmann. He shook his head, murmuring something about his being unable to get away; and then came the only thing that really scared me. 'Of course you could go in the care of some of our people, but it would be better not, perhaps; so difficult to spare our folks just now;'—all that in a sort of meditative tone, and then with a change which in some way altered his very features, he fixed me with a look which seemed to pierce like red-hot gimlets into my very brain and read every thought in it, and asked me to suggest some one else. I positively shrivelled up inside, if you know what I mean; felt like a fish on the end of a fork thrust suddenly into a blazing fire. I don't know what I said or did. It must have mesmerized me, I suppose. I think I shook my head and stammered out that I didn't know of any one else; but I can't be certain. All I clearly remember is a feeling of intense relief when his eyes left mine, and I heard him say something about seeing to the matter. I never felt anything like it in my life before; and if I gave you away, it was then."

"I've had a look from him like that and can understand how it made you feel. That's why I can't place the man. Hullo, look! There come his wife and daughter with the Countess. We'd better join up. Won't do to let them think we're too thick;" and we quickened up to Rosa as the others reached the spot, and all stood chatting. Presently Lottchen drew me aside from the rest, declaring that she never saw anything of me now, and after a moment, Nita, attracted by the child's loveliness, joined us.

I said something or other which made them both laugh, and just as the others turned round and looked at us, I had the surprise of my life.

A good-looking woman was passing, holding a tot of a kid by the hand; she glanced at me, stopped dead with a look of profound astonishment, paused to stare, hands clenched and pressed to her bosom, eyes wide, mouth agape, and every feature set as rigid as stone.

"Johann!" little more than a whisper at first, and then loudly, "Johann!" and without more ado she rushed up, flung her arms round my neck, and burst into a flood of passionate sobs mingled with equally passionate terms of affection.

CHAPTER XIV
ANNA HILDEN

"Johann! Johann! Oh, my dearest! Oh, thank God I have found you at last! Oh, my long lost darling!" raved the woman ecstatically, while her child ran up and clung to my coat, calling, "Papa! Papa!"

A pleasant situation considering the circumstances and the fact that a number of other people, attracted by the woman's hysterics, began to cluster round us.

Nita and Lottchen scurried back to our group; the two elder women were looking both scandalized and disgusted; and Nessa bent over Lottchen, scarcely able to conceal her laughter. Fortunately Rosa kept her head.

Giving me first a look of scornful indignation, she said something to her mother and the whole group moved away.

The woman's outburst of hysterical passion had quieted by then, and she just let her head rest upon my shoulder, feasting her rather fine eyes upon my face with languishing rapture.

My first thought was that she was a lunatic; so I tried to unclasp her embrace. Gently at first, but then with considerable strength, for she resisted stoutly. Next I observed that for all her hysterical sobbing, her eyes were scarcely moist; a fact which put quite a different interpretation on the affair.

"We don't want a scene here," I said.

This had comparatively little effect and she tried to wrest her hands away and begin the embracing over again.

"If we have any more of this, I shall call the police," I said sharply. This did the business. After a moment she grew less demonstrative, making a great to-do in the effort to check her agitation, and allowed me to lead her away.

While we were shaking off the crowd there was time to study her and try to get a glimmer of the meaning of it all. Now that the hysterics were over, she appeared to be less emotional than perplexed. She kept her eyes on the ground, evidently thinking intently and taking no notice of the child at all, who was as unconcerned as if she didn't belong to the picture, except that once or twice she glanced up at the woman, as if wondering what to do and looking for a lead.

A thought of the truth occurred to me and made me look more searchingly than ever at the woman's side face. Two things struck me at once. She was older than I had believed; a little make-up cunningly concealed some wrinkles, and a touch of rouge on the cheek helped to account for my mistake about her age; and closer inspection revealed some lines of grease paint close to her hair.

I put her down then as a second-rate actress, and her over-acting in the embracing scene suggested corroboration. How the ordinary woman would behave on discovering her long lost lover or husband may be a question; but she certainly wouldn't shed tears which were carefully tearless out of the fear that they would spoil her make-up. It was obviously a plant.

That wasn't altogether a comforting reflection, however. My loss of memory made it impossible to expose her, for the simple reason that any story she might choose to tell could not be contradicted.

"Now I should like to know what all this means," I began when we were free from inquisitive lookers-on.

"Do you pretend you don't recognize me?" she asked, turning her big blue eyes on me with a pathetic wistfulness.

"Do you pretend that I ought to?"

"Why did you desert me? Oh, how could you, Johann?" she wailed.

"I don't even know what you mean."

"Oh, but you must; you must. You loved me so; at least you swore you did, over and over again," she cried. "Oh, don't tell me you've forgotten me. I could bear anything but that."

This suggested von Gratzen. It was just the sort of scheme which would appeal to such a wily old beggar to trap me into admission. "Who are you?" I asked.

She clapped her hands to her face and looked like starting hysterics again. "Oh, you must know. You must. You can't have forgotten me! You can't!"

"Perhaps your name will help me."

With a very overdone theatrical gesture she stopped and stared at me and looked distracted.

"I'm—Anna. Your Anna."

"*My* Anna? I didn't know I had one;" and she clapped her hands to her face again, but not quickly enough to hide her expression, which looked uncommonly like a smile. "And the surname?"

"Hilden, of course," she said after a pause without looking up.

This gave the clue. It was not von Gratzen's scheme but von Erstein's. I remembered our interview; his persistent attempt to test my memory; his story of Anna Hilden; his genuine anger when I had not recollected her; and then the sudden change of manner which had been so puzzling.

He had put her up to play the part of the ruined maiden and had probably planned the melodramatic scene which had just taken place, knowing that, unless at the same time I gave myself away, I could not expose her. It was cunning, and put me in a beast of a mess. There seemed only one course—to prevail on the woman to admit the truth.

"You can see for yourself that this has taken me entirely by surprise," I said after a pause. "I had a very tough time of it a few weeks ago; the ship I was in was blown up and the explosion caused me to lose my memory entirely. What you have said may be absolutely true; although to me it seems impossible. What do you wish me to do?"

"I want my rights," she replied, after a slight pause.

"Well, we can scarcely discuss things here. Where do you live?"

"In the Kammerplatz. 268g. No, I mean 286g;" making the correction in some confusion.

Curious that she could not remember the right number; looked as if she had only just gone there for this special business. "Shall we go there?" I asked.

She found the question unnecessarily embarrassing, hesitated and glanced at the child with a frown of perplexity. "I can't go home yet. I was just taking my little darling to some friends."

She was certainly not a good actress, or she would never have implied that it was more important to take the child to some friends than to have an explanation with the false lover discovered after long years. "When then?" I asked, concluding that the child had been borrowed for the show and was to be returned with thanks at once.

"Come there in an hour," she said after thinking. "You won't escape me again, for I know where to find you now," she added with a toss of the head.

"I shall not try. Here's my address;" and I scribbled it on a card. "I'll turn up all right. I'm only too interested in what you've said and wish to know all you can tell me about it. I'll do the right thing by you, Anna;" and I held out my hand.

She hesitated a second and then shook hands, her look showing that my words had impressed her favourably and also perplexed her.

I spent the interval in the Thiergarten thinking over the whole unpleasant incident: the probable effect upon those who had witnessed it, and the line to take in the coming interview.

It would serve one good turn at any rate. Von Gratzen would hear all about it from his wife and it ought to put an end to his suspicions. If the woman I had ruined could identify me as the result of a chance meeting, he could scarcely fail to regard it as a mighty strong corroboration of the Lassen theory.

Both Rosa and Nessa would of course know that the story, even if it were true, had nothing to do with me, and what the Countess herself thought didn't amount to anything. The main point was what would happen if the woman stuck to it and how far she was prepared to go. That would probably depend upon the inducements or pressure brought to bear by von Erstein; and judging the man, pressure was the more likely.

It would be easy enough to knock the bottom out of the scheme by bringing the police into it; her nervousness at the mention of them had shown that plainly. But that wouldn't suit me. The less the police had to meddle with my affairs, the better. No doubt an inquiry agent could soon get at the truth so far as the woman herself was concerned; and if she proved obdurate, that might be the best course. But obviously the quickest and best solution would be to get the woman herself to own up; and that must be the first line of attack.

Her answer to my question what she wished me to do, suggested an idea. She wanted her "rights," as she phrased it; and clearly the straightforward course was to offer them. "Rights" meant marriage; and she was likely to feel in a deuce of a stew if I agreed to marry her. The farce of it was quite to my liking. To appear to force her into such a marriage with a man she had never seen in her life was rich, and at the same time good policy, as it would impress her with my honesty of purpose.

I kept the appointment punctually and found her rather breathless and flurried. It was a mean little flat; had evidently been hastily got ready; and the number of things still littered about the room, told that I had arrived in the middle of her efforts to get it in order.

She looked far less presentable without her hat and things. She was an untidy person, anything but clean, and made the mistake of trying to explain away the confusion and disorder in the place.

"I didn't really believe you'd come, or I'd have had the place tidier. When any one has to struggle alone for a living in these times, there isn't much chance of keeping the home right."

"Still I can see you've been doing your best."

"I always have to," she replied with a quick, half-suspicious glance.

"You have a hard struggle?"

"Hard enough."

"What do you do?"

"Anything and everything I can, of course. It's hard work."

Her hands offered no evidence of this, however. "Well, we must try to make things easier for you, Anna. Now let us talk it over."

"I'll wash my hands first and tidy up a bit," and she went into the adjoining room, where I heard her moving some furniture into place.

This gave an opportunity of scrutinizing the mean little sitting-room, and one fact was instantly apparent. There was not a single thing to suggest that a child had even set foot in it. On the floor close to the shabby sofa was a partly open leather bag; much too good and expensive to be in keeping with the rest, and a glance into it revealed a number of dressing-table fitments, also much better than a struggling working woman would be at all likely to own.

She had forgotten this in her confusion at my arrival and presently came out to fetch it, still in the untidy slovenly dress. "I won't be a minute, now," she said.

But several minutes passed before she returned, wearing now a well-fitting coat and skirt and cosmeticed much as she had been when we had met first.

"I try to keep my head above water, you see," she said, to account for her good clothes, no doubt.

I smiled approval and got to business. "First let me ask you whether you are absolutely certain I am the man you think."

"Do you think I should have made that fuss to-day if I wasn't? Why do you ask such a question?"

"Because I don't remember anything whatever of it, and to me you are an absolute stranger. Just tell me everything about it."

Her story was in its essence that which von Erstein had told me, repeated as if she had got it up much as she would have studied her part in a play. She was not very perfect in it, and there were just those verbal slips and trips which one may hear in a badly rehearsed play on the first night of production. Moreover, apart from her lines she was hopelessly muddled and had either been very badly coached about details or her memory was little better than my assumed one.

She judged by my looks that her story shocked me, and I sat a long time frowning as if lost in thought. "It seems absolutely inconceivable!" I exclaimed at length with a deep sigh. "Absolutely inconceivable that I could have treated you in this way; and only—how long ago was it?"

"You came straight to Hanover from Göttingen."

"What was I doing there?"

"I don't know? At least, you were always so close you would never tell me anything."

"You saw a great deal of me, of course?"

"Well, naturally. I wasn't going to marry a man I never saw, I suppose."

"No, no, of course not. Oh dear, to think of it all!" I put a few more questions which she could easily answer, and when she was growing more glibly at ease I asked: "And how old is the child?"

"Eh? I don't know. Oh yes, I do, of course. Pops was nine last birthday."

"Nine!" I exclaimed. I might well be astonished, for they had muddled this part of the thing hopelessly. The child I had seen in the Thiergarten wasn't a day more than six, probably younger even. "Where was she born?"

This rattled her. "What does it matter where she was born, so long as she was born somewhere," she said, flushing so vividly that it showed under her rouge. Clearly she did not know where "our child" was supposed to have been born. "What does matter is what you're going to do about it."

"There's only one thing any honourable man would think of doing, Anna. I shall make you my wife at once," I cried.

Her amazement was a sheer delight. It was so complete that she didn't know what to do or say and just stared at me open-eyed. "I didn't say I wanted that, did I?" she stammered at length.

"There's the child, Anna; and neither you nor I can afford to think of our own wishes;" and in proof of my moral duty in the circumstances, I delivered a lecture on the necessity of freeing the child from the stain of its birth.

This gave her time to pull herself together. "Are you in earnest?" she asked when I finished.

"I hold the strongest views in such cases. The best plan will be for me to arrange about the marriage at once, to-day indeed; and probably to-morrow or the next day we can be married."

"But I——" She pulled up suddenly. It looked as if she was going to protest she wouldn't marry a man she'd never seen before. "I'd like to think about it," she substituted uneasily.

"But why any need to think? You showed this afternoon how bitterly you resented my desertion and, unless you were play-acting, how much you still care for me. So why delay when I am willing? It is true that I can't pretend to care for you as I used, but it may all come back again to me. We'll hope so, at any rate."

"But you're engaged to that rich cousin of yours, aren't you?"

This was a good example of her slip-shod methods. As she knew that, she knew also where to have found me of course, so that the little melodramatic recognition scene in the Thiergarten had been a mere picturesque superfluity. I let it pass and replied gravely: "I should not allow that engagement to interfere with my duty to you, Anna."

"You must have changed a lot, then."

"I hope I have, if you're not really mistaken about my being the man you think. But I'll go and see about our wedding;" and I rose.

"Wait a bit," she cried, flustered and perplexed. "I didn't expect you to—to give in quite so—quite like this," she added, laughing nervously. "It isn't a bit like I was led—what I expected. Do you mean really and truly that you're ready to marry me straight off like this?"

With all the earnestness I could command I gave her the assurance. "I pledge you my sacred word of honour that if I've treated you as you say I'll marry you as soon as it can be done." A perfectly safe and sincere pledge.

This frightened her. The affair had taken a much more serious turn than she had expected. "You—you've taken my breath away almost," was how she put it; and she sat twisting and untwisting her fingers nervously, not in the least seeing how to meet the unexpected difficulty. "I must have time to think it over," she said at length.

"Why?"

"Oh, I don't know; but it's—it's so sudden."

"There's, the child, Anna," I reminded her again.

"Oh, bother the child. I mean I'm thinking of myself." This hurriedly, as she turned to stare out of the window. "Do you know the sort of life I've been living?" she asked in a low voice without looking round.

"Whatever it is, it must be my fault, and I don't care what you've been doing. I drove you to it. There's our child, remember."

There was another long silence as she stood at the window. Her laboured breathing, the clenched hands, and spasmodic movements of her shoulders evidenced some great agitation. If it was mere acting she was a far better actress than she had yet shown herself. And the change in her looks when at last she turned to me proved her emotion to be genuine.

"You're a white man right through, and I'm only dirt compared to you," she cried tensely. "Look here, I've lied about that kid. She isn't yours, or mine either for that matter. What do you say to that?" and she flung her head back challengingly.

"Only that I know it already, her age made it impossible. But it makes no difference to the wrong I did you."

"Do you still mean you'd marry me?"

"I mean every letter of the pledge I gave you just now, child or no child," I answered in the same earnest tone.

"My God!" she exclaimed ecstatically, throwing her hands up wildly, and then bursting into tears. "And they told me you were a scoundrel!" She was quite overcome, dropped into a chair and hid her face in her hands. The tears were genuine enough, for when she looked up they had made little runlets in the rouge and powder.

"Well?" I asked presently.

"I'm not fit to be the wife of a man like you," she stammered through her sobs. "I'm dirt to you; just dirt. If more men were like you there'd be less women like me."

Had the moment come to push for her confession? It looked like it; but it seemed cowardly to take advantage of her remorse and distress produced by my own trickery.

"Go away now, please," she said after a long interval.

"But how do we stand, Anna?"

"I don't know. I can't think. I can't do anything. Only that if I'd known— — Oh, for Heaven's sake go away, or I shall say— — Oh, do go!"

"Is there anything else you would like to tell me?"

"No. Yes. I don't know. Only leave me alone now."

"Then I'll come to-morrow."

"No, not to-morrow. The next day. Give me time. I must have time," she cried wildly.

I hesitated. In her present condition it would have been easy to frighten her into admitting everything; but somehow I couldn't bring myself to do it, so I left her.

CHAPTER XV
A NIGHT ATTACK

The success of my bluffing offer to marry the woman prompted some regret that the matter had not been pushed home to the point of obtaining her full confession; and it was to prove one of those disastrous blunders which come from decent motives.

I had scarcely left her before I began to see the thing clearly. It had not been difficult to persuade her, but there was von Erstein. He was not likely to believe in any readiness to marry, and would soon be able to talk her round to his view. In that case I might whistle for a confession.

All the same I had not come empty away. She had admitted the lie about "our child," and he couldn't talk that away. Moreover, it was still possible to set inquiries on foot and get the truth that way. It was all to the good that her impression of me was so favourable. There was no acting or humbug about that, and it remained to see the result. It was fairly certain that she would have little desire to carry the scheme any farther.

In the meantime what were the others thinking? Nessa had laughed at the business in the Thiergarten; but there was more than a joke in it, even when one knew the truth. Both she and Rosa would be very curious to learn what had followed, so I went to see them at once and found them all talking about it.

The Countess was shocked and very distressed. "It was such a scandal, Johann; and to happen in such a spot and with the von Gratzens there," she said.

"I need not tell you how sorry I am, aunt."

"That wasn't Johann's fault, mother," said Rosa. "He couldn't prevent the woman choosing such a public place and acting as she did."

"Why do you say choosing, Rosa? You don't imagine she expected to meet Johann there, do you? What happened after we left?" she asked me.

"My impression is that she did choose the place, aunt. I had a talk with her and afterwards saw her at her flat."

"But surely there can't be a scrap of truth in it."

"How can I say? Most emphatically I don't remember her nor a thing she told me."

"What did she tell you, Herr Lassen?" asked Nessa, her eyes twinkling. "Of course we're all anxious to hear—if you don't mind telling us, that is."

"I don't mind in the least. It's not a nice story;" and I told them as shortly as possible. Nessa had to hide her face from the Countess when I spoke of my offer of marriage, and Rosa covered her laughter under a pretence of indignation.

"You seem to have forgotten our engagement very easily, Johann!"

"Oh no. She reminded me of it; but of course she has the first claim."

"Indeed!" she cried, tossing her head.

But her mother took it seriously. "I think you were right, Johann, and I'm thankful you had sufficient manly spirit," she declared, making me feel no end of a hypocrite.

"And when are you to be married, Herr Lassen?" asked Nessa, with mischief in look and tone.

"It is not yet definitely settled."

"And your child?" chipped Rosa.

"There was a mistake there. She admitted afterwards that the child is neither hers nor mine."

"Admitted that!" exclaimed the Countess with more indignation than I thought she was capable of feeling. "Do you mean to tell us that she was brazen-faced enough to confess such a thing? She must be a regular baggage and you must be mad to think of marrying her! I never heard such a thing in all my life."

"She wasn't exactly brazen-faced when she told me, Aunt Olga. I think she was rather affected by my offer; and as an honourable man——"

"Honourable fiddlesticks, Johann! Don't talk rubbish. She's an impostor, nothing else; and I shall go to my lawyer in the morning and tell him to inform the police."

Rosa came to the rescue then. "Unless you want to get Johann into serious trouble, you won't do that, mother. You've often worried because I didn't wish to marry him, and I haven't told you the real reason; but you had better know it now. The woman's story about the sale of secret information is true. You may not remember it, Johann; but I have a couple of letters of yours in which you more than half admit it, and that it was the reason why you fled the country and never intended to come back."

"Rosa!" cried the dear old lady in deep distress. "Is that true, Johann?"

"Unfortunately, I can't say either yes or no, Aunt Olga."

"I'll get the letters," said Rosa, and she fetched them and read the portions out to us. "You can see it's his handwriting;" and she gave the letters to her mother, who glanced at them and then handed them to me.

"I don't know the writing, of course," I said. "I don't believe I could even copy it. I'm in the pothook stage still." It was a small, curiously wriggling fist, difficult to decipher, but easily identified by any one who had ever seen it. And the Countess knew it well.

"What had I better do, Johann?" she appealed.

"I leave that to you. I hope I am incapable of anything of the sort now; but if I did it, I must take the consequences."

"There is only one thing to do, mother; and that is, nothing. You don't want Johann to be shot, I suppose," said Rosa sharply.

"Don't, Rosa!"

"It's all very well to say don't; but that's what will happen if you insist on stirring this dirty water."

"But you wouldn't have him marry such a woman, child!"

"Perhaps he'd rather do even that than be shot," was the retort.

It was cruel, but effective; and after a few more words her mother gave in and went away, distressed to the point of tears.

"I'd rather have had you tell her the whole truth than grieve her like that, Rosa," I said.

"Possibly, but I wouldn't. You don't know mother, and I do. It was necessary to frighten her or she would have spread the story broadcast. I'll go and make it all right presently."

"Do you believe this story about your cousin?"

"I know it's true, and so does Oscar. He told me the moment we heard Johann was coming back."

"But he was coming back in spite of it," pointed out Nessa.

"Because of his spy work, Nessa. He was a born spy. He wormed out a lot of things in America; and the Secret Service people, seeing how good he was at the work, sent him to England and, after what he found out there, told him to come home and promised to overlook the other affair. That'll explain why I wasn't overjoyed to see you," she added to me.

I nodded. "And explain probably why von Gratzen thinks it worth while to send me back to England to recover my memory."

"Very possibly—if he really believes you've lost it, that is. Oscar says its the reason, and he ought to know. He laughed at it all; but it's no mere laughing matter."

"Better to laugh than worry," said I.

"Now tell us all about your Anna," said Nessa, who refused to consider the thing serious.

I gave them a more detailed account of the interview and answered a heap of questions about Anna, describing the change of front she had shown, the way in which she had been led to confess about the child, and my opinion that von Erstein was at the back of it.

"I shall never forget that scene in the Thiergarten to-day," laughed Nessa. "You did look so thunderstruck."

"Nothing to what I felt, I can tell you. I never felt such a fool in my life. Of course I couldn't tell whether she was in earnest or not."

"Nessa laughed and was giggling about it all the way home."

"I couldn't help it. It was so utterly ridiculous, Rosa. Her 'Oh, my long lost darling!' was just exquisite. And she did it uncommonly well."

"My laughter will have to wait till we're all out of the wood," said Rosa; "and there's a long way to go yet."

"Yours won't, will it?" Nessa asked me.

"Not a bit of it. Let's laugh while we can. But now what about the workman's card that I need?"

"Oscar's getting it," replied Rosa. "I told him to lose no time; and after this affair to-day, the sooner you're away, the easier I shall feel. It's getting on my nerves. I'd better go to mother now and calm her down."

We rose and Nessa turned to me with a mischievous smile. "You'll have me at the wedding, won't you?" she rallied.

"Whose?"

"Why yours, of course."

"Certainly. It couldn't take place without you," I replied, laughing, but with a look which made her rather sorry she'd chipped me.

"Why not?" asked Rosa stolidly. Her humour was only Teutonic. "You don't expect me to be present, I hope?"

"What do you say, Miss Caldicott?"

"Oh, don't be ridiculous. Rosa doesn't understand such stupid jokes. Good-night, Herr Lassen." She spoke indifferently, but there was a little pressure of the hand which sent me off home feeling mighty pleased with myself and thinking a lot more about her than the new complications, and so nearly brought me to grief.

It was a dark night, the streets were deserted, and I was plunging along castle-building on the foundation of that hand-pressure when, as I was taking a short cut through a square, a drunken man ran up behind, and lurched into me. He cursed me for getting in his way, and tried to close with me and, before I could shake him off, two others appeared, and one of them aimed a blow at my head with his stick.

Luckily there was just time for me to wriggle out of the way and let the first man have the benefit of the blow. It caught him full on the head, and down he went in a heap. The other two were so astounded by this that they hesitated long enough to give me a chance to attack in my turn. I went for the ruffian who had struck at me, bashed him under the chin hard enough to send him staggering back tripping into the gutter, and was ready for number three. But there was no fight left in him, and he bolted.

His companion in the gutter scrambled to his feet, but his stick had flown out of his hand in the fall, and the moment he found he had to deal with me alone without it, he also thought discretion safer and ran off after the other.

I turned to have a look at the drunken brute who had started the row, or rather the robbery, for that seemed to be the meaning of the affair. The blow had seemed hard enough to crack his skull; but when I examined him I saw that it had not hurt him seriously. I also discovered something which told me I had not appreciated the true purpose of the attack.

I recognized him at once. He was the fellow who had called on me that morning in the name of Rudolff.

He was able to get up and walk; shakily, it is true, for he was a good deal dazed, and I had to hold him up on the way to my rooms, which were close by. The stairs were a difficulty, but we got up somehow, and a drink of spirits and a rest soon brought him round sufficiently to talk.

"I suppose you were coming to warn me again, Rudolff, eh?" I said.

He stared stupidly at me.

"Don't try to fool me in that silly fashion, my friend. I know too much about you. So drop it, or you'll step out of this into the police station. You should choose companions who don't blab, you know."

That made him begin to sit up and take notice. "I've been drunk, haven't I?"

"No. Not too drunk to play the decoy, my man."

"Don't understand," he mumbled, shaking his head.

"All right. I haven't time to fool about with your sort. You can try that on the police;" and I rose and went to the telephone.

"Wait a bit," he cried hurriedly. "I'll try to remember things."

"Give me the nearest police station," I said into the 'phone, but without releasing the receiver.

That was enough for him. "Don't bring them here," he said with an oath. "I'll tell you all I know."

"I only want one thing. Who put you on to me? Tell me that and you can go."

He tried to lie and mentioned a name at random.

"You're only making a fool of yourself, Rudolff. Lies are no good to me. You came here this morning with a yarn which you could only have got from one man in Berlin, and I know all about it. You were in the Thiergarten this afternoon and pointed me out to you know whom I mean."

It proved a good shot and he squirmed uneasily, although trying a feeble sort of denial. "What's the use of lying?" I rapped sternly.

"I don't know what you mean," he muttered.

"We'll soon settle that."

Taking the precaution to lock the door I turned to the telephone again and asked for von Erstein's number; and after some preliminaries with some one I took to be his servant, von Erstein answered me.

"Who is it?" he asked sharply.

"Johann Lassen. Hope I haven't disturbed your packing."

"What do you want with me?"

"Nothing; I've had quite enough of you already; but there's a friend of yours here and he's in a bit of difficulty."

"What the devil are you driving at? Who is he?"

"The man you sent here to-day."

"I don't know what you mean."

"Oh come, that won't do. Anyhow he does, and that's enough for me." I tried to pop in the suggestion of a threat.

"What's his name?"

"You know that without my telling you; I only know what he called himself. You don't send men about the place on secret errands without knowing their names, do you?"

"Well, what does he call himself?"

"Rudolff; I don't know who he is now."

"I never heard of the man, and I've had enough of your tomfoolery."

"Just as you like. I can deal with him, of course." I heard him swear sulphurously.

"What does he want?" he growled after a pause.

"To keep out of gaol, chiefly, I fancy."

"Oh, blazes! Can't you speak plainly?"

"Yes. You see that second little practical joke you fixed up for me to-day has missed fire; he's had a crack on the head from one of your mutual friends, and I've got him here. After what he told me I rang you up to know what you'd like to do about it. As you and I are such pals, it didn't seem quite friendly to give him in charge without letting you have a chance to tell me your side. See?"

"I tell you I don't know anything about it;" angrily with an oath.

"No thoroughfare that way, my beloved."

There was no reply; he had apparently rung off. So I used the opportunity to impress friend Rudolff and lead him to understand that von Erstein had told me everything, and then hung up the receiver, paused a moment, and again pretended to call up the police station.

This was too much for the man. "What are you going to do?" he asked.

"My friend tells me that he had nothing to do with it, knows nothing about you, and that I'd better hand you over to the police."

"Who were you talking to?"

"Count von Erstein."

"Then he's a liar," he cried furiously. "He sent me here this morning so that I should know you by sight, first for that business in the Thiergarten this afternoon and then for this affair now."

"Don't tell me such lies, you murderous brute. Why, not ten minutes ago you gave me another name. Von Erstein, indeed, my friend!"

"Friend! He's no friend of yours. He's got me under his thumb for another thing and drove me to do both jobs by threatening to split on me. I can't get into the hands of the police. If you'll let me go I'll tell you all I know about it."

I shook my head and played the unbeliever till he was nearly beside himself with fright, and then told him to write down the story. This wasn't to his liking at all, but a little gentle persuasion in the shape of another pretence, with the 'phone, set him to work.

I walked up and down smoking while he wrote, glancing every now and then over his shoulder to read the result. He was not a ready penman, but he got the main facts clear enough for my purpose.

His statement was practically what he had already told me, and he added some very useful details which would help to fix it on von Erstein. But in one respect it fell short of expectation. He knew no more about Anna Hilden than his employer had told him—that I had really ruined her and that she was looking for me.

Whether he was lying or not, there were no means of deciding, and it seemed better not to question him too directly. The whole affair had shaken him up a good deal, and when he laid down the pen with a sigh he begged for another drink.

I let him have it and he gulped it down at a draught. "What are you going to do with that?" he asked, pointing to the statement.

"That wasn't in the bargain, friend cutthroat; but I'll promise you one thing, as you've seen wisdom. If I have to use it, I'll see that no harm comes to you, provided that you're ready to speak to the truth of it."

He shook his head dismally over this, and while he was hesitating, there was a nervous knock at my outer door. It flashed into my thoughts that it might be Anna Hilden. I didn't want them to meet, so I shut the room door behind me as I went out.

It was a very wild shot indeed; for the moment I pulled back the latch, the door was pushed wide and von Erstein came swaggering in.

CHAPTER XVI
A POISON CHARGE

"Where's the fellow you called Rudolff?" he demanded truculently.

My first idea was to shove him out, but it struck me that an interview between the two men might have interesting results, so I went back to the sitting-room. "Your friend's still here," I said.

Rudolff wilted at the sight of his genial employer, and as they were now two to one, both scoundrels, and capable of any violence, it was best to take precautions. Thus while von Erstein was challenging the other man to say he knew him, I crossed to a small table drawer and put my revolver in my pocket, keeping my hand on it in case of necessity.

The instant Rudolff knew that I had tricked him out of the confession he was nearly as mad as von Erstein. He couldn't well have been madder.

"A bit late, eh, beloved?" I jeered. "Had to wait for a taxi? They are rather scarce just now."

"What has this man written?"

"Just a line or two about the weather and so on."

"Let me see it."

"He can tell you, of course."

"I have a right to see it."

"Naturally. You'll see it all right—some day. What he says about atmospheric and other kinds of pressure is——"

Oaths from the two interrupted the sentence.

"Give it up," from Rudolff, and "I want to see it now," from von Erstein, came almost in the same breath.

"It pains me to disappoint such a charming pair of friends, but——" I shook my head. "Can't be done, beloved; out of the question."

"We'll see about that;" and they exchanged glances.

"Don't make asses of yourselves. One of you has a cracked pate already, and the other's so podgy that half a punch would put him out of action; so you wouldn't have a dog's chance at what I see you're thinking about."

"What do you mean, Lassen? I'm only asking to see what this man has written about me," said von Erstein, trying to fool me with an appearance of calmness, while he took his handkerchief out of the pocket of his overcoat—a suspiciously bulky handkerchief which he handled very gingerly.

"You may as well lay that thing on the table, beloved. I'm too old for that game."

He tried to laugh and suddenly grabbed the handkerchief with his left hand to free the revolver it was concealing. He bungled over it, and before he succeeded I had him covered. "I told you to put it on the table. If you lift it so much as an inch, I'll put a bullet in your head," I cried.

What a coward he was! He went as white as a sheet, tossed the weapon on to the table, and put up his hands as a shield. "Don't, Lassen. Don't do anything like that," he stammered.

I laughed, picked up his revolver, and tossed mine across to him. "That's less dangerous for you, sweetheart; it's unloaded."

Still trembling, now with more mortification than fear, however, he dropped into a chair and strafed me with fine Teutonic hate.

I turned to his companion. "Now, get out, you. Do you hear?" for he hesitated, looking to his master for orders. "It'll be bad for that head of yours if I have to chuck you out. I'll give you one minute to clear." He was no stayer and slunk out in half the time; and I followed and shut the door after him.

When I got back to the room von Erstein was on his feet also ready to go. "Oh, don't hurry away, beloved; this is an excellent chance for a pretty little love scene. Mix yourself a drink, have a cigar, and be your own cheerful sprightly self."

The scowl which greeted this was a real gem.

"What a seraphic smile! No wonder that every one loves you so and worships the ground you tread on."

"Stop it," he growled with an oath.

"Oh, you naughty darling! Did'ums," and I chucked him coyly under his fat double chin. His spasm of rage at this almost overpowered his cowardice, and he must have been within an ace of apoplexy. The blood rushed in a crimson flood to his flabby face, he clenched his fists and trembled like an aspen with the strain.

"I'm going," he mumbled thickly at last.

"Of course you are, darling; but presently." I stood with my back against the door. "I can't spare you yet. Besides, you haven't thanked me. Isn't my sweetheart grateful to his Popsy-wopsy?" I chided in a sort of Mantalini manner.

"Oh, blazes! Let me go, will you?"

"But think what I've saved you from, beloved. Why, if it hadn't been for me by this time you'd be a murderer or a thief, or both. Imagine it! The torments your tender conscience would be suffering! A murderer! My Albert!"

Another spasm of impotent rage followed, and this time, instead of cursing he groaned aloud and dropped into a chair with his hands to his head.

I locked the door then, putting the key in my pocket, took the cartridges out of his revolver, tossed it into his lap, and mixed myself a drink and lit a cigar. "Now we'll have our chat," I said, dropping the banter.

He looked up and, seeing the way to the door was free, jumped from his seat to escape; and began cursing again on finding it locked. "Are you going to stop that rot?"

"Yes, if you behave yourself; except for an occasional endearment, lest we forget how much we love one another."

"What have you got to say? Be quick about it, I want to go."

"Sit down and have a drink. It'll pull you together."

"Not here, thank you. I don't want to be poisoned."

"I didn't think of that. It's rather a good idea. I will poison you." He must be punished for that insult. I went into my bedroom and came back with a pinch of salt in a screw of paper which I opened out before him. Then I poured out his drink, put the salt into it, stirred it carefully till it had dissolved, pushed the glass across the table, and placed a chair close to the spot. "Now sit down and drink that."

"I'll see you to the devil first," he cried, trying to bluster and turning as white as a sheet.

I promptly took him by the collar of his coat and forced him into the chair and ordered him to drain the glass. His panic was pitiful. He was such a blithering ass that he never suspected I was only fooling; and was convinced I meant to kill him. The sweat of abject terror stood in beads on his forehead, he couldn't utter a word, and sat staring up at me like a paralyzed idiot.

"Drink it!" I thundered in his own bullying tones which made him jump and twitch convulsively. He made one feeble attempt to lift the glass, and then with a moan dropped back in his chair in a faint.

I was afraid at first that he was really dead; but his pulse was beating all right. It was probably just pretence; so I moved the glass out of his reach and left him to come round when he pleased. It was merely shamming, and when he thought I was far enough away, he made a grab to upset the glass.

"I think you're the biggest fool I ever met, von Erstein, but you've been punished enough for your little poison suggestion. Look here;" and I swallowed the "poison" myself. "Not enough salt even to alter the taste of it, man."

In a minute he was cursing quite as cheerfully as usual and looking just as amiable. "Well, can I go now?" he asked.

"As soon as you've answered one question. Who is Anna Hilden?"

"I don't know any more than I told you before."

"I don't mean the right one, but the mock heroine of the Thiergarten scene to-day."

"I don't know anything about her."

Taking out my card case in which I had put Rudolff's statement, I unfolded the paper and laid it on the table. "Rudolff says here— —"

He tried to snatch the paper, but I whipped it up in time, leaving only the card case in his hand. "Rudolff says here that you sent him to me so that he should point me out to her this afternoon. Now then, who is she?"

"I don't know anything about her," he repeated doggedly.

"I'll help your memory. She admitted to me that it was a put-up job and that the child was neither hers nor mine. That enough for you?"

But he stuck to his denial and nothing I could say moved him. The poison farce had apparently convinced him that his life was safe and he met all my threats with the same dogged answer.

I had to give it up in the end. "Very well, then, I shall have to get the whole story out of her. The police will do it, if I can't; so that it's only a matter of a day or two. Do you still refuse to own up?"

"I tell you I know nothing about it. Wash your own dirty linen for yourself," he replied.

I unlocked the door and told him to go. His exit was very characteristic. He stepped very gingerly toward where I stood by the door, fearing I should strike him, paused when just a couple of yards away, then darted out quickly, opened the front door, shook his fist at me and snarled out a threat. "I'll make you pay a heavy price for all this, curse you," he cried and bolted down the stairs as I made a step after him.

Except that he had been thoroughly frightened and enraged to the point of collapse, the interview had yielded little satisfaction. It was not improbable, moreover, that it had been a blunder to warn him about Anna Hilden. As for his threats, they were just laughable; but he might be able to strengthen the woman's backbone and cause her to persist in the story she had acted.

That the whole business was faked, there was no doubt at all; and if she did persist, it would only be necessary to set inquiries about her on foot. It might be as well to do that before seeing her again, as it would be a big trump card to face her with some of her own life history.

There was something to go on in the shape of Rudolff's statement; but it didn't amount to much. In all probability von Erstein would see to it that the man was got out of the way; and the mere paper itself could not carry the least weight with a soul.

Reflection suggested one exception, however. Von Gratzen might take a different view of it, if I told him frankly the whole affair. He had urged me to go to him in any trouble; and if he was not a fraud, he could help me enormously.

He would certainly want to hear from me all about the inner meaning of the scene his wife and daughter had witnessed, and it would be best to see him as soon as possible. He hated von Erstein, moreover, and might be glad to find something against him.

The next morning there was a note from him asking me to see him at his office at eleven o'clock, as he had some important news for me. Not a mere official summons this time; and this was rather a good sign.

It was to be hoped that the "important news" had to do with my leaving Berlin. The delay was irksome. Things were happening which threatened to make it more and more difficult for me to disappear without causing more fuss than would be healthy for either Nessa or myself. It all tended to force one's hand; and I began to think seriously of resorting to the "third wheel" Nessa and I had discussed together.

Von Gratzen received me with all the usual cordiality, shook hands warmly, and immediately referred to the Thiergarten affair, taking the line which I had half expected.

"My wife and Nita told me all about it, and of course it settles one point satisfactorily. It places beyond doubt that you are really Johann Lassen. Nevertheless I could wish it had been established in a less dramatic and embarrassing fashion for you."

"It was exceedingly unpleasant, sir."

"Tell me all about it."

I described it from my point of view; making much of my profound astonishment and my inability to say whether the story was true or not.

"Have you any reason to doubt it? Did you remember anything which enabled you, I mean?"

"Not a thing. So far as I know, I never saw the woman before in all my life."

"But she was positive?"

"She embraced me and called me her 'long lost darling,' and so on."

"Women are hysterical creatures, we know, and apt to make any sort of statement at such moments. Do you think she was really in earnest? Of course it's important."

"Your people could judge that as well as I, sir."

"True. Which would you rather it was—true or false?"

"False, without a question."

"Despite the fact that it establishes your identity?"

"Certainly. Any man who feels as I do now must loathe to have such a brutal thing as that dug up out of his past."

"Good. I'm glad to hear you say that." He smiled as if he was really glad, but there was something else behind his questions that left me guessing as usual.

If he accepted the woman's recognition as settling the matter of my identification as Lassen, was it better to leave it there or risk unsettling him again by telling him about the subsequent interview with her? Rather a nice point to decide. But his next question cleared the course and concealment kicked the beam.

"You'd like to have the matter investigated?"

"Certainly," I replied promptly. Very few official inquiries would give him the truth, and it was thus much better to tell it myself. "I was going to ask your advice about it. I know that part of her story is false; she owned it; and I doubt all the rest;" and I described the interview.

This appeared to both interest and amuse him, especially my instant offer to marry Anna; and he expressed his appreciation in the equivocal fashion. "It was clever, my boy; quite the best line. You must have had considerable experience in bluffing people;" and there was a glint in his keen eyes which might have meant anything. "You can act well too, or you'd never have dragged that confession out of her. She must have thought you were in earnest."

"I was, sir. If she can prove that I am the man she thinks, I will marry her."

"Good. Very good indeed. *If* she can prove it, of course. But you wouldn't relish the job, eh?"

"That goes without saying."

"Well, we'll hope she can't. We shall soon know all about her. In the meantime what are you going to do?"

"I can only wait and see."

He laughed and rubbed his hands. "Wait and see, eh? That's the English Premier's phrase, isn't it? So you've picked that up, it seems."

His comment made me wish I'd used a different one. "There isn't anything else to do, sir."

"Quite so. Wait and see. Exactly. And as an honourable man you'd prefer to get the question settled before leaving Berlin?"

The shrewd old beggar was a positive expert in sticking one in a hole. I didn't know what answer to make, so I just shrugged my shoulders and smiled vacuously.

"It's rather a pity, too," he continued after a pause. "I've arranged that matter of your leaving; in fact I intended you to go to-day. I have all the necessary papers, even tickets for you and Miss Caldicott;" and he took them out of his desk and laid them in front of me, giving me one of those wily smiles of his.

I could have cursed the luck. The sight of them, the knowledge that Nessa and I could have been out of the infernal country within a few hours but for this rotten thing coming in the way, so exasperated me that it was scarcely possible to conceal my bitter chagrin. I tried to hide it from him by taking the papers and looking them over.

"Oh dear, I've forgotten something," he exclaimed, rising. "I'll be back in a moment," and he went out of the room.

What a temptation that was! To have all I needed actually in my hands; to be left alone with them and yet not to be able to use them! I'd have given every shilling I had in the world to have stuffed them into my pocket and walked off. Did he mean me to take them? Or was it intended as a test? Did he guess what a temptation it was? Could I get away with them? He stopped out of the room long enough, and as the minutes passed, it was all I could do to resist it.

But I stuck it; put the papers down on his desk and tried not to look at them. It was a touch of sheer purgatory. His first glance, when at length he returned, was at them, and the way he looked at me made me pretty certain that he could guess something of my feeling. It looked uncommonly as if he were disappointed to find me still in the room and the papers on his table.

"I'm sorry to have kept you, my boy, but it couldn't be helped," he said as he sat down and put the temptation out of sight. "I told you in my letter that I had something important to tell you. I have, and unpleasant into the bargain. Was Count von Erstein with you last night?"

"Yes, about ten o'clock."

"Did you offer him some drink?"

"Yes, and a cigar, but he refused both."

"What was he doing there? Wait, I'll tell you first that he has made a charge against you that you attempted to poison him."

I laughed. "Of course I didn't. It was a joke."

"It may not be altogether a laughing matter; he's a dangerous man to joke with. Would you care to tell me about it all?"

"Of course. This will explain a good deal." I put my hand in my waistcoat pocket for Rudolff's statement, and then for the first time missed the card case which Rosa had given me. The loss was of no consequence, however, as I had the fellow's confession. "Before I give it you I ought to say that I promised the man who wrote this that if he was prepared to swear to the truth of it, he should come to no harm."

"That'll be all right," he agreed with a nod.

"An attempt was made on my life last night by this fellow and two others at von Erstein's instigation;" and I described the affair and all that had occurred subsequently.

"Ah, more clever bluff, eh? Upon my word I shall be expecting you to try it with me next," he said. Then he read over the confession carefully and lapsed into thought. Long and apparently anxious thought it was, too.

"I'll stand by you, my boy. I believe your story implicitly and I know von Erstein. But it was a bad mistake. He has a lot of influence in many directions. I hope you'll hear no more of it; but it was a bad blunder." He paused and, in a different and lighter tone and with a very peculiar look and a shadow of a smile, added: "It makes me almost wish you had taken advantage of my absence just now to get away with those tickets."

What on earth could one make of such a statement? If he'd given me another chance I'd have taken it; but he didn't. He locked the tickets up and sent me away, saying he would look into my affairs at once and send for me as soon as there was any need.

CHAPTER XVII
ANNA HILDEN AGAIN

It is difficult to describe my feelings when I left von Gratzen, but I think my chief thought was a bitter regret that I hadn't taken the tickets and chanced things, mingled with a disquieting belief that I was muddling matters hopelessly.

Neither regret nor self-cursing were of the slightest help, however; and after a few minutes of impotent perplexity, I realized that extremely obvious fact.

Something had to be done; and the question was—what?

It looked as if von Gratzen would have let me have those tickets if I hadn't been ass enough to tell him about Anna and play the fool about being eager to have that affair cleared up first. He had not appeared to attach sufficient importance to the poison charge to refuse them on that account.

This cleared the ground a little, therefore. Could the obstacle be removed in time to allow of my using them that night? Could I get the confession from Anna herself, this meant? It was worth trying.

She had fixed the following day for me to see her; but that wasn't a good enough reason for my not seeing her at once. My natural eagerness to have the thing settled without delay would readily account for my disregarding her wish, and whether it did or not didn't matter two straws. So I set off on the errand at once.

Persuasion was the first card to play, and if that failed, a threat of the police; but by one means or another I must have the confession to take to von Gratzen that afternoon. Everything now turned on getting it into his hands early enough for Nessa and me to catch the Dutch mail which left about eight that night.

She had her hat on when I arrived, and resented the visit. "I said you were not to come until to-morrow," she said. "I can't see you now, as I'm just going out."

"I could not wait till to-morrow. I can't bear suspense."

"I've nothing to say to you, so it's no use your coming in."

"But I'm in already, Anna, and I must speak to you." She tried to avoid me and leave the place, but I shut the door and stood with my back to it.

"Very well. Go into the sitting-room and I'll listen."

"I'll follow you," I replied drily; and with a laugh and a shrug she led the way to her room.

"You seem almost as eager to marry me now as you were before to get out of it," she scoffed.

It was an unpromising start, for she was in a very different mood from that of the previous day. "If you think a moment of all that this must mean to me, of my desperate anxiety to know the truth about the past and to see what lies ahead, you'll understand it all, Anna;" and I went on for a few moments in that style endeavouring to re-establish the former relations and work on her emotions.

"I haven't had enough time to think about it," she replied. "Of course it takes a lot of thinking about."

"Does that mean you are not sure I am the man who wronged you?"

"Why should it, pray?"

"Well, you said that you had been mistaken about the child."

"I may have said that for a purpose. You got the soft side of me yesterday, and — — But I tell you I haven't made up my mind."

"You haven't altered your opinion about my being an honourable man and wishing to do the right thing, I hope?" and I did my best to draw a vivid picture of my state of mind and appeal to her good nature.

This appeared to have a softening effect; but not enough for the purpose. "Why does one day make such a difference?"

"Every minute makes a difference, Anna. I am on the rack and it's positive torture to prolong this suspense."

"I'm sorry. I am really; but I can't make up my mind. If you could do without me all these years, another day can't matter so much. Not that I can see."

"If you had lost your memory, you'd understand."

"But that was only a week or two ago. What of all the other time, the years and years you've left me to fend for myself?"

"I can't account for that," I said, as if distracted.

"You hadn't lost your memory all that time, however."

"The shock of the explosion has utterly changed me in every way."

"It was about time, I should think, judging by all I've heard and the way you treated me. I don't deny you're a white man enough now; but what if you got your memory back? It might change you into something very different. I have to think of that, you know. You might be mad enough to—to do anything; perhaps even murder me. You're not surprised it makes me think, are you? I don't wish to be made into an honest woman only to be murdered."

This was altogether so different from her previous attitude, that it was clear some one had been coaching her; and of course it could only be von Erstein. "You need not fear that, Anna."

"Why not? How do you know what you'd be mad enough to do if you got your memory back and found you'd tied yourself to me?"

"There's a very simple way out of that. Even if you wish me to marry you, we need not live together. I should give you an allowance and you could go your way and I mine, if you preferred it."

For some reason which beat me this seemed to appeal strongly to her. She sat thinking, and there was something of her previous day's emotion in her look as she asked: "Do you mean that?"

"You little know me if you doubt it, Anna."

She got up impulsively to stare out of the window as she had done before, and after a long pause she turned. "Look here, come to-morrow."

I looked intently at her and read something in her face that gave me fresh hope. "Why not to-day? You have made up your mind, I can see that; so why not tell me now?"

She shook her head. "Not to-day. To-morrow."

"Why?"

"I can't tell you why. Don't ask me."

"But I do ask you. I beg you as earnestly as I can."

Another shake of the head; and she would not budge, so that it became necessary to try a turn of the screw.

"Your reason has to do with some one else?"

"What do you mean?" she flashed in surprise and some alarm.

"I had a visit yesterday from a man who called himself Rudolff."

"Well? What's that got to do with it?"

"With two companions he tried to murder me."

She caught her breath. "Is that true?"

"As you see, the attempt failed and the man himself got the blow intended for me. I took him to my rooms afterwards and—well, here's his confession."

Her interest was keen enough to quicken her breathing as I took out the paper; and her fright deepened as I read it, and she began to tremble violently. "As you hear, he was the man who pointed me out to you yesterday in the Thiergarten."

For a few moments she was too overcome to speak. "What—do you—think it all means?" she stammered brokenly.

"Do you know Count von Erstein?"

Her hand went to her throat as she tried to reply, making a swallowing, half-choking motion. "You don't believe—that I had anything—to do with all that?"

"Oh no, Anna. I am sure you had not. I have told the authorities——"

"The police?" she broke in. It was almost a scream.

"Not the police. But, of course, a man can't let any one attempt his life and just sit down under it. I have a very influential friend——" I paused intentionally.

"Who is that?" came like a pistol shot.

"Baron von Gratzen; and he——"

"Did you tell him about me?"

"He knows of it. He is greatly_interested in me because this unfortunate affair about my treatment of you will affect all he can do for my future. His wife and daughter were present yesterday when you recognized me. Of course he questioned me all about it and declared that he would have the fullest investigation made at once."

That seemed to break her right up. Von Gratzen's reputation caused the collapse. She had stiffened in alarm at the mention of his name, had listened with parted lips and straining features to every syllable about his interest in me, and when she knew that his people were going to take up the investigation, she was utterly overcome.

With a muffled cry of despair, she fell back in her chair in a half-fainting condition, her hands pressed to her face, moaning distractedly. She remained in this state for several minutes, the effort to regain self-control being quite beyond her, and at length sprang to her feet, saying she must go out at once.

"You'd better tell me everything before you go, Anna," I said. Knowing that she had been driven into the deception by von Erstein, I pitied her sincerely. She was like a wild thing in her panic, shaking her head and flourishing her arms hysterically.

"No, no. To-morrow."

"It may be too late then. I have great influence with the Baron and can put the matter to him in a way to help you. It will be useless to try that to-morrow."

"Not now. Not yet. I can't. I can't. Let me go. Let me go, I say!"

I persisted, however; and at length she consented to my seeing her again that afternoon at five o'clock. I had to be content with that, and as soon as we reached the street she hurried off.

She was going to von Erstein of course, and I would have given something to be able to hear what passed. She was in deadly fear of him. Her manner had shown that; and considering what the man was, her news would probably give him an equally bad attack of nerves. He would not relish von Gratzen's intervention any better than she had.

On the whole the interview had turned out well enough. It would have been better if I had been able to drag the truth out of her at once, of course; but I was confident that I should get it all in the afternoon. That would still give me time to carry the news to von Gratzen and satisfy him that the obstacle to my leaving was removed.

The "third wheel" must none the less be in working order. Nessa must be prepared to leave, and I went to the Karlstrasse to see her. She was out with Lottchen, however, and I only saw Rosa, who was delighted to hear that von Gratzen had arranged for us to leave.

"It's very lucky, too, because Oscar has left Berlin for a day or two without having been able to do anything about the other scheme. You won't need it now, of course."

"I wish I was sure; but I'm not. Von Gratzen may still raise some objection; things are so mixed up. But I mean to go to-night in any event, with or without his permit. Rotten luck that Feldmann's away."

"He was afraid you might do something like that, so he gave me the name of a man who can do what you want, but I wasn't to tell you about it unless it was absolutely necessary."

"It is necessary, as you can see for yourself. Who's the man and what is he? I'll go to him straight off."

"David Graun is the name; he lives at 250, Futtenplatz. He's a Jew; a very shady character, and Oscar said you'd have to be awfully careful how you handled him."

"Where's the Futtenplatz?"

"It's in a low quarter across the river;" and she told me how to find it. "Oscar says he bears the worst of characters and does all sorts of shady things under the cloak of a second-hand clothes' dealer."

"He's sure that the man can get me what I want?"

"Oh yes; positive, if you handle him right; but you must be awfully cautious. He'll ask much more at first than he expects."

"He's a Jew, of course."

"It isn't only that. It's his way of testing any one who goes to him. If you agree to pay it, you won't get anything out of him except promises. Oscar said I'd better tell you this to put you on your guard; and you mustn't let him think it's for yourself under any circumstances."

"Do you know how much I ought to pay him?"

"Only a few marks, ten or fifteen at the outside. He'll probably ask a hundred or even more."

"I understand. But it's odd that Feldmann should know all this about him."

She smiled. "That's what I thought, and Oscar said I might tell you the real reason. The fact is this Graun works with the police. He got into trouble once and they made things easy for him on his promise to act as their spy. There's a lot of this false identification card business done, and he reports every transaction to them, and they are able to watch all the people who go to him. When any one is wanted, they give him a description, and he just keeps the man waiting while he communicates with them."

"That's cheerful. He'll tell them about me, then."

"Oscar says you needn't worry about it. So long as any one is not known to be an alien or a criminal, nothing happens; but you're to be careful to get the things at once."

"I don't quite see why."

"I didn't quite understand it, either. Oscar only told me at the last minute just as he was hurrying away. I fancy he said something about a second visit being risky, lest the man should have one of the police there to have a look at you."

"I'll be off then. Tell Nessa I'll see her as soon as possible and tell her everything."

"Oh, I do hope you'll get away safely. If the Baron lets you have the permit and tickets, I'll never say another word against him as long as I live," she declared as we shook hands.

"It will be all right one way or the other."

"Yes; but if you could really travel by the mail a few hours would end everything. I shall be so anxious."

"Of course your mother mustn't know anything about Nessa leaving."

"She's in bed, after yesterday's upset. So that will be all right."

"Not really ill?"

"Oh, no; only a bad headache. Nessa and I are booked for a concert this evening, and I shall tell the servants not to sit up for us, so that she won't be missed till to-morrow morning; and by that time you two ought to be in Holland;" and with that I set off to interview the tricky old Jew in the Futtenplatz.

CHAPTER XVIII
A SINISTER DEVELOPMENT

On the way to the Futtenplatz I made up a little fairy tale to account for my visit to the Jew, Graun. I didn't like the job, and what Rosa had told me about his relations with the police didn't make it any pleasanter.

A very little knowledge of German police ways was enough to render it quite credible. It was just the sort of low cunning which would chime with their methods. There were plenty of people, besides aliens, who were anxious to get out of Berlin at such a time, and it would suit the authorities admirably to have this secret means of finding out who they were and acting accordingly.

Rosa's description of the Futtenplatz was well deserved: a squalid, dirty place, with mean shops of the poorest sort. The Jew's second-hand clothes shop was one of the meanest and dirtiest, and Graun himself fitted thoroughly into the picture.

When I entered he was bargaining with a man who wanted to sell him a coat, and while the transaction proceeded—while the old Jew was beating down the price to the last pfennig, that is—I had ample time to observe him.

Red-haired, with red tousled beard and whiskers, pronounced Hebraic features, small suspicious eyes, and filthy from the top of his narrow forehead to the tip of his clawlike finger-nails, he was one of the most repulsive specimens one could wish to avoid.

"What do you want?" he asked in a high-pitched rasping voice, squinting at me, when his customer went out, cursing him for the smallness of the amount he had received for the coat.

I told him straight out. The remembrance of Feldmann's tips was one reason, and my desire not to stop one unnecessary moment in such unsavoury surroundings was another.

He shook his head. "You've come to the wrong shop, my man. Given up all that sort of thing long ago. Too risky."

"All right; sorry to have troubled you. Good-day," I replied casually, and turned to leave.

He let me get to the door and then called me back. "Wait a moment. Who sent you here?"

"No one in particular. It's pretty well known, isn't it? Good-day."

"Here, wait. Come here; I know some one who might be able to do it for you."

I didn't go back. "It isn't of the least consequence," I said with an airy wave of the hand. "I told the man he'd better go to the police and just tell them how he lost his card."

"Come in here a minute;" and he shuffled off to a door at the back of the shop.

I hesitated, took a couple of paces toward him, stopped and shook my head. "No. I don't want to have anything to do with it, if there's any risk attached to it, as you say."

This worked all right. "When I said that, I thought you wanted it for yourself," he said slily.

I burst out laughing and turned again as if to go away. "Good-day, my friend. That's rich and no mistake."

"Here, don't be in such a hurry," he said, coming a step toward me. "If your friend's in any trouble, I might— —"

"What the devil do you mean by that?" I cried, and cursed him royally for the suggestion.

He came up and laid his filthy claw on my sleeve. I shook it off with another choice epithet or two. "Come into my room a minute and we'll talk it over. Don't lose your temper."

I allowed myself to be pacified: not too quickly, of course; and with a great show of reluctance allowed him to take me into his room, which was, if possible, filthier even than the shop and smelt vilely.

"Now, tell me all about it. Of course most of those who come to me are in trouble of some sort or other and I have to be careful. If the police knew anything, well— —" and he gestured to indicate the trouble it would mean for him.

"All right, but don't try that rot with me. Either you can sell me what I've asked for, or you can't. So out with it. I don't care which way it is; and this place of yours stinks so that I don't want to stop in it and be suffocated."

He leered as if this were rather a good joke or a compliment. "I might be able to manage it, but — —"

I broke in with an impatient oath. "I don't want any 'might be.' Can you or can't you? Be quick about it, too. If you can, how much?" This was evidently the right line with him and he grinned appreciatively.

"That's the way to talk. Shall we say 150 marks?"

"How much?" I cried with a regular spasm of astonishment. "Say it again, man."

"A hundred and fifty marks."

I sat back and stared at him. "Do you think I want to deal wholesale and set up in the business myself? I only want one, you infernal old humbug;" and I roared with laughter.

He was accustomed to being abused and joined in the laugh, combing his tousled red beard with his filthy fingers. "Well, how much then?"

"Oh, a couple of marks or so."

He threw up his hands, gesticulating violently, as if the offer was an insult, appeared to work himself into a furious rage, and fumed and fussed and stormed, until I got up. Again he tested me; let me leave the room and reach the door of the shop, following with a mixture of lamentations and appeals to Heaven to bear witness to my lunacy.

I did not so much as turn round, remembering Feldmann's caution, and I was all but in the street, before he changed his tone, apparently satisfied that I was sincere.

"It's no use to part like this. Come back and talk it over again." Once more a similar pantomime was played; but this time I was much slower to give way. "It can't be done at the price. Impossible. Think of the risk I should — —"

"Then don't do it. I tell you if you mean there's any risk in the thing, I won't touch it with a ten-foot pole. I thought a few marks was all that would be necessary; but if you offered to give it me for nothing and there's any risk I wouldn't take it. Get that into your head."

"Do you think I give things away?"

"Not I, seeing how you cling to the dirt on you."

This was also accepted as a joke and he wagged his head and winked. "It takes too much time to clean things; and time's money," he replied, with one of his repulsive leers. "But I like you. You say what you mean. I'll take a hundred marks from you."

"Will you? You'll be cleverer than I take you for, if you do."

"But there's the— —" He was going to repeat about the risk, but checked the word as bad business; and a long chaffering began in which he tried to squeeze me first to seventy-five marks, then to fifty, coming down by tens and fives to twenty-five.

He stuck at that point a long time; and lest he should think even that sum suspicious, I held out at the five marks to which I had increased my offer during the bargaining.

Once more he let me all but leave the shop, and when he again called me back I refused to go and struck out a fresh line.

"I'll tell you why I've stopped so long as it is, Graun," I said. "I've never met any one quite like you before, and you're a very interesting character. I do something at times in theatricals and you're worth studying; but I've had enough of you now. It's been worth a few marks to have such a chance as this, and, while I don't care two straws whether I get what brought me here or not, I'll give you five marks for the fun I've had," and to his consummate astonishment I put the money in his dirty palm. "If I were you, I'd spend it on soap or something that will get rid of some of this beastly stink."

"You give me this?" he cried in amazement.

"Yes, give it you. Good-day."

It was the turning point of the conference. He clawed hold of my arm. "You can come and study me any time you like at the same price," he said with a grin. "I don't mind how often. And look here, you shall have the card if you'll make it ten marks."

"Another five, do you mean?"

"Oh, no. Oh, no. Another ten," he cried greedily.

I shook my head at first and then smiled. "I tell you what I'll do. I'll give you the other ten, if you'll throw in another cursing and lamentation scene, like the last. Five for that and five for the card. You do it so beautifully, Graun; and it's all put on, I know."

He grinned, but shook his head. "It wasn't put on."

"You're a dirty, stinking, money-grabbing Jew, Graun," I cried, with every appearance of fierce earnestness.

He seemed to take it as meant, and he did repeat the cursing scene with the utmost energy and wild gesticulation, to my intense amusement.

"It wasn't quite so good as the first, Graun, but it's worth the money all the same. Here you are; get me the card. I believe you're quite a decent sort really and just put on this manner for business."

More leers as he shuffled off, and in a minute or two later I left with an identification card in the name of "Johann Liebe, mechanic."

Whether he would tell the police of my visit, I neither knew nor cared. He was obviously satisfied that things were pretty much as I had pretended, and the little hint that I might wish to "study" him again was quite likely to make him hold his tongue.

I had all that I needed; the way to leave was now open; and in a very few hours Nessa and I would have seen the last of Berlin for many a day.

The interview had taken longer than I had expected, however, and after snatching a hasty meal in the first decent place I came to, I hurried to the Karlstrasse to fix up the final arrangements for our departure.

Nessa was as jubilant as I at the news of my success. "Rosa told me all you said and where you'd gone and that we were to go to-night. Oh, isn't it splendid!" she exclaimed.

"You'll be ready?"

"Oh, no. I shall take care to miss the train, of course. Make a point of it," she cried, her eyes as bright as diamonds. "I shall have a cab, tell every one I'm going to England and — — How can you ask such a silly question, Jack?"

"Steady. Not that name till we're in Holland anyhow."

"Do you expect me to be steady at such a time, Herr Lassen?" with mock emphasis on the name.

"I shan't be Lassen after this, mind. This thing I've got in my pocket christens me Johann Liebe."

She laughed. "Let me look at it. I declare I could almost kiss it," she exclaimed, when I showed it to her. "And now we'll be sensible. What are my marching orders?"

"Flying orders, we call them. Well, I still hope we shall travel in state under Government patronage, and — —"

"I hope not," she broke in. "I'd much rather go on the 'third wheel,' you know. It would be glorious fun. I don't want to have to scrap my disguise and have had all my trouble for nothing."

"That's all right; but the other wheel's both safer and quicker, thank you. All the same you'd better bring the props along in case things go wrong. One never knows. Do you want to bother with any luggage?"

"A comb and a toothbrush, a few hairpins and a pair of scissors. That too much?"

"Rather not; but why scissors?"

"You don't want your assistant to have long hair, do you? And it might be injudicious to worry a barber."

We both laughed. "I never thought of that. By Jove, it would be a beastly shame to have to cut off that lovely wig of yours." She had most beautiful hair of a rich dark auburn.

"A thousand times better than an internment camp," she replied, sobered by the mere thought of it. But only for the moment; she was too wildly excited at the prospect of going home for anything to damp her spirits. "Why, I'd do it only to play the part of Hans Bulich for an hour."

"Who's Hans Bulich?"

"Your assistant that hopes to be, of course. You're surely not going to begin by forgetting essentials?"

"I had forgotten for the moment."

"Well, don't forget again. Shall I spell it for you?"

"Don't give me any of your lip, 'Hans,'" I retorted smartly.

"All right, matey, keep your hand on the brake," she replied in her excellent assistant's tone; and worked in a number of motor parts to show she had been swotting them up as I had suggested.

"You'll do, boy," I said, laughing. "And now let's remember this isn't going to be all mere chaff," and I told her my plan. She was to be at the station a quarter of an hour before the train started and look out for me in the waiting-room. "If things go right with von Gratzen, that'll be the ladies' room; if not, then the third class. I'll manage to 'phone you in time for the necessary make-up. As for the rest, it's up to us to manage the best we can."

"If we have to go disguised, are you going to risk the mail train then?"

"There won't be any risk to speak of now that I've got this;" tapping my pocket. "Of course we can't go all the way because I haven't a passport; but we'll get as near the frontier as we can. Osnabrück, probably; but I'll have the tickets all right. And now I must be off."

"I wish my silly heart wouldn't beat like a racing 40 h.p., but I'll have it in good order when we meet again."

"It's a good thing I don't make it beat, eh?"

"Hands off, matey," replied "Hans," but with a very un-boylike blush.

"You must drop that habit, young 'un. You've got to think about other 40 h.p.'s, you know;" and with that I went, little thinking of all that was to happen before we met again.

I hurried to my rooms to put the final touches to my preparations; pack the one or two trifles I needed for the journey; make sure that no inquisitive eyes had discovered my hidden suit case; and have everything ready for instant departure.

This did not take more than a few minutes, and I had just finished and was replacing the suit case in its hiding place, when the telephone rang.

"Hullo?" I asked, wondering who could want to call me up.

"Herr Lassen?" came in a woman's voice I did not know.

"Yes. What is it?"

"I'm to tell you Anna Hilden wants to see you at once."

"Who is it speaking?" There was no answer, and none again when I repeated the question. Who could it be? And the meaning of it? It certainly wasn't Anna's voice, although the 'phone has a trick at times of changing the voice considerably.

It was still nearly an hour before the time she had fixed for me to go to her, and I couldn't understand how she could have got hold of my telephone number. But she wouldn't have telephoned if it hadn't been urgent. It looked as if she had made up her mind at last to admit everything, and the sooner I had the confession the better chance there was of catching von Gratzen at his office. So I hurried off, was lucky enough to get a taxi, and reached her place within ten minutes of getting her message.

To my surprise the door of her flat was ajar. Not perhaps an unusual thing, considering that she was a somewhat casual person. I pressed the electric bell and heard it ring all right; but she didn't come to the door. Probably slipped out for something, I concluded; and after a second ring, I pushed the door wide and went in.

She was not in the sitting-room, and I was just dropping into a chair to wait for her, when a glance through the open door of the adjoining bedroom brought my heart up into my mouth, as if I'd come on an air pocket a thousand feet deep.

She was lying asprawl on the bed in a most unnatural attitude.

In a second I was in the room and knew the truth.

She was dead, and the marks on her throat could only mean one thing.

"Murder!"

CHAPTER XIX
MURDER

Some horror-filled moments passed before I grasped the full significance to me of the unfortunate woman's death. I turned dizzy and bewildered like a drunken man, and could do nothing but just stare at the body, literally stupefied by the suddenness of it.

It wasn't the fact of death that startled me; I had seen too many dead bodies at the Front to be much concerned.

But I made a big effort to pull myself together. I examined her to be certain that she was really dead, for the body was still warm. There was no doubt about it. The poor thing had been choked, and the marks of the murderer's fingers showed on her throat.

There had been a struggle in the room, and some of the wretched furniture had been overturned. My wits were beginning to clear by that time; and I was glancing about the room wondering who had been brute enough to commit the murder and what I had better do, when I made a discovery that told me everything and turned the blood in my veins icy cold.

In examining the body I had disarranged the bedclothes slightly, and by the side of the neck, just where it would have fallen from the murderer's finger, lay a ring.

Von Erstein's! The puzzle ring he had once shown and explained to me! It was impossible to mistake it; and there was probably not another ring like it in Berlin.

I didn't lose my head that time; the instinct of self-preservation was too strong to allow of any other feeling. My one absorbing thought was to get away before any one could come.

I darted back into the sitting-room and snatched at my hat which I had left on the table. In my flurry I fumbled. It fell to the floor and rolled under the table; and when I grabbed for it again, the quaint little card case which Rosa had given me lay open just beside it.

Too obsessed by the desire to get out of the place, I had no other feeling than a faint satisfaction at finding it again; not realizing for an instant the full significance of the incident I pocketed the thing, picked up my hat and left the flat. I took care to shut the door; this would serve to postpone the discovery of the murder; went down the staircase without undue hurry, made sure there was no one to see me leave, walked leisurely away until I turned the first corner and then made off at a rapid pace.

A sensation of profound relief that I was safe for a time at any rate was followed by some minutes of acute reaction in which I was incapable of consecutive thought. A mental blank from which I awoke pretty much as a man might wake from sleep-walking. I gazed about me unknowingly, and seeing the gate of a small public garden close at hand, I went in and sat down.

I soon began to get my wits in working order and bit by bit pieced things together. Curiously enough, almost the first thought was about the comparative trifle of the card case. I remember that I took it out and looked at it, wondering stupidly when I could have dropped it in Anna's room. Then I recalled that I had missed it in the morning when with von Gratzen. It couldn't have been in my pocket therefore when I went to Anna; and in a few seconds I understood.

The last time I had touched it was on the previous night when I had taken Rudolff's statement out of it to show von Erstein and he had tried to snatch the paper away and had only got the little case. I remembered that he had thrown it down close to him and had fiddled with it nervously afterwards.

It was clear that he had taken it away with him and had intentionally left it in Anna's room to shift his villainous deed on to me. It was worthy of him; and it would have succeeded but for that wonderful slice of luck— ineffably blessed luck, indeed—by which I had found the card case.

That helped me to piece the rest together. Panic-stricken by what I had told her about von Gratzen, Anna had no doubt threatened to expose everything; Erstein's whole scheme would be ruined the moment she opened her lips: and this had roused the brute in him until he had been driven to strangle her. The ring had slipped from his finger without his noticing the loss of it in his rage. Then he must have tossed my card case down under the table to connect me with the crime.

He had obviously left the door ajar for the same reason; had probably rushed to the first public telephone box and called me up in a voice which was enough like a woman's to mislead me; and intended to send some one to catch me red-hot on the scene of the crime.

Two points were not clear. Why no one had caught me? There had been ample time, supposing that he was hiding in wait for my arrival. And why had the murder been committed in Anna's room, seeing that she had gone from me to find him?

One of two suggestions seemed to answer the last question. Either she had not found him at first and had left a sufficiently urgent message to make him hurry to her, or that after a first interview he had induced her to go home and had followed at once. The plan to kill her must have been in his mind then, and obviously he couldn't do it in his own rooms.

The first question—why I had not been caught—wasn't so readily solved; but the ring might well account for it, if he had only discovered the loss of it in the interval of waiting for me. With that damning bit of evidence against himself, the bottom had dropped out of his scheme against me, and he would not dare to try and have me caught in the act.

And now I had fortunately shut the door against him. He couldn't go back for the ring even if he had the pluck, which I doubted.

This was another stroke of luck, indeed; and it was needed in all truth, for the mess was bad and black enough to need a heap of it, if I was to escape being charged with the murder. Such a charge would ruin me lock, stock and barrel. Even if I could clear myself—and that was almost impossible— all the truth about myself would be ferretted out, and it was thousands to one that I should be shot for a spy.

Only one expedient occurred to me at first—to bolt. But that looked hopeless in the new circumstances. It would be tantamount to a confession of guilt; von Erstein would tell some plausible lie about the ring belonging to Anna; and it would be believed easily enough if suspicion were lifted from him by my flight; the hue and cry would be raised all over the country; old Graun would tell his story—that I had a workman's papers in the name of Liebe; and my arrest would be a matter of hours possibly, certainly one of days at the outside.

That idea had to be set aside, therefore. Before there could be any thought of flight suspicion must be fastened on von Erstein. But how? Not by sitting on a public seat and nibbling my nails; so I got up and started back to the centre of things.

I had completely recovered from the disturbing panicky condition which had so confused me in the first rush of things. I don't think I was even afraid. My chief feeling was that I was in the very devil's own mess and that I should go under, unless my own wits could save me. If Feldmann had been in Berlin I should have gone to him; but he wasn't, and it was no use wishing he had been.

There was only one other man in the whole city—von Gratzen; and the moment that became clear and plain, I hailed a taxi and was driven straight to his office.

He was still there, but refused to see me, sending von Welten to ask my business. I said that it was on personal business I wished to see his chief.

This didn't work, however. Von Welten returned, saying the Baron was exceedingly busy and would I state my business in writing. This looked ugly; but after thinking a second, I wrote on my card: "Please see me for the sake of the Untergasse affair;" placed it in an envelope and sent it in. If anything would induce von Gratzen to have me in, that would.

I was right. Von Welten came back smiling. "The chief will see you in a minute or two, Herr Lassen. I'm glad." He was an exceedingly pleasant fellow and stayed chatting with me until von Gratzen's bell rang and I was shown in.

"You're giving me a lot of trouble, young man, as you can see," he said, pointing to a portfolio in which there appeared to be a lot of papers on the top of which were the coveted tickets for Nessa and me. "And now what about this Untergasse affair? Found anything out that's valuable? I can't give you many minutes."

"I'm in a devil of a mess, sir, but it has nothing to do with that. I wrote that because I was compelled to see you."

"I agree with you. You've been in one ever since you reached the city, it seems to me, indeed. Nothing fresh, I trust?"

"There is, and the worst of all, sir. I'm in danger of being charged with murder."

"With what?" he cried in amazement. "Phew! Well, tell me."

"When I saw you this morning I gathered that the reason those tickets for Miss Caldicott and myself could not be used was because of the trouble about the woman, Anna Hilden."

"True, but you yourself said you wished it cleared up first."

"So on leaving here I went to see her again."

"Good God, you don't mean to say you lost your head and laid hands on her in this awful way?" The thought of it appeared to affect him deeply.

"Oh dear no, sir. I hope I'm not capable of such a thing. From what she said, I became certain the whole thing was a fraud and ——"

"So it is," he interposed, nodding. "You are right. We know all about the woman already. Go on."

"I tried persuasion first; but that was no use, so I let her know that the matter was in your hands."

"I hope that frightened her."

"It did, sir. She was almost out of her wits and promised to tell me everything this afternoon. I was to call at five o'clock."

"Where did you go next?" he shot in abruptly.

"To the von Reblings."

"To tell Miss Caldicott about these, I suppose?" holding up the tickets.

"Yes. I knew she would be very anxious."

He put the pinned set of tickets, etc., into the portfolio, under a couple of papers, and leant back, with his fingers interlocked, and stared at me with frowning intentness. "You're not a fool, my boy, and you must see that your zeal on that young lady's account is likely to rouse a lot of suspicion. What do the von Reblings say about it?"

"They are extremely anxious that she should be allowed to go home."

"Umph!" a grunt and a nod, both of which were repeated. "And where did you go next after leaving them?"

I started and hesitated.

"Are you going to tell me the whole truth? We get to know many strange things here, you know."

"I went to see a man named Graun ——"

"I know you did. You were followed and he was questioned. I won't ask you why you got what you did from him; but don't attempt to use it. Now go on about this other affair. Just everything; everything, and quite frankly."

"I will, sir. Let me get my thoughts in order again. You've taken me considerably by surprise." I paused a few seconds and then told him exactly what had occurred, from the moment of my receiving the telephone call, down to my discovery of von Erstein's ring under Anna's body.

He jumped up excitedly at that. "Why didn't you tell me that first?" he cried. "There isn't a moment to lose. I must see about it instantly;" and he hurried out of the room.

For the second time the tickets were within reach and I was alone in the room. He had apparently forgotten them in his excitement, and that I had only to stretch out my hand and secure them. Or had he gone out deliberately intending to give me the chance? He knew how eager I was to get away; the old Jew's tale must have shown that.

I didn't hesitate this time. I whipped them out of the portfolio and pocketed them. Had I better bolt, or stay to face him? A mighty difficult question. If I ran away, he might suspect; if I stayed, there was a chance that he might not miss them. If they were missed, they wouldn't be worth a pfennig. We should certainly be stopped at the station; there would be a scene and Nessa would be hopelessly compromised. That was unthinkable.

There was nothing for it, therefore, but to stay and face it out. It wasn't easy to do; and nothing in the world except the thought of the consequences to Nessa, could have glued me to my chair for the minutes I had still to wait for von Gratzen. It was a positive relief when the strain ended and he came back.

He was looking very grave and stern, and there were still traces of the excitement he had shown when he had left me.

How I watched him! The next moment would decide everything for me. He was thinking closely, paused with his hand to his forehead when halfway to the desk, nodded in response to a thought, and went on to his chair. I had to hold my breath, as he sat down and laid his hand on the portfolio. I was ready to throw up the sponge as he slightly lifted the top paper and toyed with it.

The thought flashed through my head that the only thing left was to admit everything; who I was; why I had come; why I was so eager to get away; and then ask him to help me in return for what I had done in the Untergasse affair.

But the moment for that hadn't come yet at all events. Whether he noticed the absence of the tickets it was impossible to say. He appeared to be entirely lost in thought; he was staring abstractedly at nothing; not once had I seen his eyes drop to the desk; not so much as a side glance came my way; but then he was such a wily old beggar that that might all have been pretence to mislead me.

After a time that seemed hours to me, he nodded to himself again, took the hand from the papers to pass it across his forehead, and smiled. A smile of infinite meaning it was too. Then he closed the portfolio and put it away in a drawer.

"Now tell me the rest, boy," he said, turning to look at me for the first time. "Hallo, you look a little done up. Room too hot? Open the window a bit."

I jumped at the excuse to get out of range of his keen eyes for an instant. He might well say it was hot, for the strain had brought the perspiration in great beads on my forehead.

"Stand there a while and get a breath of the fresh air. A thing like this is sure to shake you up," he added.

Did he know? Was this intended to give me an opportunity of pulling myself together? Had he noticed everything and been thinking out some further subtle move in the game? Who could tell?

"Better?" he asked, as I returned to my seat. "There's no hurry. I've put off my other matters and shall have to keep you here for an hour or so. I'll tell you why presently. Oh, by the way, you'd better give me the card you got from old Graun. It may help you if I'm able to say you gave it to me; and, of course, it's no use to you now."

Was this his way of telling me that he knew? was the question in my mind as I gave it him. Then I resumed the story of the afternoon.

"You brought that card case away?" he shot in when I mentioned it.

"Yes. I have it here. Will you take it?"

"Perhaps I'd better," he replied after a pause, and then opened the drawer containing the portfolio, tossed it in carelessly, and let me finish the rest of the story without interruption, when he once more lapsed into close thought.

Von Welten came in before he spoke and handed him a note. "Not a second later than seven o'clock, mind, von Welten. Not a second, mind," he said when he had read the letter. "That'll do;" and we were alone again.

"Now I'll tell you something in my turn," he said. "You have rendered us a very great service; a much greater service than you can imagine. You have only made one mistake, for you ought to have hurried to me as fast as possible from that woman's rooms; but you're evidently lucky, for no harm has been done."

"I don't quite understand, sir," I stammered in surprise.

"I'm going to explain it to you. In the first place let me tell you I believe absolutely that you have told me the truth—about this murder, I mean—perhaps not in everything else."

"There is only one thing, and if you wish— —"

"Don't interrupt me, boy. I don't like it," he exclaimed testily. "It puts me out. Now about this affair. We know all about this woman, Anna Hilden. That isn't her name at all; but that doesn't matter now. She is, or was, one of von Erstein's mistresses; not the only one, by the way. The real Anna Hilden was another—years ago, of course—and that is how he knew all about that sale of the secret information to France."

I had not said anything about that and he noticed my start.

"You needn't be astonished. I tell you we know many things here. It is our business to know them. The man who betrayed us in that affair was von Erstein himself, and you, if you are really Lassen, were merely the go-between and scapegoat. But he was too cunning for us to be able to prove a thing against him. There are many things we think we know about him and can't prove, and others we don't wish to prove," he said, with a very meaning side glance.

"I can understand that."

"We'll hope you don't come under either head, my boy. Well, we've been waiting for von Erstein, and now, thanks to you, we've got him. This woman went to him to-day after you left her; she was with him a considerable time; she left in great agitation; and he followed later to the flat which had been taken for this affair of yours. That he murdered her, there is no doubt, after what you've told me; but it's got to be proved. You won't be sorry if it is, probably."

"He ought to be hanged," I exclaimed impulsively.

He fixed his keen eyes on me, and in an instant I saw what I had done and that this was one of his infernal traps.

"You're either forgetting yourself, or beginning to remember things, aren't you?" he asked deliberately, with one of his queer inscrutable smiles. "It's in England that they hang murderers, you know."

I could have cursed myself for the idiotic slip, as his eyes bored right into my brain.

CHAPTER XX
VON GRATZEN'S WILINESS

Abashed and confused by this unexpected trap, I sat cudgelling my wits for something to say, and at last stammered out, "I—I meant lynched, hanged on the nearest lamp-post, sir."

It was the lamest of lame dogs; but he appeared satisfied. He leant back in his chair. "Oh, I see. Yes, of course. Your American experiences, I expect. Well, we can talk about that another time. I was going to say that in von Erstein we have to deal with a very cunning individual indeed, and I shall expect you to help us. One of the necessary steps may be your arrest."

"Arrest!" I echoed in dismay.

"I said arrest. It may be necessary. It is essential he should not believe that a jot of suspicion attaches to him. You'll appreciate that?"

"I can appreciate it perhaps, but——"

"Don't be alarmed. I promise you very good treatment."

"But I thought you wished——" I pulled up on the brink of blurting out about my going to England.

"No matter for the moment what I wished, my boy." I was beginning to hate that term of familiarity, for I knew now what it covered. "Everything must wait upon this now," he continued. "The arrest will not be made at once, however, as there is one thing you have to do first."

This was better. If it wasn't done at once, it never would be done, I was resolved. "What is that?" I asked.

"You must return that ring to von Erstein."

"Do what?" I cried aghast. The ring was the only evidence against him!

"Do try to listen carefully. You must return it to him and lead him to believe you brought it away from that room. Let him snatch it from you while you are threatening to denounce him; or give it him as the terms of a truce between you; anyhow you please. But mind, it must be done so that he is convinced no eyes but yours have seen it. That's vital."

The light was beginning to break through even my thick skull then.

"We have it here; our people found it exactly as you said."

"Then the murder is known?"

"Oh, yes; the police have it in hand by this time; but they know nothing about that ring. We sent two men to the place who are suspected of being in his pay; and they will be able to report to him that nothing of the sort was found on the spot. We have taken every precaution, of course. It has been photographed from a dozen different points and a replica is being made. I am waiting now for the impression of the mould."

"It has occurred to you, of course, that he may destroy it?" I suggested.

He shook his head. "There's no fear of that. For one thing he's much too proud of it; there isn't another exactly like it in all Europe, probably not in the whole world; for another, he looks on it as a sort of mascot; there's some kind of legend or other about it; and lastly, if you do your part well, he will feel he can keep it with absolute safety."

The scheme was subtle enough to be worthy even of von Gratzen, and it increased my dread of his almost diabolical cunning. "When will you make him account for it?"

"That depends. He's a vindictive devil and is sure to denounce you for the murder, the instant he thinks he can do it safely. The most effective moment to deal with him would be when we get him in the witness box, giving evidence against you. But we shall see."

"And when am I to be arrested?"

"As soon as he lays the information against you, unless I find on consideration we can avoid quite so drastic a step. It is not altogether impossible; but the pith of everything is that you get the ring back to him as soon as possible."

A pleasant look-out for me—to be charged with murder of which he knew I was innocent in order to help him carry out plans. "You will scarcely expect me to be deliriously joyful at the prospect of being tried for my life," I said with a feeble smile.

He didn't like that at all and frowned at me. "Worse than that might happen to you, perhaps; and in the end it would be immensely to your advantage," he replied with unpleasantly deliberate significance.

I dropped that line like a hot coal. "I'm in your hands, sir."

"I'm glad to hear you say that. Of course, as I said just now, it may not come to that; I have another possible plan, indeed. But the other part is essential. You will give me your word of honour to carry out my instructions faithfully?"

"Yes, I give you my word of honour. Would it be sufficient if I were to let him have it with a letter?"

"Why?" Like a pistol shot came the question and his eyes snapped.

"I might bungle the personal business. I'm not much of a hand at acting, I'm afraid."

"I see," he replied; nodding; and something uncommonly like a smile hovered about the corners of his mouth. "I thought you said something to that Jew about theatricals and your studying his character. I have looked on you as a particularly good actor, my boy. But let's think. It would depend on how you worded any letter."

He considered for a while, started suddenly, nodded to himself, smiled, wrote hastily, and handed me the paper. "Just memorize that."

"Von Erstein, you will know where I found the enclosed just as I know why you left what I found there. You think to ruin me. I am not the man you believe me to be and can prove my innocence by means of which you can have no conception. Enough that I tell you I have sufficiently recovered my memory to protect myself against your devilish malice. The enclosed proves I am ready to cry a truce.—Johann Lassen."

What I felt as I read this under the keen piercing gaze he rivetted on me the whole time, no words can describe. "Well, my boy?" he asked.

"I—I'll memorize it, sir," I stammered to get time to think.

"Just read it out. Let me hear how it sounds."

Fortunately, or intentionally, I couldn't determine which, he put his hand before his face as I read it in none too firm a tone. "It'll do. Oh, yes. The recovery of your memory seems to explain the word 'means,' and he'll think you are only bluffing him. He'll never dream you've told me all about it; and, of course, that's what I intended. You understand I much prefer your seeing him; but if you can't, you can send that letter."

I began to breathe freely again. "I'll see him to-night, if possible," I replied.

"I'm sure you will. It's now all but seven. He generally goes to dinner at eight, and between now and then you ought to be able to catch him at his rooms. Mind, I depend on you."

"You may, sir."

"They ought to be ready for us now," he said; and as he rang his bell von Welten came in, bringing the ring, the replica and the photographs; and we all scrutinized them carefully.

The facsimile of the ring was absolutely perfect. It was either in wax or some harder material and had been gilded, and as it and the original lay side by side on the table it was impossible to distinguish the one from the other.

"Very good indeed. Clever work, in the time," said von Gratzen. "Of course he understands that the finished facsimile must be in gold and will take to pieces in the same way as the original."

"Oh, yes. He has a number of small moulds of the individual parts. Would you like to see them, sir?" replied von Welten.

"Not necessary at all. He knows his job. That'll do, von Welten. Leave the real thing with me;" and he picked it up and examined it with a gloating and almost satanic smile, as von Welten left the room. "At last!" he murmured under his breath.

Then he wrapped it up and handed it to me. "You see how I trust you, my boy. I know you won't fail me, too. And now you had better go. Just a last word. As soon as you've returned that to him disappear for a time. Leave Berlin and go, oh anywhere; the farther the better for the time; and don't on any account come to me again until I send for you."

Utterly mystified by all this, I ventured: "But can I go away without a permit?"

Another of his queer inscrutable smiles greeted this. "Perhaps it would be better; but you haven't any too much time to spare—if you're going to catch von Erstein," he added as an afterthought. He rang his bell and wrote furiously. "Get that stamped officially at once. As quick as you can," he told von Welten, who hurried away. "He'll give it you as you go out," he said to me, rising and gripping my hand. "And now, good-bye, my boy—for a time at any rate. You're a good lad, and whatever happens, if you do what I've asked, I'll always stand by you."

Von Welten met me with the permit as I left the room. "You're in luck to have got on the right side of the chief in this way," he said, as we shook hands.

Were they all living enigmas? was my thought as I left the building, for von Welten's manner was as veiled and significant as his chief's. Did von Gratzen know that I had taken the tickets? Had he worded the letter I was to write to von Erstein in order to tell me that he knew my lost memory was a fraud? Did that remark, "You haven't any too much time to spare," refer to my having to catch the mail? He had qualified it by saying something about seeing von Erstein; but that had seemed to be just an afterthought.

It was beyond me; and I was even more astounded when I read the paper which von Welten had given me. It was much more than a mere permit. It amounted to an official authority that I was travelling on business of State; was to go where I would and when; that all assistance was to be given to me; and any inquiries were to be telegraphed straight to von Gratzen.

I was indeed lucky, as von Welten had declared. He little guessed what luck it was! Or did he? Was it all intended to make my path to the frontier clear?

There was no time to puzzle about it then, however. I could write and ask for the reply to the riddle when Nessa and I were safely in Holland or home in England; what I had to do now was to get this business with von Erstein finished as quickly as possible.

I drove to his flat; but he was not there, and I could not learn where to look for him. I was rather glad of this. It would be much easier to write the letter arranged. I went then to the Karlstrasse to tell Nessa that she could travel in her own character.

Rosa was with her, and both were nervous at not having heard earlier how matters were going, for it was then more than a quarter past seven.

"I've been worrying awfully," said Nessa. "Is anything wrong?"

"Not a bit of it. Everything's gloriously right. I've got our tickets, and all you've to do is to be at the station."

"But what's happened?" exclaimed Rosa.

"I haven't time to tell you now. I'm sorry; but I have to rush back to my rooms and get something.—By Jove!" I broke off in a cold sweat as the meaning of von Gratzen's look at my suggestion about writing dawned on me. I had told him before that I could neither write nor read writing! I had even given him a specimen of my new pothook fist! Of course I must keep it up, and it might take me Heaven knew how long. "I must go this instant," I said, and shaking hands with Rosa I rushed away to my rooms and set to work at once.

It was a deuce of a business. Every letter had to be printed in clumsy fashion; my fingers were trembling under the stress of my impatience; I made blunders and had to begin all over again, and every lost minute was of vital importance.

If I hadn't given my word of honour to von Gratzen I'd have wrapped the beastly ring up, scribbled a word or two and have left it at that. It was on the table by the side of the paper as I wrote, and I had just started on the second edition absorbed in the work, when a hand was stretched over my shoulder and grabbed the ring.

It was von Erstein; I was never more glad to see any one in my life. I could have forgiven him everything for such a service.

"Very good of you to leave the door open, Lassen," he said, with a sneering laugh. "Just going to return it to me, eh? I thought I'd dropped it here last night."

There were still minutes enough left for me to put up a show of a struggle, and get in an explanation. So I grabbed hold of him, taking care that he should not get away and also that he kept possession of the ring.

"I *was* going to send it you, von Erstein. You can see I've begun the letter there."

He stooped to read it and was puzzled. "What the devil does that mean?" he growled.

"I'm willing to come to terms. We both know where I found it."

"How do I know where you put it?"

"Don't lie, man. You know very well that it was on your finger when you left here last night, and"—I paused for the sake of emphasis—"two people saw it there this morning."

This hit him hard, and he winced and drew a deep breath. "Rubbish!" he muttered.

"I've made sure about that. I've just come from your flat, remember," I said meaningly.

"Have you been spreading that lie about me?"

"Do you take me for an idiot to let any one want to ask where I found it?"

He was satisfied, and his relief showed itself in his immediate change of manner. "All right, we'll bury the hatchet if you like," he said with a very poor attempt to hoodwink me.

"You can go then;" and I moved to let him leave. I was anxious to get rid of him now, as it was time for me to be off to the station. I must have betrayed my impatience somehow, for he started, stared a moment, and sat down. "You're in a deuce of a hurry."

"Dinner time, and I'm hungry. Clear out."

"Nice room you've got here, Lassen," he answered, squinting round, and started again as his eyes fell on my suit case. "O-ho, that's the game, is it?" he chuckled. "Going to bolt? No good, my friend, no good at all."

His fat insolent chuckle roused the devil in me. "You'd better drop that tone with me, von Erstein, and not interfere with my movements."

"Shall we go and dine together?" he sneered. "It'll be safer, for there are a few inquisitive friends of mine waiting outside."

I had noticed one or two men hanging round the building as I entered, and it wouldn't do to be shadowed. So I went out, locked the front door and put the key in my pocket.

"What's that for?" he growled uneasily.

"So that our chat shan't be disturbed. I've sampled your friends already, remember," I said drily.

"Let me go," he cried in a dickens of a stew.

"You wanted to stop, and stop you shall."

To my intense joy he came for me and thus saved me from the unpleasant job of knocking him out in cold blood. I did it quite satisfactorily, and as he fell he struck his head against the corner of a writing desk and saved me the trouble of hitting him again.

Then I collared my suit case, clambered out of the bathroom window down by the fire escape, and got away by a passage into a side street. A single glance satisfied me that none of his "friends" saw me, and I rushed off to the station.

I reached it with only a few minutes in hand, and Nessa was waiting for me in the door of the waiting-room.

"I was afraid you'd be late and that something had happened," she said nervously.

"It's all right. We've plenty of time. Don't be nervy and not too friendly yet. There may be eyes about. We'll find a carriage at once."

It was all right enough to tell her not to be nervy, but I was on pins and needles, wondering if my theft of the tickets had been discovered, whether at the last moment we should be stopped, and a hundred other wonderings.

My eyes were all over the place as we walked to the train; and to my infinite dismay I caught sight of the old Jew planted close to the barrier through which we had to pass. That was not the worst, moreover, by any means. He was talking to a man who had policeman written all over him.

And then, as if that wasn't bad enough, on the platform just beyond von Welten was strolling up and down smoking.

CHAPTER XXI
OFF!

The sight of the old Jew, his police companion, and von Welten knocked me all to pieces for the moment. We were done. That was a certainty. I could have bluffed the Jew, probably, with the official authority which von Gratzen had given me; but von Welten was what Jimmy Lamb would have called a very different proposition.

"I think I'll have a cigarette," I said; and pulled up to light it and try to think what to do.

"Whatever's the matter, Jack?" whispered Nessa. "Your hand shakes like anything and you're looking awful."

"Nothing to what I'm feeling. I'm afraid it's all up. I can't tell you all about it now. Just shake hands with me and trot back to the waiting-room. If you see me stopped—wait till the train has actually started, of course—make a bee line back to the von Reblings. If it's all right, I'll beckon to you."

"But if there's any trouble why should I leave you in it alone?" she protested, like the brick she was.

"Let me be boss now. If you're with me, you may never get away at all; and if you're not, it may only mean a postponement. Be a good sort. Good-bye, Miss Caldicott;" and I held out my hand.

She took it reluctantly. "I'd rather be with you," she replied with a glance for which I could have kissed her. Then she did as I wished.

I put as bold a face on things as I could, walked quickly up to the barrier, putting my hand in my pocket as if for my ticket.

"Good-evening, sir," said the Jew as I approached.

"Hullo, you here, Graun?" very much astonished.

"Herr Johann Lassen?" asked his companion.

"That's my name, certainly. Who are you, and what do you want? I'm in a hurry to catch the train."

"I'm a detective and have to ask you a few questions."

"Fire 'em out, quick as you can, please."

"There's no such hurry as all that. You can't go by this train. You paid a visit to this man to-day."

"We shall be here half the night at this rate. I went to purchase an identification card and he sold me one in the name of Liebe."

"Your object?"

"That's my affair. I haven't it with me and am not going to use it."

"That's your story. I don't believe it. Give it to me."

"I've told you I haven't it."

"Give it to me."

"I would if I had it. As it is, I can't."

"Give it up at once," he repeated very sharply.

This looked like a deadlock and moments were flying fast. There was nothing for it but to try the effect of my official authority, and I was fingering it, when von Welten caught sight of me and hurried in our direction. I threw up the sponge. To produce the authority in his presence would be only to make bad worse, so I put it in my waistcoat pocket.

The detective knew von Welten and saluted him.

"Well, Grossbaum, what is it? How do, Herr Lassen?"

"This man had a deal with Graun to-day and is travelling— —"

Von Welten interposed angrily. "Hold your tongue, you fool. I've always thought yours was the woodenest head in the force. I suppose you brought this disreputable old scoundrel here. Get away, both of you. Think yourself lucky if I don't report this last cleverness of yours. Be off, I say;" and the precious pair slunk away like a couple of whipped curs. "I'm awfully sorry about this, Herr Lassen; but why on earth didn't you show the fool that paper the chief gave you?"

"I was going to," I stammered, utterly bewildered by the turn of affairs and gaping in wonder what would happen next. I was prepared for almost anything except what did happen.

"I knew you would travel by this train and thought I'd like to be certain that everything was all right about the ring;" and he dropped his voice to a whisper.

"Yes. He came to my rooms and I gave it him."

"The artful devil! Of course he's planted some of the woman's things there. I told the chief I thought he would; and I'll see to that in the morning. But where's Miss Caldicott?"

"Eh?" I asked stupidly.

"Do you mean to say she isn't going after all?"

"N-no. I mean—yes. She's over there," I stammered.

"Well, she'd better be here if you wish to catch the train. There's only another minute and they'll start on the tick."

Oh, I was surely dreaming. In a dream I beckoned to Nessa, who came hurrying up; in a dream von Welten was introduced and rushed us through the barrier to a compartment he'd already secured for us; in a dream he stood by the carriage door till we started, saying he thought it better for us to travel alone; and in a dream we shook hands out of the carriage window, and he waved to us as the train steamed out of the station.

Even when we quickened up speed through the outskirts of the city, I had hard work to wake up from that tremendously splendid dream. But Nessa was very much awake and boiling over with excitement, curiosity and delight. "What's the matter with you, Jack? Aren't you just mad with joy? I am."

"That's all right," I nodded.

"But you look so odd."

"Only intoxicated a bit."

"Surely you haven't been taking some drug or other! You came along the platform as if you were walking in a dream."

"Are you sure it isn't one? Are we really in a railway carriage?"

"Of course it is, and a very comfortable one too. But whatever do you mean? Are you trying to frighten me or just fooling as usual?"

"I don't know, but I simply can't believe it all yet."

"Why? Do you understand that I'm bubbling over with curiosity? Do wake up and make haste and satisfy it, if you don't want to drive me out of my senses. Good heavens, you're on fire!" she exclaimed in alarm, as she wrapped her hand in her cloak and pressed it against my side excitedly.

That roused me effectually. My waistcoat was smouldering and I plunged my hand into the pocket and discovered the reason. In my stupid absent-mindedness I had shoved the lighted end of my cigarette into the pocket and it had set fire to a couple of papers and singed the cloth.

"Nothing to worry about," I said. But there was. When I unfolded one of the papers, I found that it was the authority von Gratzen had given me. A fair-sized hole had been charred right through the folds and the tinder dropped as I opened out the sheet. It was hopelessly unreadable and thus useless. "I didn't think I could be such a gorgeous idiot," I exclaimed staring fatuously at the ruin.

"It's serious then?" asked Nessa, who had watched me anxiously.

"Try if you can make anything out of it."

She studied it and shook her head. "A word or two here and there are readable. That's all. What is it?"

"The proof that I ought to be shut up in a lunatic asylum. But it *was* something that would have taken me anywhere and everywhere through this beastly country and forced every one to help me."

"That's delightfully intelligible," she cried, laughing. "Are you going to keep this up much longer, or tell me things?"

"I'm going to tell you everything; but that silly ass trick of mine has knocked me. I'll smoke a cigarette. You don't mind?"

"Providing you don't put the end in another pocket," she quizzed. "I thought it was agreed we were not to take things too seriously," she added as I lit up.

"I've learnt my lesson." I had indeed. It had cost me the best safe conduct a man could have wished for, and if any unexpected trouble arose, there was now no possibility of undoing the mischief. As the guard passed along the corridor a little later, I decided to report the loss at once, and beckoned to him. "I've had an unfortunate accident," I said. "I'm travelling on special State business and have burnt this very important paper;" and I handed it to him.

He looked at it, turned it over, and shrugged his shoulders. "I'm afraid I can't be of much help, sir."

"It is my authority signed by Count von Gratzen; you can just make out a part of the official seal; and you will have seen that Herr von Welten was on the platform when we left Berlin."

"Yes, sir. He gave me orders to reserve this compartment for you, but——"

"You can't do anything, I know; but I wish you to make a note that I told you of the loss. That's all."

"Would you telegraph to his Excellency, sir?"

"Where's the first stop?"

"Not till Hanover, sir; but as it is State business and so important, I could stop at the next station for you to send a message, and you would have a reply wired to Hanover, or Osnabrück, if you are going so far."

"A good idea, guard. I'm much obliged to you. I'll think about it; just give me a form." He took one from his pocket and went off, saying he would come back for the message.

Nessa had listened in the greatest amazement. "Who on earth am I travelling with?" she cried. "Do you mean that you are able to have trains stopped at your mere nod?"

"I'll tell you who you're travelling with in a moment, but let me think whether I dare send that wire." It wasn't long before I decided to risk it. Von Gratzen himself had suggested I should get out of the way for a time: even go to a distance: and would understand the importance of the ruined authority, since I could not return when he needed me without it. He would therefore wire me all I should require, pending the receipt of a new authority. That was all clear enough.

But there was a fly in the ointment. He might have discovered the theft of the papers. But even in that case there wasn't very much risk, as the von Erstein affair was so vastly more important that he would hesitate before sending any instructions to get me into trouble. So I wrote the message and gave it to the guard, with a ten-mark tip, and the train was accordingly stopped for it to be despatched.

Then I was ready to satisfy Nessa's acute curiosity. "Now you want to know who your fellow traveller is, eh? I'll tell you. He's a composite individual: an Englishman, a German, a State official, a spy, a thief, and an alleged murderer. I hope you're proud of him."

"I don't care what he is if he's going to get me out of Germany. I needn't know him afterwards, I suppose."

"If you're disrespectful and don't behave yourself I'll—I'll— —"

"Dock my wages, mate?" she popped in in her slangy voice.

"That reminds me. There's a little thing to be done in case of accidents;" and I took her bag from the seat.

"You don't mean to tell me you're going to keep me waiting any longer!"

"I'm not going to have young Hans' clothes found in your possession; much too risky;" and I packed them into my suit case.

"But your risk?"

"There's none for me. I'm travelling on business of State and may need disguises of any sort. And now I'll read you the riddles; but we shall have to be quick about it."

"If you dare to hurry over it and not tell me every little detail, I'll never speak to you again, Jack," she declared with great energy.

"We must drop that Jack business, and speak in my language. And I have to be quick because it's nearly bedtime."

"You don't imagine for an instant I'm getting into any sleeping berth to-night surely! I couldn't sleep a wink. I want to do nothing but talk."

"All right, let it go at that;" and I began the long story. It is needless to say that her interest was acute. She was literally hungry for every detail and interrupted with innumerable questions, so that it took hours to tell, and I hadn't quite finished when we reached Hanover, where I broke off to get something for us to eat.

A number of officers and soldiers were on the platform there, many of whom stared pretty hard at me; surprised probably to see a man of military age in civilian clothes. I did not take any notice of them; but there was a rather unpleasant incident on my return to the carriage. A couple of officers were in hot altercation with the guard because he would not allow them to enter our compartment.

They grumbled, declaring there was no room anywhere else; but he stood his ground, and in the end they went off in just such a rage as one might expect Prussian officers to show.

Nessa was greatly relieved to see them go, and as soon as the train started we commenced our meal.

"I'm only a nervy idiot," she said; "for I declare I was awfully scared and couldn't help thinking they knew about the tickets. Do you really believe von Gratzen didn't know you took them?"

"I'm absolutely fluster-bustered about it. Sometimes I thought he knew I was a fraud; sometimes that he didn't; he acted both ways, and——"

"But that von Welten was at the station," she broke in.

"Evidently he knew I had them, but must have thought old Gratz gave them to me. He said he had come to make sure I had planted the ring on von Erstein, all right. Otherwise, he'd have stopped us; but he actually asked where you were. It knocked me bang over."

"I'd bet he knew all about it, and so did von Gratzen. I expect the truth is that after you'd saved his wife and Nita that day, he guessed everything and determined to give you a chance to get out of the country. Why, he almost told you to take them when you were with him in the morning. And then that authority he gave you! It's as plain as a pikestaff he meant that to get out of any bother on the way; and, as if that wasn't enough, there was von Welten at the station to see that we got away without any trouble."

"Let's hope you're right."

"Of course I am. Naturally in view of all that happened he couldn't give you the things openly or he might have got into a mess over it which couldn't be explained away. But everything else could. His plan about von Erstein, the brute, gave him an excellent excuse for allowing you to leave Berlin; in fact you can see he was clever enough to cover his tracks at every step. Surely that's clear enough."

"It may be to you, but I gave up long ago trying to understand him, and if you'd seen as much of him as— —"

"I don't want to see him, not till after the war anyhow, although he's just the dearest old thing in Germany. If I ever do see him again, I shall want to hug him."

"Hug him as much as you like, by all means; all I wish is that he won't hug me in the way he probably would if he got the chance. And now hadn't you better try forty winks?" I suggested.

"What time is it?"

"Nearly one o'clock."

"What time shall we cross the frontier?"

"About an hour after we leave Osnabrück, and we get there at half-past three."

"Then I'll go to sleep at four o'clock. Not a moment before. I simply couldn't. Oh, to think that in four hours all the suspense and horrors of the last months will be at an end! When shall we reach home? Think of it, Jack! Home!"

"Depends on our getting a boat. We'll go right through to Rotterdam and shall reach there by nine or ten to-morrow morning, say before midday anyhow; but we may have to wait for a boat."

"I shan't mind that. We must wire to mother as soon as we're over the frontier. Not likely to have any bother there, are we?"

"Can't think of any. We've got all the necessary papers."

"How perfectly glorious! And to think that I owe it all to you."

"That rather takes the cream off, doesn't it?"

"Don't fish. I might say something to make you blush. I'm quite capable of it and not a bit responsible for what I say. I want to revel in the thought of it all."

"State business, is it? What do I care about State business? I want a seat and I'm going to have one," broke in a harsh ill-tempered voice from the corridor.

"Going to have travelling companions to Osnabrück," I said. "Some of those officers who got in at Hanover. Better let them come in."

There was no question of letting them. The man whose voice we had heard came in. "We've got to sit here; there's not another seat in the train," he said bluntly.

"By all means," I agreed. There was nothing else to do.

"Come on, you fellows," he called, looking out into the corridor. "Plenty of room here."

I stiffened as I caught a glimpse of one of his companions. He was a man named Freibach who had been at Göttingen with me, and both Nessa and I had known him in London before the war. I tried to warn Nessa, but it was useless; and her start as she saw him was enough to give everything away.

Would he recognize us? If he did—what?

A minute settled it and judgment went dead against us. He knew us both.

"Hullo! This is a surprise if you like. How do you do, Miss Caldicott, and you too, Lancaster?" he exclaimed in English, and after shaking hands with Nessa held out his hand to me.

CHAPTER XXII
CHECKMATE

I'm not a particularly blood-thirsty person, but considering the hosts of Freibach's countrymen who had fallen in the war, I certainly did bitterly regret that he had been spared.

Poor Nessa! Just when she had been at the height of ecstatic delight at the near prospect of escape, this infernal thing had come to plunge her back into the abyss. It seemed to break her up.

And well it might! If it had been almost any other man than Freibach it might have been possible to face it out. Indeed, if he had been alone, or had even thought what he was doing, I believe he would have been decent enough to hold his tongue. But his surprise had betrayed us.

And that we were betrayed his companions' looks proved plainly. The man who had come in first looked up with a scowl as I shook Freibach's hand.

"What's that, lieutenant? Do you mean to say these people are English and dare to try and keep us out of here with a pretence of State business? What's the meaning of it, and what the devil are you doing here?"

My friend realized then the bad turn he had done us and looked the regret he dared not express.

I put the best face on it I could. "There is no need to adopt that tone with me, sir — —"

"Isn't there? Oh! I'm accustomed to use what tone I please with you English. I'm Major Borsch of the 23rd Potsdam regiment; and it's my business to know all about you both." That he was a bully of the best Prussian type was evident. "What was that humbug about State business?"

How I regretted that burnt authority at that moment! "This lady, Miss Caldicott, is on her way to England. She has been in Berlin since before the outbreak of the war and is returning by the order of Baron von Gratzen; and acting under his instructions I am escorting her to the frontier."

He burst into loud coarse laughter which made Freibach wince. "A pretty tale, but not good enough for me. And who are you, pray, that you are detailed off as escort?" The sneer on the last word was worthy of even von Erstein.

"I am travelling as Johann Lassen. I have all my papers here. I am on a special mission for Baron von Gratzen, who gave me a written authority for that purpose."

"Did he indeed? Very nice of him. I should like to see that special authority. A swine of an Englishman on a special State business! What next, I'd like to know."

It wasn't easy to keep one's temper with this sort of brute; but there was Nessa to be thought of. "Unfortunately I have partially burnt it."

"Dear me! What a misfortune, eh?" he sneered. "Let me look at the precious fragments and your other papers."

I handed over the burnt paper. "I have already reported the accident to Baron von Gratzen by telegraph." I dragged in the Baron's name as much as possible, for I had noticed that the mention of it had had some impression even on him.

He scrutinized the authority and shook his head over it. "A forgery, of course;" and he was going to tear it up when I interposed.

"I shall have to report the destruction of it to the Baron, of course," I said quietly.

The officer who sat next him whispered something and the paper was not destroyed. "And your other papers? I must see them."

I did not reply, and he repeated his demand angrily. But I had taken his measure by this time. He had not ventured to destroy the remnant of the authority; and although its destruction didn't matter two straws either way, it mattered very much to see that he was sufficiently in awe of von Gratzen to abstain.

"Do you want me to take them from you?" he thundered.

"Do so, if you think it safe," I said in a very different tone.

"Don't you dare to threaten me, you swinehound," he roared.

"Go to blazes!" I answered in much the same tone. "Who the devil are you to come blustering in here in this way? I'm on Baron von Gratzen's business, not yours; I've no instructions to show his papers to any and every boorish clown who dares to ask for them. If you want to see them, telegraph to him, and when he instructs me to tell you his business I'll do it, and not before."

I fired this at him with all my lung power and tried to look even more angry than I felt, and shouted him down when he tried to interrupt me once or twice.

He cursed volubly.

"If you don't behave yourself I'll have you put out of the carriage," I cried. "Do you imagine that Baron von Gratzen sent his confidential secretary to secure this compartment for me and this lady that we might be insulted by such a foul-mouthed brute as you? Ask your questions civilly, and I'll answer them; but don't imagine you can bully me."

That his three companions relished all this was apparent in their looks; but the effect on the bully himself was a sheer delight to witness. He tried to bluster, but he was frightened. The sting of my attack was the reference to von Welten's reservation of the compartment, and I promptly drove it home by asking Freibach to have the guard called.

He hesitated; the other man was his superior officer, of course, and looked to him. "He'll be able to confirm what I say," I added.

The major nodded and nothing more passed until the guard arrived.

"Who saw these people off at Berlin?"

"Herr von Welten, sir, and he told me that the compartment was to be strictly reserved for them by Baron von Gratzen's orders. I explained that the train was sure to be full; but he said that under no conditions was I to allow any one to enter it."

The major's face dropped at this. "You can go," he ordered.

"Wait a minute, guard. Tell Major Borsch about the telegram."

The man told his story succinctly; and it had an excellent effect upon the bully, and a whispered conversation followed between him and the man next him. I began to hope. The worst was over for the moment, apparently; and the next scene was likely to take place when we reached Osnabrück. What would happen there was on the lap of the gods.

The only thing that really mattered was to contrive somehow that Nessa should be allowed to continue the journey, and it wasn't impossible that Freibach might be able to see to that. He would be willing enough, because he had been very kindly treated by the Caldicotts in London. Moreover, he had got us into this mess and was obviously distressed about it.

The whispered conference at the other side of the carriage ended by the major jumping up and leaving the carriage, muttering something about not being able to breathe the same air with us, and then his companion turned to me.

"You will appreciate the seriousness of the position to us, Herr Lassen, and that we are compelled to investigate it," he said. His tone was somewhat curt, but more official than offensive.

"Certainly."

"We are to understand that Baron von Gratzen has employed you on a special mission, knowing that you are an Englishman?"

"I have already given you the facts, but of course I am not at liberty to explain to you all his Excellency's reasons. He would not have given me that authority otherwise."

"It is unfortunately too mutilated to be intelligible."

"It was couched in the widest terms. It was to notify to all concerned that I was to be allowed to go where I pleased and that every assistance was to be afforded me. You can still see a part of the official stamp."

"It is most extraordinary. Incomprehensible."

"Not if I were free to explain why it was given to me."

"Who gave it you?"

"Baron von Gratzen wrote it himself in my presence. If you know his handwriting, there is enough of it left unburnt for you to identify it."

"I do not."

"Again in my presence he handed it to his secretary, Herr von Welten, to be stamped, and von Welten gave it to me as I left the office. You have heard that he was at the station and himself reserved this compartment for Miss Caldicott and me."

"That's the most remarkable thing of all."

"On the contrary, it was a perfectly natural step. There was a matter I had to arrange before leaving, and his chief was anxious to know that it had been done exactly in accordance with my instructions."

"What was that?"

"That is a question to be put to the Baron. My lips are sealed."

"And you an Englishman! It sounds incredible."

"Do you suppose I should have telegraphed to Baron von Gratzen if it were incredible?"

This worried him not a little, and he sat thinking with his hand pressed to his head. Not having the key to the riddle, he might well be baffled. "And your companion, Miss Caldicott, is going to England?"

"Certainly. You have been quite courteous and I have no objection whatever to show you her papers;" and I took them out and handed them over. "You will see that they also bear the official hallmark of Baron von Gratzen's office."

He was obviously impressed. "Both tickets are through to Rotterdam, I notice. Are you going to England also?"

"My instructions are to see Miss Caldicott across the frontier, and to return to Berlin as soon as my task is finished, unless his Excellency sends for me sooner."

It was such a lovely mixture of the truth and the other thing that it appeared quite flawless, and he couldn't make head or tail of it. "Of course you understand that you will have to remain at Osnabrück while this is being investigated?" he said at length, returning the tickets.

"That is for you to decide, and so far as I myself am concerned it is not of the least consequence. But it's different with Miss Caldicott. It is essential that her journey should not be interrupted."

Nessa started at this and spoke for the first time. "I shall not go on without you," she protested.

"I must ask you to recall that, Miss Caldicott, if you please. I shall, of course, be placed under some sort of restraint until this gentleman——"

"I am Captain Brulen," he interposed.

"Until Captain Brulen has satisfied himself. His Excellency's instructions are that you proceed at once; and for you to remain there would be extremely invidious and possibly unpleasant."

"I shall not go on if you're stopped," she insisted. It was like her to wish to stick by me in the coming trouble, but impossible, so I adopted an official tone.

"If you persist in your refusal, Miss Caldicott, it will compel me to take a line I should deeply regret. My instructions *must* be carried out; they were very peremptory."

"I don't care what you do. I won't go on without you," she declared.

"Any delay at Osnabrück will render it impossible for me to see you across the frontier personally, and I shall have to ask Captain Brulen to detail some one for the purpose, Miss Caldicott. I can, of course, rely upon your doing that?" I asked him.

The poor man didn't know what to make of this little interlude and replied with a perplexed gesture.

"I won't go," cried Nessa obstinately. "And if you send me as a prisoner, I'll come straight back. I've made up my mind absolutely."

This dogged attitude was growing dangerous and it became necessary to explain it, so I asked the Captain to come into the corridor, and he complied after a slight hesitation.

"I had better explain one point to you in reference to that young lady. Until quite recently I have been living in London—on Baron von Gratzen's instructions, of course. I met Miss Caldicott's friends there frequently; they are influential people and were extremely useful to know, you will understand. They have always regarded me as an Englishman, and at one time there was a sort of engagement between us. That was when your fellow officer, Lieutenant Freibach, met me. He also takes me for English. You will now understand her attitude just now."

He swallowed it like mother's milk. "Why on earth didn't you tell us all this before?"

"Partly because of Major Borsch's disgusting manner; but mainly for the reason which is on the surface, surely. It is not impossible I may receive a wire to go on to England. You see my meaning. Under no circumstances must either of them know what I have told you. You will now see why Miss Caldicott must go on to-night and must not be allowed to return. The whole of my work in London would be utterly ruined if she and her friends knew I was a German."

"Of course. I am at liberty to tell Major Borsch this?"

"Emphatically not. It is for your own ears solely. I never trust that type of man. Personally, all I care about is to get Miss Caldicott off my hands; and the sooner the better. This business about me will be cleared up in half an hour when we reach Osnabrück; but not in time for me to continue in the train, probably. There will be a wire from the Baron; but that may not be considered sufficient. I don't blame you in the least; but I shall certainly report the Major's conduct."

"I can probably get Freibach to see to Miss Caldicott."

"Nothing could be better. Please von Gratzen immensely," I replied, smiling. "And if you leave us two alone again, no doubt I could persuade Miss Caldicott to agree."

He did this; and as soon as Nessa and I were alone I told her the arrangement and began the persuasion campaign.

Her reception of the news was just what might have been expected. She was furiously indignant. Was that my opinion of her, she demanded. Did I think she was a German and likely to desert any one who had run all this risk to help her? Did I take her for a despicable coward? Was she so abominably mean a thing in my eyes? And a great deal more to the same effect.

It's always best to let that sort of thing empty the petrol tank; so I just listened with becoming meekness which appeared to keep the engine running long after the tank was exhausted. Then: "And how do you think you can help me?" I asked smoothly.

Another vigorous outburst. She didn't care about that. No one should be able to say she had run away in such a case; and so on.

"Now do listen to me a moment. I don't think anything of the sort. It's splendid of you, Nessa. But— —"

"I can't leave you in the lurch, Jack, and I won't," she broke in.

"If there was the faintest use in your stopping, I wouldn't ask you to go. There isn't. On the contrary, it would make matters infinitely more awkward. It was getting awkward just now, and that's why I took that man out. I've told him that you take me for an Englishman, and that Freibach knew us in London when we were engaged, and— —"

"That's true."

"Yes; but he understands it differently—that I was in London as a German spy."

"He doesn't!"

"Indeed he does, and it altered his tune entirely. I said I wanted to get you off my hands as soon as possible— —"

"Is that also true?" she interposed, with such a smile.

"At the present moment, yes."

"Thank you. Almost enough to make me say I'll go," she cried with a toss of the head.

"Naturally. But it is true, for this reason. When we get to Osnabrück there will probably be a telegram from old Gratz; these people are likely to want something more than that, however; and I am sure to be detained while they communicate with him. But he can't let me down, even if he guesses I've helped myself to those tickets, because I'm necessary to him for the von Erstein affair: a much more vital matter to him than the tickets. The whole thing will be cleared up and I shall be able to follow you home. Very likely catch you up before you leave Rotterdam."

"Then if it's going to be so easy, why shouldn't I stop?"

"For the simple reason that the papers for you are only to be used on this particular date, and there would be no end of a fuss in getting any others."

"You really and truly wish me to go on?"

"If you care a rap for my safety you won't hesitate another moment."

She looked very troubled. "If I do, I won't go a step farther than the first town across the frontier, and if you don't join me soon I shall come back," she declared. "I shall. I'll tell every one that you've got into all this solely on my account and that I'm quite ready to go even to an internment camp."

Knowing her detestation of such a thing, I could appreciate all that lay behind this statement. It touched me too closely for me to reply immediately. Thank Heaven, she wouldn't be allowed to come back; but there was no need to tell her so. "Let it go at that, Nessa. The first town you'll stop at will be Oldenzaal, and I'll come to you there. You're due there about five in the morning; but you won't get there by that time if we keep stopping in this fashion. It can't be Osnabrück yet; there's half an hour before we're due there. I wish they'd hurry up."

We had stopped at some station the name of which I couldn't see and stuck there some minutes.

"Can't be anything wrong, can there?" asked Nessa nervily.

"Probably a troop train. It's all right, we're off again."

But it was not a troop train that had stopped us. It was a very different cause, as we soon knew, for the brute of a major burst into our compartment flourishing a telegram and cursing me volubly.

"So we've got the truth about you, Mr. Englishman, at last. You infernal scoundrel," he cried viciously. "You wanted a telegram from your friend and patron, von Gratzen, did you? Well, read that!" with another string of oaths.

He held the message up and I did read it, with feelings which may perhaps be imagined although I can't describe them. It was to the guard.

"Detain passengers Johann Lassen and companion. Suspected of murder. Acquaint police at next station and have them arrested.—Von Gratzen."

CHAPTER XXIII
WITHIN A HAIRSBREADTH

Major Borsch stood gloating over me as I read the telegram. "Well, what do you think of your friend the Baron, now?" he sneered.

He expected me to be completely crushed, so I shook off my first feeling of dismay and looked up with a bland smile. "I'm much obliged to you for showing it to me," I replied, as if it were the merest trifle. I must have done it pretty well, for even Nessa, who had been overwhelmed by the news, was surprised and pulled herself together.

"Perhaps you'll also be obliged for what will follow," he roared, aggravated by my coolness.

"What an exceedingly unpleasant person this is," I said to Nessa. "I'm sorry he can't behave himself; but you must try not to let it worry you. I suppose he can't help it."

"He doesn't worry me in the least, thank you," she replied contemptuously.

"You hold your tongue, you baggage," he shouted, turning on her.

"Major Borsch!" I cried, rising.

"Sit down, you infernal swinehound! And as for you, you——"

The sentence was not finished. My temper flew out of the window. If I was to be charged with murder, a little extra such as a smack on the mouth of even a major wouldn't make much difference, so I gave him one, and put enough behind it to knock him down.

An involuntary scream from Nessa was drowned in his yells for his men; and two of them rushed in and seized me. He didn't get up until I was thus rendered helpless and then kept far enough away, pouring out a torrent of cursing abuse while he staunched the blood on his cut lips.

Captain Brulen arrived in the middle of it, with Freibach close on his heels; and the bully declared I had tried to murder him in order to escape. It was such a palpable absurdity that Freibach turned his face away to smile.

"This man was insulting the lady in my charge and I struck him, Captain Brulen," I explained. "You probably know him well enough to understand it is just what he would do."

"It is a very grave position," he replied. "Very grave indeed."

"You mean because of that telegram? Nonsense. It's a palpable forgery."

The major burst out into raucous laughter. "Forgery! Forgery, is it? Well, forgery or no forgery, you'll answer for that attack on me. Search him, and if he resists knock him on the head," he ordered the two soldiers.

"Is this man the senior officer on the train, Captain Brulen?"

"Hold your insolent tongue; and, Captain Brulen, stay where you are. Do as I told you," he ordered the men.

It would have been madness to resist. There was nothing on me of any consequence; and as Nessa was sitting on the suit case with her dress entirely covering it, nothing of importance was found, except the passports and our tickets. These the bully promptly pocketed.

"Can I speak to you a moment, Major?" said Brulen then.

"No. Mind your own business. This is my affair, not yours."

"Very good, sir," and with that he and Freibach went away. Both looked very disturbed, although for quite different reasons, as I knew.

"Take the man to the other end of the carriage; see that the two prisoners have no chance of speaking to each other; remain between them in the middle until we reach Osnabrück, and if any attempt is made to escape, use your bayonets. You're answerable for them."

"I'm going to sleep," said Nessa as the brute was leaving the carriage; and she put her legs up on the seat with excellently acted unconcern.

"Good idea, so will I," and I threw myself full length on the seat.

"Silence," roared the brute. "If they speak, club them both," and with this amiable command to our guards he left us.

The men would in all probability have obeyed him to the letter, so we prudently gave them no occasion.

Except for the desire to try and reassure Nessa, there was nothing to be said. The disastrous telegram had ruined everything. What did it mean? It didn't seem possible that von Gratzen could have sent such a message. It was too blunt, too crude, and altogether too brutal a thing to fit with all I had seen of him. He was wily enough in all truth, but such a method was so lacking in finesse, so devoid of cunning, that I could not believe it had really come from him.

It was possible that he had been infuriated at discovering I had stolen the passports; but even then he would have resorted to some far more adroit means of arresting me. There was another consideration, too. It was not in accord with his plans to denounce me as the murderer in this fashion. His object was not to have me accused, but to catch von Erstein in the web so subtly woven.

At the same time it must have been sent by some one having high authority, because the train had been stopped in order that it might be delivered to the guard. The police could have done it. The detective at the station had probably reported my flight, and, if von Erstein had already accused me to them, they might resort to such a means to have me arrested. But in that case the message would not have been sent in von Gratzen's name. That killed that theory therefore.

There was only one alternative suggestion—that the telegram was a forgery and that von Erstein had ventured to use von Gratzen's name, relying upon his influence to get him out of trouble for it. He had guessed I was going to bolt, and he would have little difficulty in finding out where I had gone; I might even have been followed to the station without knowing it; and it was just such a step as would appeal to his cunning vindictive nature.

The truth would soon be out, as a few minutes would see us at Osnabrück at the pace we were rushing through the night; and until we reached there, nothing could be done. Despite the mysterious telegram I still had faith in von Gratzen's concluding assurance—"Whatever happens I'll stand by you, my boy."

All the same it was a deplorable business, especially for Nessa; and that worried me desperately. We were both sure to be locked up; and Germany is one of those insalubrious countries where it's very difficult to get out of gaol when once the doors have closed on you. Even if the thing were explained at Osnabrück, it would be impossible for her to continue her journey that night; and when she would be able to do so, Heaven alone knew.

It was such a devil of a mess that no amount of wit-racking suggested a way out which did not involve a heap of delay and trouble. But the knot was cut nevertheless, in the most unexpected fashion.

We were nearing Osnabrück, running at some thirty or forty miles an hour, when the engine whistled furiously, and we were far enough in the front of the train to feel the grinding of the brakes quickly applied. Before they could do much to reduce the speed, however, there was a tremendous crash, the heavy carriage collapsed like a card house, the lights were extinguished, and the coach rocked a moment, seemed to rear right up, and then toppled over on its side.

I was flung half a dozen ways at once; against the opposite side of the compartment, then back again and next down, so that I lay sprawling across the door. Something hit me a smack on the head and something else came floundering down on top of me, amid a shower of splintered glass and other fragments.

The "something else" turned out to be Nessa as I discovered when I called out to her in deadly fear that she had been killed. Thank Heaven we were both unhurt, save for the few bruises and slight cuts caused by the shuttlecock shaking we had experienced.

We owed our escape to the fact that we had been lying with our legs up. The result to our two guards showed that. They had been pinned down and lay groaning and moaning piteously in desperate agony.

Nessa was too overwhelmed by the shock to be able to move for a time. But she was awfully brave; not a cry had escaped her lips; and although she was trembling so that she could scarcely speak, she assured me she was not hurt in the least. "I shall be all right in a moment, Jack. I'm not hurt. I was afraid you were killed," she stammered.

It was then I found that the first something which had hit me was my suit case; and never was anything more welcome. There was a flask of brandy in it and a flash lamp, and I managed to get them both. The spirit soon revived us, and I flashed the light round the compartment and took my bearings.

It was a gruesome sight. The two unfortunate soldiers were unconscious; fearfully injured, bleeding terribly, and in such a mess as made one think of the trenches. The carriage lay on its side and the corridor over our heads. That offered the only way of escape, and to reach it I had to stand on the men's bodies. By this means I succeeded in getting a grip on the side of the doorway opening into the corridor. I pulled myself up and scrambled through the opening. Everything was smashed to splinters; there was an ominous smell of gas; part of the train was already on fire, the flames lighting up the weirdly awful scene; and the wind was blowing them right down on our carriage. There wasn't a second to lose if we were not to be roasted alive.

Lying at full length to get a purchase for my feet among some of the wreckage, I leant down to help Nessa out.

She kept her head splendidly. She had presence of mind to remember the suit case, handed it up to me, caught my hand, and I swung her up beside me. It was touch and go even then, for the flames leapt the intervening space at that moment and a flare of gas soon set everything in a blaze.

We had still to get off the carriage, and, although people were hurrying up with assistance, there was no time to wait for them. Crawling over the wreckage to a spot where the side of the carriage had been shattered, I threw the suit case out, sprang after it, and held out my arms, calling to Nessa to jump. She did it without a second's hesitation, falling right on top of me with sufficient suddenness and force to send us both sprawling to the ground.

We were up again in a moment. Nessa laughed strangely and hysterically. "I'm all right, Jack," she cried breathlessly. "Mind the suit case;" and then clutched me convulsively and fainted.

It wasn't surprising, considering that we had had so narrow a squeak for it, and I could estimate the effect upon her by my own general shakiness. What amazed me was that in such a crisis, when death had been a matter of seconds almost, she had seemed to think more about that blessed suit case than her own safety. But she told me the reason afterwards; and of course it was on my account.

I wasn't sorry she fainted. The whole scene was so painful and horrible, that it was a mercy she was spared the sight and smell and sounds of it. Then again it helped to rally me, as I had to see to her. I picked her up and carried her right away to a distance where neither sight nor sound of the disaster was likely to be too obtrusively harrowing, found a shed, and gave her some brandy, and had a swig of it myself.

She soon came round, but was much too overcome by the shock to be moved for a long time, or even to talk. So I let her lie where she was, wrapped her up in some of the clothes in the suit case, lit a cigarette, and set to work to think what our next move had better be.

It wasn't the easiest of problems. There was no chance of getting across the frontier that night, for we had neither tickets nor passports. That bully of a major had kept them. What had happened to him in the smash couldn't be even guessed, of course; but whatever it might be, there was no recovering our papers. That was a certainty.

Could any others be got? Not at Osnabrück. That telegram had been sent to the guard of the doomed train and, if he was alive, he would undoubtedly inform the police; and the instant I turned up as Lassen, we should both be clapped into gaol.

It looked as if it would be extremely unhealthy to attempt to ask for any message from von Gratzen. A very aggravating poser. It was galling to think that a message might be waiting which would clear the road for us effectually, and yet be unable to go for it.

There was the unpleasant contingency that it might not be there, moreover; in which case I should have to put my head in the lion's mouth, with a great probability of the jaws closing on it. A very awkward risk. It didn't affect me so much as Nessa. Even if the police held me in custody as a suspected murderer, it would only be a temporary trouble. But Nessa? What would happen to her it was impossible to foresee; so I ruled out that course.

If we were to get out of the country it must be done under strictly unofficial patronage. Our own. The less we bothered von Gratzen or any one else, the better. That meant going on in our disguises; and then I realized how invaluable Nessa's thought of the suit case had been.

It wasn't a particularly cheerful outlook; but there was one big thing in our favour. Our carriage had been burnt; scarcely any one had been on the spot at the time; certainly no one who could possibly recognize us; and the conclusion every one would draw was that we had perished in the flames. That was another virtual certainty; but in our favour.

There was more than enough on the other side of the ledger, however. I had no identification card; Nessa was in rather a bad shape, and it looked as if she would have to go to bed and stop there for a time, whereas if we were to get away, we ought to be some miles from Osnabrück before daylight; and to go to any hotel or other place for the purpose was very much like asking for more trouble when we had quite sufficient already.

At the same time her safety was the pivot on which everything else turned; it would be idiotic to try and get away, if it meant knocking her up permanently; and that must be the first and prime consideration. She lay so still and seemed so weak and done up, that it was clearly necessary to do something instead of merely thinking about it.

"Can you make an effort, Nessa?" I whispered, bending over her.

"Make an effort? Of course I can. I thought you were bowled over. That's why I kept quiet. I'm all right," and to my surprised relief she sat up at once. "What shall we do?"

"I thought you were almost down and out," I exclaimed.

"Because I fainted? That was the reaction, I expect. I've never done such a thing before that I can remember. But I'm all right again now. I've been thinking."

"I've been doing a bit of that myself. Are you sure you're fit?" It was difficult to believe it after what she had gone through.

"Of course I am, except for being a little shaken. It was an awful business while it lasted; but it's over and got us out of all that trouble. Of course every one will believe we were burnt alive;" and she shuddered. "I suppose it's an awful disaster."

"Better not think of it. The last glimpse I had showed that our carriage and the one behind it were in flames. You can see the glare through the door there."

"Oh, Jack! And they were crowded with people!"

"We can't do anything to help, and we'd better think of ourselves," and to distract her thoughts from the horrors of the train wreck I told her the reasons against venturing into Osnabrück.

"I've been thinking the same. Surely there's only one thing to do?"

"Well?"

"The 'third wheel', of course. It's been in my mind from the very moment of the collision. I don't know how it was, but that rushed into my head instantly; and when you weren't hurt, I could think of nothing but that;" and she pointed to the suit case.

"It was the last word you spoke before fainting."

"And the first when I came round. I was so thankful when I saw you'd brought it away all right. I didn't care after that. You didn't seem really hurt; only shaken; I knew I should be all right soon; and I felt a sort of certainty that the third wheel would carry us into safety. Hadn't we better go?"

"Yes, if you feel fit to do a few miles before daylight?"

"You'll soon see that, if you'll go to your own room and change and leave me to do the same."

My "room" was the back of the shed outside, and I lost no time in getting off my own clothes and putting on the workman's dress over what my flying friend had called the "tummy pad." Then I lit up and waited, thinking what a plucky soul Nessa was, until she called to me.

"How's this, matey?" she asked in her new character and laughed.

It was a wonderful transformation indeed! I should never have recognized her; and the few little scratches on her face from the broken glass in the collision, combined with some artistic smudges she had added, made her into a lifelike young workboy.

"What have you done with your hair?" I exclaimed.

"Just messed it up under the cap. Of course it'll have to come off; but we'd better not waste any time about it now, had we? We can see to it later in the morning."

"Righto," I agreed; and we set to work to finish the other preparations. We had to dispose of our own clothes, of course; so we rolled them up tightly, put the overalls in the suit case, and were ready.

"Now for the frontier," I said. "Let's hope the luck's with us."

"Cheero, matey; if it isn't, you'll get us through somehow," she replied with the most plucky confidence.

I loved her for that, for I knew that she understood the difficulties and risks that lay ahead quite as well as I did. I lost my head for a minute then; and just as we stood on the threshold of the dingy little shed, I put my arm round her, drew her quickly to me and kissed her on the lips.

She held to me for an instant, kissed me in return, and then drew away quickly.

"Not so much of it, matey. Do you take me for a girl? You've knocked my cap off, clumsy," she cried, laughing and blushing, as her glorious hair fell over her shoulders and down to her waist.

"A fine sort of a girl you'd make, and no mistake," I replied, picking up the cap and giving it to her.

In a few moments she had it in place again, pulled the cap down over it and was once more ready.

"Come on, clumsy," she called, stepping out into the night.

And in that way we started on the journey to the frontier.

CHAPTER XXIV
NESSA'S DOWNFALL

The chief event of the hours following the railway smash was histrionic rather than serious, although Nessa regarded it as both humiliating and tragic. And tragic it might easily have been.

Her courage was wonderful. Nothing could damp her spirits nor lessen her high confidence. She laughed at the idea of risks or danger, scoffed at difficulties, and made light of every obstacle as if ours was a mere holiday jaunt. An optimist to the very tips of her pretty fingers.

To be Hans, the mechanic, was just a delightfully farcical joy; she took pride in her skill in playing the part, and was so eager to show me how carefully she had studied it that I hadn't the heart to be a candid critic and point out that it was one thing to act a part for an hour or two on an amateur stage or when we were by ourselves, and quite another to keep it for days in circumstances when even a slight trip might spell grave trouble.

And that our situation was full of difficulties and even dangers was certain. She was still suffering from the inevitable shock of the railway smash; she was done up and sorely in need of rest; it was out of the question to think of seeking a lodging in Osnabrück; the best we could look for was to shelter in some barn or out-of-the-way shed; fifty miles or more lay between us and the frontier, any yard of which might bring some incident which would involve discovery; and even if we got through safely, the job of crossing the frontier would be the most difficult and dangerous of any.

The little incident in the shed as we were leaving kept us both silent for a while. It was the first sign since we had met in Berlin to suggest the renewal of our old relations; and it was not until we reached a good spot for ridding ourselves of our own clothes that the silence was broken.

We struck out to the north of the town and turned along a footpath which would lead us round the outskirts. This took us across a broad stream, and Nessa pulled up on the bridge to suggest we should sink the clothes. We made them into two parcels, put some heavy stones in each, and I sunk them under some trees which overhung the stream a little distance along the bank.

"And when do you propose to put your thinking cap on about our plans, Jack?" she chipped when I rejoined her.

"I'm not going to think of anything else from this minute."

"Hear, hear. The 'anything else' must wait, eh?" she cried, with one of her bright silvery laughs.

"That's not very much like a German hobbledehoy's laugh, is it?"

"Righto, matey, I forgot. That was Nessa; this is Hans;" and she guffawed in her best Hans' manner.

"Not so much of your forgetting, young 'un. This may be no mere picnic."

"Keep your hair on; but I'm going to have the time of my life. By the way, what's your name?"

"Been christened so often lately that I'm not too clear about it. You can call me boss."

"Boss, eh? Then you expect to be master, I suppose?" with a mischievous meaning chuckle. "Am I to keep it up always?"

"Jack's the English for it."

"Anything else?" she chuckled again.

"Wait till the time comes, my lad;" and she decided to drop the chaff.

"And what about our plans, boss?" she asked after a pause.

"I don't see anything for it but to tramp it, if you can stick it."

"How far?"

"The nearest road to the frontier is about thirty odd miles; but as we can't take that, we can put it down at fifty, say. There's no need to rush things, and if we can manage ten or fifteen each day, it ought to do the trick."

"Nothing in that to hurt me, boss. I've often padded twenty or twenty-five in a day, looking for a job, you know. But what's waiting for us at the end of the tramp?"

"I wish I could tell you. My rough idea is to make for a place called Lingen. There are two little dips in the Dutch frontier which come down close to it, and it looks like a fairly good jumping-off place. I'm out of it, if we don't run against some of the smuggling lot there, and the best plan I can think of is to try and join up with some of them and get across in that way."

"Looks all right. If we can get there, that is."

"Needn't worry about that, young 'un. We can tramp it at night, at the worst; but we're not likely to be interfered with. We can always be going to a job just a few miles farther on. I always thought of Osnabrück as the place where we might have to start our tramp, and I've a road map. What we want at the moment is a place where we can rest for an hour or two."

We plodded on steadily, avoiding the roads as much as possible, until we had left Osnabrück well in our rear, and then Nessa pointed to a cottage on the fringe of a wood, which appeared to be deserted.

"Looks like the very spot for us, young 'un. Stop here and I'll go and have a squint at it."

"Look sharp about it, boss, I'm getting a bit leggy and could do with a doss for an hour or two."

I reconnoitred the place cautiously from the back, where there was an untilled garden patch, and first made enough noise to rouse a dog, if there was one. All remained quiet; so I slipped along the garden and flashed my torch lamp through a broken pane of a back window. The room was quite bare, and I opened the window and went over the cottage.

It was deserted right enough. A four-roomed shanty, dirty and dilapidated, but good enough for a shelter; so I fetched Nessa. "A rough shop, young 'un, but better than none."

"Better quarters than those English swine get in the concentration camps, I'll bet," she said as we went up the ricketty stairs to an upper room.

"Bare boards only. It's a good thing you can rough it."

"Nothing to what our brave fellows have to put up with at the front," she replied; and without more ado she lay down with the suit case as a pillow and was soon fast asleep.

I crept out of the room, lit a pipe, and strolled round the cottage trying to think out a definite plan of operations. The most practical question was that of supplies. There would not be any serious risk of trouble with the police even if we kept to the main roads; and this would both shorten the tramp and enable us to get food at out-of-the-way inns.

The one thing that offered difficulties was Nessa's disguise. She was overacting her part considerably and, what was much worse, involuntarily had dropped now and then into her own dear self. The boy business was a blunder. She must turn woman again. It would be much safer if she passed as my sister or even my wife, or perhaps both at turns, according to circumstances.

She would probably kick against it a bit, considering the trouble she had taken and the pride and pleasure she felt in the part. But safety must come first. There was another consideration. If we were stopped, I should be asked for my identification card; and the lack of it might mean trouble. As my wife she wouldn't need one. I must therefore be re-christened and become Hans Bulich.

Over a second pipe the prudence of the change became more obvious, and I regretted the hurry we had been in to get rid of her dress, realizing the difficulty of replacing it without rousing suspicion. We should come across plenty of places where such things could be bought; but for a man and a boy to buy such things were almost certain to lead to awkward questions, especially anywhere near the frontier.

It was broad daylight before I finished wrestling with these new problems, and, as it was better not to run a risk of being seen about the cottage, I went into a little shed belonging to it, propped myself in a corner and dozed off. I was tired and must have slept heavily, and was awakened by a kick and the angry shout of a man asking what the devil I meant by sleeping on his premises. "Get up and be off with you, you lazy tramp," he said, when I rubbed my eyes and blinked at him.

"I'm not a tramp, guv'nor," I protested, getting up.

"Then I'm no farmer, you skulker;" and he looked like repeating the kick.

"Steady, man, steady. Keep your temper. I'm a mechanic on my way to a job in Osnabrück. My boy and I lost our way in the wood yonder and came here to ask the road. Finding the place empty, we decided to doss it till daylight. My mate's only a youngster and was regularly done up."

"You look dirty enough for a tramp anyhow," he growled. "I'm pestered with them. Got any money on you?" A rough-and-ready test of his tramp theory.

"Hope so. More than enough to pay for this sort of bed. Times are pretty good with us chaps now;" and I pulled out a handful of money.

His surly look cleared. "I don't want any of it. What sort of a mechanic do you call yourself?"

"Motors and aeroplanes and that sort of thing."

"The devil you are!" he exclaimed, and, after a pause: "Care to earn a mark or two?"

"Don't mind if I do? How?"

"My motor's in the lane yonder, and something's gone wrong with it. Do you think you could patch it up?"

"I'll have a look at it for you. I'd better get what tools I have with me. They're with my lad."

He opened the front door of the cottage and I ran up to fetch Nessa, fastening her hair up tightly. I told her about the farmer, and found him waiting for us at the bottom of the stairs. He squinted so curiously at Nessa that I feared he suspected her sex.

"My name's Glocken," he said as we went to the car.

I didn't respond to the evident invitation. "Farmer are you?"

He nodded. "Got a couple. One here; the house is just over the hill yonder;" jerking a thumb in the direction; "and one out Lingen way."

"That's where we're padding it, ain't it, boss?" asked Nessa.

A nasty slip, but my fault, for I had not told her I had said I was going to Osnabrück. The farmer noticed it, of course. "Thought you spoke of a job at Osnabrück?" he said meaningly.

"Did I? Must have been half asleep, I suppose. It's Lingen we're bound for."

"No concern of mine. Here we are. Now let's see what you can do."

It was a curious composite; a cross between a touring car and a delivery van. The seats of the tonneau had been taken out to make room for goods, and there was a moveable arrangement for raising the sides at need. There were a few swedes and a tiny truss of hay in it, suggesting the use to which it was put; but there was something else which prompted very different thoughts.

"They've taken all my horses, so I have to fall back on this, to carry the fodder round," he said, noticing my curiosity.

I nodded and threw back the bonnet to find the trouble. It was a splendid engine, 40 h.p. but very dirty; and the dirt had caused the stoppage. Half an hour would put everything right; but I tinkered and fussed over it, as I wished to investigate what I had noticed in the tonneau.

The farmer watched me for a time; then talked to Nessa, who made great play with the Hans impersonation; and I found my chance. I was right. The farmer fed his cattle on very original diet; coffee, sugar, and cocoa seemed to be considerable ingredients, judging by the evidences I found under the swedes and hay. And his other farm was at Lingen! And Lingen was close to the Dutch frontier!

If circumstantial evidence went for anything, this meant that the chief use of the car was for smuggling, and that the agricultural produce was to pull the wool over the eyes of the curious.

I finished my work quickly, trying to see how to turn the knowledge to the best account. It looked like the chance of chances for us, for he might be the very man we wanted to find near the frontier.

"She'll do now, farmer," I called, and started the engine to prove it.

"You know your job, I see," he said, highly pleased, and gave me five marks, which I pocketed.

"She wants cleaning badly if you don't want to have her break down in running to and from that farm of yours at Lingen."

"No fear of that, is there?" he asked in concern.

"I wouldn't answer for her any time in the state she's in."

"Could you do the job for me?"

"Not now; but I may have a bit of spare time when I get to Lingen. I reckon you pack some weight into her at times, too. Groceries tot up, you know. Which is our road for Lingen?"

"What d'ye mean by groceries?"

I gave him a smile and a wink. "No concern of mine, farmer. I never talk about other men's business."

"I'll come along the lane and show you a short cut," he said and went off. "What are you two after?"

"Grub," exclaimed Nessa promptly. "Ain't had a bite since yesterday forenoon, 'cept some berries I picked to give my belly something to do." It was very naturally said, but a blunder, of course.

"Funny. You must have been off the track a lot," he said. "There's plenty of places everywhere. Which way did you come?"

"It's which way we've got to go, that matters now, farmer," said I.

"That's true, and here's the footpath. You strike me as the sort of man one could work with. Come and see me when you get to Lingen;" and he told me how to find the farm and offered his hand.

He let us get a few yards and then called me back. "It's no concern of mine, but that's a delicate youngster of yours; any one would more likely take him for a wench than a lad, when he's off guard. Anyhow, come and see me at Lingen;" and without waiting for my reply, he walked off.

"What did he want?" asked Nessa.

"Spotted you for a girl."

"Jack! He couldn't!" she protested indignantly.

"He did;" and I used the fact as a text to urge the change I had in my thoughts. She did kick at it, as was to be expected; but a little later we had a powerful practical proof of its necessity.

We turned into the first inn we came to for some breakfast, and I was talking to the woman of the house, a very kindly-looking motherly person, about it when there was a commotion outside. I ran out to find Nessa being rough-handled by a man who was trying to snatch her cap off. A word or two stopped any mischief, but it also drew the woman's attention very pointedly to Nessa.

"You can have your breakfast in my room, if you like," she said, and, when I thanked her, led the way to it, and closed the door and stood with her back to it. "You've taken your cap off, can't the lad do the same?" she asked very meaningly.

"Got a sore place on it, mum; 'fraid of a chill," said Nessa.

"I'm good at curing places of that sort, let me have a look at it."

"No, thank you, all the same, I don't take kindly to coddling," replied Nessa, colouring.

The woman smiled. "You do it very well, my girl, but I'm a woman myself and know my own sex," she replied drily. Then to me: "You're an honest man, I'll wager, by your looks. Hadn't you better tell me what it means?"

"She's my wife," I said. "She's English and——"

"Glory be to God!" she interposed excitedly, in English, with a strong brogue. "If I didn't guess it the instant I clapped eyes on the both of ye!" and the tears welled in her eyes as she rushed to Nessa, took off the cap and kissed her. "Ah, ye poor Mavourneen, ye! And, saints alive, look at the lovely hair it is. And to think ye're from England, only I wish it was dear old Oireland, that I do! Whisht now, or Oi'll be making an ould fool of mysilf. We'd best just shpake in German. That I should live to see the day! And out in this divil of a hole of a place! It's making for the frontier ye are, of course! And it's glad that I am I can help ye, so I can. And it's breakfast ye want, is it? Sure I'll see to it; but I must dry my eyes first and get sober."

She kissed Nessa again and almost kissed me also in her joy, wiped her eyes, looked in the glass to see that all was right and bustled out to see about the breakfast.

"Something like a stroke of luck, this," I said; but Nessa was too cast down at her failure in the part to answer, so I looked out of the window to give her time to get over it.

She rose presently and I felt her hand on my shoulder. "I'm a failure, Jack," she said wistfully, struggling to smile at it.

"And thank Heaven for it, sweetheart."

"But even that brute of a farmer found me out. I wouldn't care so much if it had only been this good soul."

"She spotted me as English too," I reminded her.

"I know. You're trying to make it easier for me; but that man didn't spot you, the beast!" She smiled then at her own vehemence. "Well, it's good-bye, Hans, I suppose," she said with a sigh.

"And good riddance, too."

"And yet you said I was doing it so well."

"And so you were, child, for the stage, but this is different."

"It's taken all the fun out of the picnic for me."

"What? To be my wife?"

She laughed and shook her head. "Well, there's one thing, you won't be the boss any longer."

"We'll see about that, young 'un."

"Don't, Jack. Don't ever dare to refer to this again or I'll—I'll—I don't know what I'll do!" she cried with a stamp of the foot. Then she caught sight of Han's cap. "It's that horrid thing that's the cause of it all;" and she picked it up and flung it from her.

That was the overt act of renunciation of the part; and as she turned to me I put my arm round her and kissed her.

"I thought there was to be no more 'anything else,'" she laughed.

"Mustn't a man kiss his own wife?" I cried.

"That hopes to be, Jack," she whispered.

And that was Hans' funeral ceremony.

CHAPTER XXV
A FRIEND IN NEED

When the woman returned to us she had quite thrown off her emotional outburst at our meeting, and her first words were a warning not to speak another word of English.

"I couldn't help it at first, I was so excited; but it would ruin me if it was known that I'm British," she declared, and over the breakfast she told us her story.

She was from Cork, where she had married a German baker named Fischer, had come to Germany a few years later, had been a widow for five years, and had continued to carry on the business of the inn. She was very curious to learn the truth about the war; and when I had satisfied her, we settled down to the consideration of her own affairs.

We returned confidence for confidence: that Nessa and I were engaged to be married; how I had come from England to find her; the plight she had been in owing to von Erstein's persecution; that we had been in the train smash, and had escaped with our lives, but had lost the passports.

She knew the von Erstein type of German well enough to sympathize deeply with Nessa and listened in tears to that part of the story.

"I can help you both, and I will; but you'll have to be as cautious as a pair of wild birds. They're just grabbing the men into the army with both hands, for one thing, and they'll take you at sight, and then what would she do, poor thing?"

"But aren't a lot of mechanics exempted?"

"Do you know anything about such things really?"

"Most there is to know about motors and aeroplanes."

"Oh, that's better," she cried, rubbing her hands. "They're making that sort of thing now at a place called Ellendorf, out Lingen way; and they're wanting men badly. You can say you've heard of it and are on your road there, and it may help you through. But understand that all strangers about here are suspected and the police are mighty curious; and it's worse the closer to the frontier you get. Have you thought how you're to get across?"

"If we're as lucky there as we have been here, it mayn't be so difficult. My rough idea was to join up with some of the folk who are smuggling things over and look for a chance to slip across."

"I'd thought of that, too, and I can help you," she said, and then explained her plan.

She declared that nearly every one near the frontier was taking a hand in the smuggling game and that the authorities, both police and military, not only winked at it, but secretly encouraged it. Lately, however, owing to the more drastic rounding up of men for the army, there had been a good deal of the slipping over which we wished to do, and stringent measures were being taken in consequence.

"That makes it more difficult," she continued; "but my late husband's brother, Adolf Fischer, lives there. I'll give you a note to him and he'll help you."

"Is he one of them?" I asked.

She smiled and nodded. "He's getting rich at it and has several people working with him. I'll have to lie for you; but I don't mind. I'll tell him I know all about you and that you want to join him; but don't say a word about skipping over, or he'll put the police on you. He's very thick with them, but that needn't scare you. They won't touch one of his men."

"We're awfully obliged to you."

"I only wish I could do more. Of course, I'll find some clothes for you," she said to Nessa. "They'll only be rough working things; but then nothing else would do; and if you'll both be guided by me, you won't think of risking the walk to Lingen. What you'd better do is to stop here and rest till to-morrow morning, get away early and foot it to Massen; it's only a matter of four or five miles: and catch the train there; and it would be all the better if you were to wear overalls. I can get you some."

"I have some already," I put in.

"All the better, but whatever you do, don't carry that grip with you. Might as well write who you are on your back. Much better carry a tool or so in your hand as if you were off to a job in a hurry; and she might have a small market basket. She'll be your wife till ye reach Lingen; and don't forget that most Germans treat their wives pretty gruffly. There are plenty of spies about with sharp eyes for trifles of the sort. They might even see that you don't eat like them. I should have known you by it," she declared.

We both laughed as we thanked her again; and soon afterwards she took Nessa away to see about the change of dress.

We had fallen on our feet in all truth. Her help was literally invaluable. Every one of her suggestions was practical and opened my eyes to the many little difficult details and pitfalls which had never occurred to us when planning our escape.

An hour or two later she came back saying she had left Nessa making some few necessary alterations in the dress and wanted to speak to me alone. "Just like me, I've put my foot in it with her. I told her what's only the truth, that you'll never be able to get over the frontier together, and she swears nothing shall make her go alone. You must talk her round or— —" and she shook her head doubtfully.

"That'll be all right."

"Perhaps. She's just the bravest darling in the world, but my, what a will!" and she threw up her hands and smiled. "The frontier men will always wink at a woman crossing, but if they catch a man trying it they shoot him and done with it. Now what'll you do if she won't give in?"

I shrugged my shoulders.

"Well, I'll tell you. Go to that factory at Ellendorf and get a job. You'll both be safe there; they'll find you a cottage, and you'll have to wait till a chance comes to get away together. Tell my brother-in-law you're going there and that you can do his work from there. But if she sticks out, don't try anything from Lingen; he's sure to hear about it, and then you may look out. Don't forget that and think that because he speaks you fair, he's soft. He isn't. He daren't be, either."

She went on to give me a host of details about the smuggling, and I took an opportunity to ask about the farmer whose car I had repaired.

"Old Farmer Glocken, you mean. He's deep as a well and as dangerous as St. Patrick found the snakes. If he can make use of you, all right; he'll do it so long as it pays him; but he'd sell his own wife, poor wretch, for a few marks. Don't go near him."

"He does a little smuggling?"

"A little! He's in it up to his eyes. He could get you both across easily enough, if you paid him, supposing he didn't take your money first and then sell you. And that's as likely as not."

Some one knocked at the door then and she went out, returning with a servant who clumped noisily after her and began to lay the cloth for dinner.

"Be careful, Gretchen," she said sharply as the girl nearly let some glasses fall. She was a stoutish, rather slatternly girl, with particularly grimy finger nails, and a shawl over her head which concealed most of her face. She was very clumsy, too, and set everything down awkwardly with a guffaw.

"What do you think of Gretchen?"

I started and they both laughed. It was Nessa, of course, and she whipped off the shawl, clapped her hands, and turned completely round so that I might study her get-up.

"Better than the boy, eh?" laughed Mrs. Fischer.

"It's wonderful. I should have passed her in the street with that shawl over her head."

"It's how the workgirls wear it."

"Look at my boots, Jack," cried Nessa, holding up a foot. "Aren't they just lovely?" Great clumsy thick-soled things they were.

"Her own were just danger signals. But she'll do as she is. Now, I've told my servants you're old friends of mine, and that you'll be here till to-morrow morning. You had better not go out. A day's rest and a long night's sleep won't hurt either of you;" and with that she hurried away.

"Isn't she a dear old soul? She's been mothering me up there, as if she couldn't do enough for me, and ransacked every nook and cranny to fish out these things."

"She's a very shrewd old party, too."

"And are you proud of your wife, or sister, whichever I'm going to be?"

"Which would you prefer?"

"Don't be silly. Don't you think this is ripping? And she's been drilling me about how to behave. I think she's wonderful."

"What sort of drilling was it?"

"No end of things. How to eat; what to do; how to walk; always to have my knitting in hand; not to talk to strangers, especially women; one or two phrases I was to use; how to carry my market basket; a regular rehearsal of everything, and we're to have another this evening. Look at my hands;" and she held them out.

"I saw your nails when you put the tray on the table."

"Yes, but look how she's managed to make them coarse. We scrubbed them all over with bath brick and then rubbed in the dirt. They're smarting, as if they were chapped. And look at my hair, plastered right down on my head. Did you ever see such a fright as I am? And then this bunchy business on my hips;" and she laughed as she looked at herself in the glass.

"That all?"

"Not a bit of it. There was a regular lecture on the proper behaviour of working men's wives; sort of fetch and carry dogs with the tails always between their legs and never a wag except when the master condescends to give them a nod or so."

"Going to do it all?"

She was fingering her hair and started, glancing sharply at me in the glass. "Sisters don't, by any means. But I know that tone of yours. You mean something. What is it?"

"Mrs. Fischer told me she had been giving you some hints."

She paused and then turned and faced me, putting her hands behind her back with her head thrown well back—a pose I knew well. "I think I know what you mean and I'm not going to do it, Jack."

"Do what?"

"Innocent! But it's no use, Jack, I won't."

"Very well."

"You don't mean that a bit. I know. You mean just the opposite. It's about my getting over the frontier alone. Isn't that it?"

"She said something to me about it."

"Of course. She tried all she knew to persuade me and now she's been at you, of course. I'm ready to listen to you; but I warn you it won't make a pennorth of difference."

"Very well."

"Oh, don't 'very well' me in that tone. You don't expect me to desert you when you've done all this and got into this mess solely for me, do you?" she cried vehemently.

"We won't worry over it now; but there's just one point you might keep in mind. It may turn out to be necessary for my safety. What then?"

Her face clouded at that. "How could that be?" she asked.

"We can answer that better later on," I said with a shrug. "But if it should be?"

"Did Mrs. Fischer say anything about that to you?"

I nodded. "Said it might be easy enough for you to get over, but very risky for us both to try it together. Suggested that if you held out I had better get a berth at Ellendorf; but there's the question of my leave. It's nearly up, and either you or I must be able to wire explanations from Holland within the next day or two."

"I never thought of that. What would happen?"

"Possibly nothing; but it doesn't help a man to play the absentee. They've a nasty term for that in the army."

"You always mean such a lot when you speak in that casual tone of yours," she exclaimed. "Of course, if my stopping meant any sort of trouble to you, it would be different. Nothing else would make me go. And if you're only saying it to force me you're—well, it's cowardly and you ought to be ashamed to do it."

"Well, think it over, and we'll see how the cat jumps. I promise you this, faithfully, I won't ask you to do it if it isn't necessary."

She paused and then came and laid a hand on my shoulder. "You won't ask me to go unless it's necessary for your sake, will you, Jack? It would be awful for me to feel that you were left here in danger. I know you're thinking all about me and not about yourself, and—oh, Jack, I don't believe I could bear it."

"We won't worry any more about it till the time comes. I think it's splendid of you to want to stick it, but it's better to tell you;" and we let the matter drop.

But Nessa did worry about it exceedingly for the rest of the day. She spoke very little and appeared to have lost interest in things; and just before she was going to bed she came with a suggestion that we should make at least one attempt to cross the frontier together. I yielded very reluctantly, as it meant the hash of a great part of our plans. But she was so downcast, so troubled, and pleaded with such wistful earnestness, that I hadn't the heart to refuse.

Mrs. Fischer declared it was rank madness; that if we tried it, we mustn't go near her brother-in-law; and that we had better go straight to Ellendorf.

Nessa was in much better spirits early the next morning when we bade good-bye to our new friend.

"How are we to repay you for all this?" I asked.

"It isn't money you mean, is it?" she asked, almost indignantly, although she was so affected at parting from us that the tears were in her kind motherly eyes.

"No money could repay all your kindness and help."

"Then don't offer it to me. Sure, it's enough that we're all of the same blood, and all I'll want is to know that you get home safe and sound. I'd like to know that," she said wistfully. "Sure my heart's still over there. There, be off with you, or I'll be making a fool of myself."

"I'll write to you, Mrs. Fischer," said Nessa, kissing her.

"Not on your life, child. It's in gaol I'd be in no time, the divils that they all are!" she exclaimed, relapsing into English.

"We'll manage to let you know," I promised, shaking her hand warmly; and we were turning to leave the room when Nessa had a most happy thought.

"We'll send you a sprig of shamrock, dear."

The thought of it broke the dear soul up entirely. "Oh, the blessed darlin'!" she cried, seizing Nessa and kissing her again. "What my ould eyes would give for a sight of it!" and she burst into a passion of sobs. "Go now, go, the pair of ye, or I'll— —" Sobs choked her utterance and she leant her head on the table, motioning us to go.

Nessa touched my arm and we stole out, both of us deeply moved by the emotion which Nessa's offer had stirred in the heart of the lonely Irish exile.

CHAPTER XXVI
THE HUE AND CRY!

On the walk to Massen we concocted our story. I was to be Hans Bulich and Nessa my sister; we were alone in the world except for an aunt in Holland; Nessa had recently lost her lover on the Russian front, and her supposed grief at this was to account for her gloomy silence; I was likely to be called up, and as this would leave her without friends or money, she was anxious to get to the aunt in Holland.

They were parts easy to play, thanks to our warm-hearted Irish friend; we looked the characters quite well enough to pass muster. The absence of any luggage, my overalls and tools and a big German china pipe, and Nessa's market basket and knitting were shrewd little touches of realism which carried us through the preliminary difficulties without any trouble.

There were several people in the carriage with us, one of whom, an old man who sat next me, was going as far as Lingen. The men were soon talking and the one subject was the food supply, which was evidently becoming a serious matter. I didn't pay much attention until a question was asked about the frontier smuggling. The matter interested them all keenly, and I threw in a remark now and then to draw the rest.

The old fellow next me seemed to know a good deal about it, and when we three were left alone in the carriage he let drop a remark which showed he had noticed my interest in the subject, and then asked if I'd been at the front yet.

"They think I'm more use at my trade," I replied, making play with the spanner in my hand.

"Engineer's mechanic, may be?"

I nodded. "Motors and aeroplanes and so on."

"Going to Lingen, aren't you?"

"Yes. How far's Ellendorf from there?"

"A matter of a league or two. I hear they're making these new aeroplanes there. Got a job there?"

"Shan't know till I get to Lingen; have another little matter to see to first, anyway."

"A good few people have little matters to see to there, these days," he replied drily, with a suggestive glance out of the corner of his eye. "I live there, and you can take it from me that if you're any good at your job, there's plenty of work waiting for you."

"Government work?"

"If they weren't all blind, yes;" and he launched into a description of the extreme difficulty of getting repairs done. "Can't get so much as a screw driven in without one of their infernal permits. I've been to Osnabrück about it now trying to get a man. Might as well have asked for the moon!" he said disgustedly, and went on grumbling about it, at intervals, for the rest of the journey.

When we reached Lingen he said he'd like to have a chat with me and suggested we should go to his shop. "Won't do you any harm to be seen with me, either; I'm well known; and what with escaped prisoners and our skulkers trying to jump the frontier, the police are pretty curious about strangers of your age and build especially."

He was well known, as he had said. Several people nodded to him on the platform, and one man came after him. "Good-day, Father Fischer, can I have a word with you?" and they stopped to talk together.

"Hear that, Nessa?" I asked excitedly. "By Jove, we're in luck if it's our man!" and when he rejoined us I asked him if he was Adolf Fischer.

"I am. Every one in Lingen knows Adolf Fischer."

"Have you a brother out Massen way?"

"I had, but he drank himself to death five years or so back, poor fool. Why do you ask?"

"I've a letter for you;" and I gave it him.

He read it and pocketed it with a chuckle of pleasure. "Couldn't be better. Friends of Martha's are friends of mine. Come along."

We had not left the station before we had a proof of our good luck. We were in front of him as we went out and the police sergeant at the door stopped us and was beginning to question me, when he intervened.

"It's all right, Braun. They're friends of mine. A stroke of luck, too," he said with a wink, which suggested there was a mutually satisfactory understanding between them.

We were allowed to pass at once, and he stayed talking to the sergeant for a couple of minutes. "Lucky you gave me that letter when you did," he said when he caught us up. "They've been ordered to keep a special look-out for a couple such as you. But they won't worry you while you're with me."

Ominous news in view of what had occurred just before the train smash outside Osnabrück, and it made me more anxious than ever to get Nessa safely over the frontier.

"You'll bide with me, of course," he said when we reached his house, a flourishing grocer's store in the main street of the little town. "I don't have any one in the house nights. We'll have a bite of food and then talk things over."

He was silent and thoughtful during the meal, and the trend of his thoughts was shown in a question he put.

"There's nothing black against you, is there?"

"Nothing to make me afraid to face any man in the Empire," I replied positively. It was the truth, if not quite as I meant him to understand it.

"I only asked, because I have to be very careful," he said; and nothing more passed until we were smoking, while Nessa had resumed the knitting which she had kept up incessantly in the train.

"Now, you'd like to tell me your story," he opened.

I told him the tale we had prepared and he put a question or two which were easily answered.

"I'm sorry for you, my lass," he said to her. "Very sorry; you're only one among too many thousands; and you shall get away all right. They're not particular about women and girls, you know," he added to me. "But it's different with men. Their orders are to shoot first and ask questions afterwards. Three were found trying to jump the frontier last week and were shot. Two the week before; and one of 'em was our only engineer. So if that's what's brought you here, I can't help you. We'd all the trouble we wanted over the last affair."

"I'm no skulker, I assure you. If they call 'em up, I'm ready any time."

"You'll give me your word to stop here then?"

"Unless I have to go anywhere else. I'm pretty handy at my job, you know."

He seemed satisfied, and then told me his plans.

Nessa was to leave that night. He had a nephew in the Landwehr regiment at present guarding a part of the frontier, which was especially promising for the scheme, and we were to run out there in his car. I was to stay with him in Lingen, partly to help in the smuggling operations but largely to keep in order his and his associates' motors. There were a number of Lingen people in the thing, which was winked at by the authorities, who would not ask any questions about me if I was known to be in the swim.

He gave me a host of details, took me out later to see the place where I was to work; a very well-equipped place it was, too, but with only a lad and a doddering old fellow as the staff: explained that they often lost considerably by breakdowns; and then left me to return to Nessa, saying that he must go and arrange about the night's venture.

I found Nessa very dejected, buried in thought, with her knitting on her lap.

"Looks good enough, eh?" I said to cheer her.

It wasn't a success. She did not answer for a while. "Do you trust him?" she asked, looking up at length.

"Why not? He was frank enough; and we should have been in a deuce of a mess without him. It can't be worse even if he gives us away. But he won't. I'm sure of that."

"But about you?"

"Meaning?" I knew what was coming, however.

"You heard what he said about those men being shot. It brought my heart up in my mouth."

"It's no more than we heard at Massen."

"We agreed to try together, remember."

"I haven't forgotten. We'll see what happens to-night."

"You don't want me to go by myself? You promised, Jack."

"Better one than neither of us, surely. That reminds me. You must have some money in case I fail;" and I offered her some notes.

She shook her head and pushed them away. "I have more than enough for my purpose."

I knew what she meant. She was resolved not to go alone, and it worried me considerably. It was splendidly staunch and lovable and brave, but none the less quixotic and a serious blunder. "You heard what that police sergeant had told old Fischer?"

"Of course," she nodded casually, as if it didn't make the least difference.

"You shall settle it for yourself, Nessa." There was nothing to be gained by trying to dissuade her then, so I left it until the moment for action should arrive. After my promise, it was impossible for me to think of going with her.

Fischer came back chuckling. "We're in luck," he declared. "I met my nephew, Fritz, in the town just now. He'll do it all right. He'll be on guard at one of the roads; the very spot of all others for us; near a little thicket they call the Pike Wood. We're to be there about nine. I explained everything to him, and of course I've pledged my word that only your sister's going over. That's right, eh?"

"Quite," I assured him.

Nessa's needles stopped clicking for an instant and I heard her catch her breath. It augured badly for the night's enterprise; but if I had wished to renew the attempt to persuade her, I could not have done it, as we were not left alone altogether again until the time came for us to set out.

I drove the car with Fischer at my side, and by his instructions, Nessa lay on the bottom of the tonneau which was constructed much like that of the farmer's I had mended at Qsnabrück. She was hidden under a rug and a tarpaulin, and he told her to cover up even her head if any one spoke to us on the way.

We had some dozen miles to run, and for the greater part of the way no one attempted to interfere with us. The old fellow seemed to be hugely pleased by the way I handled the ramshackle machine; and even more so when I explained the reason of some of the queer noises and jumps which the engine developed. "You're the man for us!" he exclaimed more than once.

When we reached the outskirts of a village close to the frontier, he bent over and told Nessa to hide herself completely. "We shall be questioned here; but it won't matter. Go slow for a bit," he added to me; "and pull up at once if they order us."

The village was full of soldiers, and I began to realize in earnest then the difficulties of our escaping without his help. We were pulled up twice in the village, but allowed to proceed the moment he was recognized and produced some authority he had.

After we left the village behind us there were plenty of people, both men and women, all with their faces turned frontierwards. "What are all these doing?" I asked.

"Crumb-hunters, we call 'em." Descriptive enough, too; and he told me they were out in all weathers to pick up any trifles from the Dutch side, and that passes were given to them for the purpose.

"And what about the Dutch guards?"

"Getting fat on it," replied Fischer, rubbing his palm and then putting a finger to the side of his nose. "Bleed us to a tune, too. Their people try to stop it; change the men often enough; but it only means that Peter gets a greasy palm instead of Paul. We turn off into the next lane on the right: it runs across the frontier; the Pike Wood's just there; but you'll have to stop a little short of it to turn the car."

We ran about half a mile along the lane to the spot where I turned and we all got out. He led the way across a field or two, and, as we were rather before our time—nine o'clock—he posted us at a point in the thicket from which we could see the guards at the gate which marked the boundary on the German side, and then left us.

I was beginning to get a little excited by that time, but Nessa seemed quite unmoved, except that she shivered once or twice, for the night air had a nip in it. Whether she persisted in her intention not to go without me, I could not say. She had heard me tell old Fischer that I wasn't going; but she maintained a sphinxlike silence all the time he was away.

He went up to the guards and I could just make out their figures as he stood talking to them; and presently he disappeared into the darkness through the gate. A minute or two later some shots were fired from the other side of the barrier; soon afterwards a loaded wagon came dashing from that side, the three horses galloping at full stretch, and a man I took to be Fischer jumped from it.

An exhibition of organization followed. A number of men sprang up from nowhere; the wagon was unloaded almost instantly; and they scuttled off into the night with cases and barrels and packages of all descriptions and sizes. It was done like a flash; and the wagon was galloped back across the frontier. It had just disappeared when an officer rode up, presumably to learn the cause of the firing. Just then Fischer rejoined us, out of breath, but hugely pleased.

"A near thing," he panted. "If that officer had been a minute earlier he'd have commandeered the lot. He's a swinehound. You must lie doggo till he's gone; but it's all right. Fritz will give you the tip. You're to go forward the moment you hear him whistling 'The Watch on the Rhine.' Don't lose a second. Give him a twenty-mark note; it's for his two pals. And now I can't stop with you, I must see to things. I'll wait for you at the car."

"What was that firing?" I asked as he turned away.

"To fool the Dutch officers," he said over his shoulder as he went.

Nessa's intention was still a riddle. She stood leaning against a tree, motionless as a statue and up to this point as silent. But the time had come when I must know what she meant to do.

"You're going, Nessa?" I whispered.

No answer; not even a shrug of the shoulders.

"Nessa, dear, you're going?"

"Are you?"

"No. I gave my word. Besides I've half a notion that this is a sort of test. Fischer has told the men that I am not, and even if they didn't shoot us both, I should be ruined with him. And you can see for yourself there isn't one chance in a hundred of our getting through."

She listened but made no reply.

"We shall have that signal in a moment. That officer is riding away."

A long tremulous sigh from her. "Do you wish me to go, Jack?"

"Yes, most certainly. It's the luckiest chance in the world."

"Is it?"

"You can see it for yourself, dearest." I tried to put my arm round her, but she drew away.

"Don't, Jack! After what you've just said."

There was a pause in which we could catch the guttural tones of the guards and hear them stamping their feet. Precious seconds were flying and I was getting into a positive fever of impatience and anxiety.

"I'm only thinking of you, Nessa. You know that. Do make up your mind to go. You must surely see that it's the one course for you. There's the road to England and your mother and——"

"And you're to stop here in all this danger alone."

My patience began to give out. "I know you're thinking of me, but I can get out of it all ever so much better alone. But there, if you won't, you won't, and there's an end of it."

"You promised to make an attempt together. Have you done it?"

"For Heaven's sake, Nessa, don't let us split hairs at a moment like this. Here's the chance of chances for you, and you may never have another. If you wish ever to see England again, or at all events until after the war's over, you'll take it."

"That shows what little chance you think you have of getting away," she retorted, and made me wish I'd said something else.

"I didn't mean anything of the sort, only that it will be infinitely easier for me alone."

She didn't answer, and in the pause the first bars of the "Watch on the Rhine" were whistled in a low cautious pitch.

"Come, dearest," I whispered and put my arm about her.

"Oh, I can't go, Jack. I—I can't be such a coward!" she whispered, trembling in her agitation.

"For Heaven's sake, dearest!"

The whistling had ceased, but she still hesitated.

After an interval, very short, the whistle came again, slightly louder.

There was only one last plea I could think of. "It may cost me my life if you don't go, Nessa."

I felt her shudder convulsively as she yielded, and clung to me for an instant. "I'll go. Oh, God!" she moaned piteously under her breath.

I hurried her across the intervening field, and as we reached the other side of it, the man at the gate called to us impatiently to hurry.

But Nessa stopped. "I've forgotten, Jack," she whispered. "I must have that money after all."

I had it ready, thrust it into her hand, and helped her over the field gate. In her agitation she fell and dropped the notes. It was as dark as pitch on the ground at that spot and I had to grope with my hands to find them.

The man called to me urgently to come at once, and I had just found them when we heard the sound of a horse galloping in our direction.

"Back to the wood," growled the man almost fiercely. "If the captain noses you, you'll be shot."

I lifted Nessa over the gate and we darted back to cover, as the officer rode up. We waited for some breathless anxious minutes for him to go, hoping that the signal could be repeated.

But he did not go; and soon afterwards the guard was changed.

The chance was gone and there was nothing for it but to return to the car.

The failure was bitterly disappointing, but Nessa was glad, and laughed. "Here's the money, Jack," she said as we left the wood.

I pocketed it in silence.

"I suppose you're awfully angry and disappointed and all that, but I'm not. The only thing I regret is that I was persuaded to go."

"I'm not angry about it. It's a great pity; but the only thing to do is to wait for another opportunity. I dare say Fischer can manage it."

"You needn't look for one, if you mean me to go alone. I won't do it. You'll never get me to consent again; and you said I was to settle it, remember."

"I remember," I replied.

"I'm absolutely determined," she declared; but something was to happen that night which shook that determination to ruins.

Fischer expressed great surprise at seeing her; but I explained that at the last moment the money had been lost and that the officer had come back in time to prevent Nessa's escape.

The car was now loaded with some of the spoils from the wagon and Nessa had to ride in front with us. We made a quick run back to the town, where I helped in the unloading, and then with Nessa took the car to the place where I was to overhaul it in the morning.

"I feel a thousand times more light-hearted, Jack," she said slipping her hand in my arm as we walked back to Fischer's shop.

"That's as it should be. I was rather bearish over it, I'm afraid; but it was such a chance."

"You won't ask me again to—— Good heavens, look, Jack, look!" she broke off, her voice shaken with agitation as she clutched my arm convulsively and pointed to a small poster outside the police station.

She might well be agitated. The poster was headed:

MURDER
1,000 Marks Reward

The murder was that of Anna Hilden and the reward was for my capture.

Two portraits were in the middle. One an excellent reproduction of Nessa with the words: "Nessa Caldicott, Englishwoman," beneath it; the other a villainous splash drawing: "Johann Lassen, German"; who were "known to have left Berlin together on the night of the 23rd in the train which had been wrecked outside Osnabrück."

CHAPTER XXVII
FARMER GLOCKEN AGAIN

This "Hue and Cry" poster alarmed Nessa intensely. Her fears were all on my account, however; and so far as concerned herself, she did not even then seem to regret that her chance to cross the frontier had been missed.

As we hurried to Fischer's I tried to reassure her that the trouble was not so serious as it looked at first blush; for the reason that the photograph of her was so good that no one would recognize her in her present make-up, while mine was execrable enough to amount to a positive disguise. But this did not allay her agitation; and after we reached the house, there was no opportunity for further discussion.

We both realized that the consequences might be very serious; and after she had gone to bed, I sat racking my wits over the perplexing problem. It was either von Erstein's doing or von Gratzen's; and in the end I put it down to von Erstein, whose influence was quite sufficient to enable him to stir up the police in this manner.

For me there was only the risk of arrest and trial for the murder; hugely unpleasant, of course, but not dangerous, because von Gratzen knew who had killed the woman and had the proofs. It was very different for Nessa, however, although she had, of course, nothing to fear in connection with the murder charge. But she would certainly be kept in the country; and Heaven alone knew what the consequences would be and what price she might have to pay for her fatal hesitation at the frontier that night.

I had no chance of speaking to her about it until about noon the following day when Fischer sent her with some lunch for me to the shed where I had put his car into shape again. As the "staff" — the gawky lad and the decrepit old man — were present, it was difficult to say much to her, but I managed at intervals to let her know what I thought.

To my concern, however, she was determined to stay in the country. Instead of regretting her refusal to go, she appeared to glory in it. If there was to be trouble for me, she was resolved to share it, declaring that she could help me by confessing her part.

I was still doing what I could to shake this determination and show her the fallacy of it, when there was another unpleasant surprise.

Fischer arrived bringing the farmer Glocken whose motor I had mended at Osnabrück. If there was one man in all Germany I wished to avoid at that moment, it was certainly Glocken.

"Hullo! so it's you, is it?" he exclaimed.

Fischer was obviously as much astonished at the recognition as I was concerned. "You know Bulich, then?" he asked.

Glocken paused and appeared to sense something of the position and answered with a cunning squint at me: "I know him for a first-class workman."

"You're right," agreed Fischer, and then explained the object of the visit. Glocken was in the smuggling ring and looked after a very important and profitable branch—the smuggling of chemicals for ammunition. These were brought by aeroplane; it being deemed too risky to resort to the ordinary method. A consignment had arrived the previous evening, the pilot, a Dutchman named Vandervelt, had had an accident in landing, and I was wanted to put the thing right.

There was no way of getting out of it, and what objection there might have been was more than compensated for when Fischer drew me aside and told me he had arranged with Glocken that if my sister would venture the flying trip, she could go with the Dutchman. I agreed without asking Nessa; and as Fischer's car was now ready for the road we drove away in it.

Glocken sat in front with me and promptly started his questions. Very awkward questions some of them were too: about our former meeting; why I had not mentioned I knew Mrs. Fischer at the inn; why I had said I was coming from Osnabrück, when old Fischer had told him a very different story; and at last enough to show that he had seen the murder poster and was inclined to connect it with me.

Having in this way thoroughly scared me, as he thought, he broached the subject of Nessa's flight and asked what it was worth, hinting that Vandervelt was something of a bloodsucker. I had still an ample supply of money; about a couple of hundred pounds, some four thousand marks; and being prepared to part with every pfennig to get Nessa away, it was a considerable relief to find that it was to be a matter of bribing.

"Couple of hundred marks, enough?" I suggested.

"You don't know Vandervelt, or you wouldn't offer a trifle like that," he said, shaking his head.

"How much then? I'm not yet a partner in Krupp's, remember."

"What's it worth to you?"

"Fischer was going to do it for nothing last night. He's almost as sorry for my sister as I am."

"Vandervelt isn't Fischer," he replied drily. "Doesn't a thousand marks strike you as cheap?" he said with a wily significant leer. That was the amount of the reward!

"Out of the question, Glocken. She must have something in her pocket when she lands; and in any case Fischer's going to arrange it in a day or so."

"Hadn't she better be off at once? Delays are apt to be dangerous sometimes, you know."

"Why?" I asked, turning to him.

Our eyes met in a mutually intent stare, and his dropped first. "You know your own business," he muttered with a shrug. "But you'd better give the thousand, if you want her to go."

It was clearly best to haggle, so I advanced to five hundred, then to seven hundred and fifty, and at last to a thousand, protesting it was an imposition. He pretended to fire up at the word; but it was only the preface to asking for the money to be paid at once.

It was all going into his own pocket, of course; and after more words I agreed to give him half the amount when we reached his farm if I found my sister would risk the venture, and the remainder as soon as she was safely off.

I broached the matter to Nessa as soon as we arrived, and she met it at first with a flat refusal. "I won't go, Jack. I thought something of the sort was meant when you asked me to come here. I don't care what happens to me. I cān't go."

"But I want you to care, Nessa. It's——"

"Well, I don't—and I won't."

"You're not afraid of the trip?"

"I'm not that sort of coward, thank you," she retorted sharply.

"I'm going to arrange with the pilot, Vandervelt's his name, for him to look after you when you land and see you to some station."

"I'm not taking the least interest in all this."

"You'd better book right through to Rotterdam and go to our Consulate, and I'll look for you there."

"I'm not going, Jack."

"You'd rather be clapped into an internment camp?"

"I don't care for fifty internment camps. They can do what they please with me, but I won't be coward enough to desert you."

"You can tell everything at the Consulate and——"

"Is that a Home for strayed cowards?" she cried, springing up and stamping her foot, her eyes flashing indignantly.

"No, it's the best meeting place for us and a safe refuge for quixotic girls."

"They're welcome to it, then. I shan't disturb them. If you wish to make me hate you, you'll persist in all this."

"I'd rather have you hate me than that you should stop here."

"How can you say such a thing as that?"

"Because I mean it; every syllable of it, Nessa, on my honour."

This appeared to make some impression. She winced and paled slightly. "I've never been thought a coward before," she said after a pause, but without so much of the former snap.

"What I do think is that if what you talk of doing is cowardice, I'd rather be thought a coward than anything else."

"That means that you approve of it then?"

"On the contrary. Don't let us get at cross purposes. I must be off to this job. The thing is this. If I'm alone here, I can get through everything without risk; and I can't if you stop. It's splendid of you to wish to stick it with me; but it'll be fatal to me; fatal to both of us, indeed."

"I don't care about myself."

"Then care for me. Do it for my sake."

"How would my stopping hurt you?"

I lost patience then. "There isn't time to go over it all again, Nessa. But if you persist in this, there's no use in continuing a useless struggle to get away. I've made the arrangement; and if you won't leave, I shall go straight from here to the police, tell them I'm Lassen, and leave them to do what they will."

"You wouldn't be so mad! You're only saying it to force me to give in," she exclaimed, firing again.

"Call it what you like; but I shall do it. Keep that in mind when the time comes for you to decide;" and without waiting to give her time to reply I left her. It went against the grain to have to use such a threat, knowing that her motive was nothing but a chivalrous regard for me; but persuasion had failed, and matters were too serious to be over nice in the choice of means to convince her.

There wasn't much wrong with the bus. Vandervelt, a very decent fellow, was a good pilot, it seemed, but not much use as a mechanic. A couple of hours or so sufficed for the job; but as I hoped that Nessa would be his passenger, I went most carefully over every part and made tests until I was satisfied. This occupied a considerable time, so that I had not finished until late in the afternoon.

The arrangement was that Vandervelt should start about sunset, as that would give him time to reach his landing place before dark. He agreed readily to get Nessa to the nearest station and to see her safely off for Rotterdam. If all went well, she ought to reach there somewhere about noon the following day.

He said nothing about the passage money for Nessa, and I avoided the subject. So long as Nessa got away, it was nothing to me whether old Glocken swindled his companion or not. They could settle their own differences; and it would have been the act of a fool to set them by the ears at such a moment.

All I saw of the farmer tended to confirm the Irish-woman's estimate of him. He had blackmailed me in the matter of the payment for Nessa, and I had very little doubt that, having scooped in a thousand marks for her, he would start another attempt with me on the same lines.

He watched me at work for most of the time; joined with Vandervelt in praising my skill; repeating with unnecessary frequency something about what extraordinary good luck it was for them that I had come to Lingen, and his hope that I should remain with them a long time.

He didn't mean a word of it, of course, and for a long time left me guessing as to his motive for all this waste of breath. At length, however, it struck me that all this rot was intended to keep me slogging away because he was anxious about the bus and that he wished to have it in good shape before something was to happen which he had up his sleeve.

He had my five hundred marks in his pocket, and, if he broke the contract and refused to let Nessa go at the last minute, he might be getting the thousand for the reward instead of only the balance of five hundred from me. I knocked that little dodge on the head, therefore.

Waiting for a repetition of his oxish praise of my skill, I laughed and said: "You're right, farmer; you've got to know how to handle them. They're difficult enough to repair sometimes, but easy to damage. A blow or two with the hammer in the right spot, and I could make this old bus fit for nothing but the scrap heap;" and I gave him a meaning look and raised the hammer as if going to smash things.

He tumbled to my meaning right enough and grabbed my arm. "Mind what you're doing, man. Do you know what that thing cost?" he cried.

"Oh, yes. A good deal more than a thousand marks. I was only showing you how easy it would be to make it worth about as many pfennigs."

He laughed uneasily and went off, grunting something I didn't catch. But he knew now what it would cost him to earn the police reward.

Half an hour later came the confirmation of my suspicion. The police sergeant from Lingen, Braun, arrived and Glocken took him into the house and then brought him across the fields to us. I was making great play with the hammer when they reached us.

Whether the old beggar had brought him there to arrest me, I couldn't tell of course, but no hint of the sort was dropped; and after a few questions about the bus, the two went off and I saw Braun start on his return to Lingen. Without me, thank goodness.

It was now nearing the time for Vandervelt to start, and I had still to see Nessa and get her final decision. Suspecting treachery, I tested the engine to show Vandervelt that it was all right, and then without his knowledge, manipulated matters, pocketed a small bit of the engine, so that she wouldn't move, and went into the house to Nessa.

Her mood had changed meanwhile; she was abjectly miserable and woebegone.

"I wonder you think it worth while to come to me again," she said.

"Time's nearly up, dear, and Vandervelt is getting ready."

No response except a desolate gesture.

"I hope you've been thinking over all I said."

"I've been thinking of part of it—the last part; the cruel part."

"I'm sorry you look at it in that light. It wasn't meant to be cruel, Nessa; but there, you know that. Have you decided?"

"Have you succeeded in forcing me, you mean?"

"I told you no more than the plain truth. The position's bad enough as it is, without anything more. For me I mean."

"As if I didn't know that! And as if it isn't that which is driving me distracted!"

"There's no time to go into things again, dear. I said it should rest with you to decide."

"Yes, and then used threats to force me!"

"I haven't threatened you, Nessa."

"It doesn't matter what you call it. The change of a word doesn't change the act. It's what you're doing, not what you're saying, that I care about."

"Are you going? That's what I care about."

"Shall you go to the police if I don't?"

"Certainly."

"Do you understand that it's just breaking my heart to go—unless you wish to break it?"

"Will you give me a chance of mending it when we meet at Rotterdam?"

She leant back in her chair, elbow on knee, and rested her chin on her hand. "We shan't meet there."

"Nessa!"

"You will never get there. I shouldn't care so much if——" She dropped her eyes to the floor and left the sentence unfinished.

I knelt by her side and took her hand. "You must go, dearest," I urged.

She flung her arms round my neck and clung to me. "Don't make me go, Jack! Don't, if you love me," she pleaded. "I—I can't bear the thought of leaving you."

"It's because I do love you with all my heart that I wish you to go. It's the only way in which our love can ever end as we wish." I pressed my lips to hers. She was trembling like an aspen.

"Bulich! Bulich! Are you ready?" It was the farmer's voice, and Nessa shuddered convulsively at the sound.

"You'll do this for me, dearest?"

"Oh, God, if there were only some other way!" she moaned.

"There isn't, sweetheart. It's the only one in which you can really help me. We shall meet again in a day or two. That's all."

"I shall never see you again."

"You may not unless you go. You're ready?"

Her grasp tightened on me and she did not answer.

"Bulich! Bulich!" came Glocken's voice again, more insistently.

"In a minute now," I called in reply.

"How shall I ever know what happens to you?"

"I'll tell you all about it myself in Rotterdam; we shall just laugh over it together."

"Laugh!" she echoed. "I shall never laugh again. I shan't be able to bear the suspense, Jack. I know I shan't. I shall come back."

"Well, give me a week's grace, before you do."

"I may come back then?" she asked, looking up quickly.

I knew that she would not be allowed to recross the frontier; but it seemed a case where the truth would do no good. "Yes," I said.

"Promise?"

"If you won't come earlier."

"Oh, what a week of suspense it will be!" she moaned.

"Come along, Bulich. Vandervelt's getting restless," called Glocken.

"I'll go, Jack." It was no more than a whisper, but it meant so much. Of her own dear will she kissed me again and again with more passion than she had ever shown, and then made a desperate effort for composure. "What an end to our picnic, Jack!" she said, trying to smile. A brave effort, but a failure; and she began to tremble again, closing her eyes and clenching her hands tightly under the searching strain of it, and turned away.

For a full minute she stood in this tense silence, until Glocken called again. The sound of his voice roused her, and when she faced me again, she had regained self-control.

"I'm ready, Jack," she said steadily.

I pushed some notes into her pocket.

"What's that?"

"Money. You must have it, dearest," I said, as she seemed about to protest. "And now, good-bye, for a day or two."

"Good-bye. Don't kiss me, or I shall break down again;" and with that we went down to the two men who were impatiently waiting for us.

"You've been a long time," said Glocken in a surly tone. "There's something gone wrong with the machine."

"How do you know?"

"I tried to start," said Vandervelt. "Glocken told me your sister had decided not to go with me."

"That was a misunderstanding. I forgot I had this in my pocket;" and I showed them the little part I had brought away. "Rather lucky, wasn't it, Glocken?"

He looked as if he would gladly have struck me, and muttered something about being sorry for the mistake.

Nessa did not speak a word as we crossed the fields, dropping a pace or two behind us, and keeping her eyes on the ground. She could scarcely have been more dejected had she been on her way to the scaffold.

I repeated the instructions to Vandervelt about Nessa, and again he promised to carry them out faithfully. When we reached the bus a minute or two put her in trim again, and I made a final test of the engine. Then I got down, helped Nessa into her place, fastened the strap round her, and held her hand while the Dutchman climbed to his seat.

She returned the pressure with a choking sigh, but could not trust herself to speak.

Then I shook hands with the pilot, thanked him, and at the same time punished the farmer for his intended treachery. "I know you'll take good care of my sister, Vandervelt; and don't forget I'm paying Glocken a thousand marks passage money. Good luck."

"What's that?" he asked sharply.

"You can settle with him on your next trip. You won't get in before dark if you stop to discuss it now."

"I will," he said, with a muttered oath and a glance at the discomfited farmer.

Then he set the engine going, we stood back, Nessa waved her hand to me, and they were off.

I watched the bus across the field, rise, circle round on the climb up, point her nose frontierwards, and I strained my eyes after her until she entered a cloud and passed out of sight.

CHAPTER XXVIII
RECOGNIZED

Glocken was furious at the trick I had played him. "You think yourself mighty smart, don't you?" he said with an oath as we went back.

"One too many for you, eh?" I chuckled. Relief at Nessa's safety made me comparatively indifferent about everything else. The job which had brought me to Germany was done, and for the moment nothing else seemed to matter.

"I'll make you smart in another sense, I promise you," he snarled.

"You can't do it, Glocken, and you'd better not make a fool of yourself. There's a lot behind all this you don't understand. Here's your money;" and I gave him the balance.

"Where did you get it? In Berlin—Johann Lassen?"

"You don't look pretty when you snarl like that, Glocken; and if you believe I'm Johann Lassen, you're a braver man than I think. We're alone here; and if I were that man, do you think I'd let you live to tell the police when a tap from this spanner of mine would silence you for ever?"

That hadn't occurred to him and he jumped away from me as if dreading an instant attack.

"I'm not going to touch you, man; on the contrary I'm going to make it easy for you. I'll give you a lift into Lingen in Fischer's car and we'll stop at the police station, if you like. I saw your game in a second this morning and it suited me to play up to it. I was told you were a treacherous skunk, but I didn't think you were such a gorgeous fool. Come along and we'll have that chat with the police."

He hung back, either because he was afraid to trust himself in the car with me or because my bluff puzzled him. It turned out to be the latter.

"I don't want to do you any harm, Bulich," he muttered.

"You wooden-headed ass, do you think I'd let you, if you could? Come to the police and tell your story; but I warn you beforehand that if you dare to utter a word against me like that, you're a ruined man, lock, stock, and barrel. Behind me in this affair is one of the most powerful men in the whole Empire, whose arm is long enough to reach even cunning Farmer Glocken, squeeze him to a jelly, and leave the remnants to rot in gaol. And he'll do it, Glocken, as sure as my real name isn't Hans Bulich, the instant I tell him the scurvy tricks you've tried with me to-day." I said this with all the concentrated sternness at my command, and it went right home and frightened him through and through.

"What—what is your name, then?" he stammered.

I shoved my face close to his. "Look at me, you clown, look at me well, and then ask it—if you dare."

It was a beautiful bluff. Whether he thought he recognized some one of the innumerable princelings of the Empire or not, I can't say; but he drew back and doffed his hat, with a muttered: "I beg your pardon, sir."

"That's better. Now I'm Hans Bulich again; and don't forget it," I said with a change of manner and tone, as I climbed into the car and beckoned to him to get up beside me. We ran back to Lingen in silence, and I pulled up just before reaching the police station. "Here you are," I suggested.

"I'm going back by train, sir, if you please," he answered with delightful deference; and I took him to the railway and dismissed him with a last sharp caution to hold his tongue.

I was well over that fence and, if the rest could be as easily negotiated, I should soon be after Nessa. Glocken was the only man I feared, because he had seen us so close to Osnabrück. The fright he had had would probably keep him quiet for a day or two, until he had had time to digest the matter; and the interval must be turned to the best account.

Old Fischer was glad to see me, asked about the day's happenings, and was relieved to know that Vandervelt had been able to make the return trip. During the evening we discussed our plans; and after a really refreshing night's sleep, I went off to the shed to continue the work there.

Fischer was so elated by his discovery of a mechanic that he brought several people in during the morning; members of the smuggling ring, I gathered, for they seemed as pleased about it as he was: chatted to each other and to me as they watched me at work, asked all sorts of silly questions about cars and engines and parts; each of them fussing over me like a hen with one chick.

About midday I knocked off to dine with Fischer, and we were smoking a pipe afterwards when the police sergeant, Braun, arrived in a somewhat excited mood and called the old fellow out of the room.

"I'd better be getting back," I said; but Braun stopped me, saying he had come about me.

This gave me a twinge, and I passed a decidedly uncomfortable ten minutes while they were jawing with their heads together in the shop. But there was no cause for alarm, it turned out.

Fischer explained it all. My fame as an aero mechanic had reached the ears of the proprietor of the Halbermond Hotel where an army flying man had arrived, and when he had inquired for a man of the sort, the proprietor had mentioned me, and I was ordered to go to him.

Fischer didn't like the business at all, fearing that it might interfere with his plans; and it was this which he and Braun had been discussing so earnestly.

"You'll have to be very careful, Bulich. If he thinks you're half as good a hand as you are, he's likely to want you for the army."

"I'll be careful. Do you know what the job is?" I asked Braun.

"Pulitz didn't know either," he said, shaking his head.

"Who's Pulitz?"

"The blabber who keeps the Halbermond," replied Fischer irritably. "He must have lost his head to say a word about you. It wouldn't matter if you were twenty years older; but there, he was always a fool and always will be, I suppose."

"Who's the flying man?"

"I don't know. Stranger here; just driven up in his car. If he'd been any one any of us knew, we might have done something."

"Doesn't the Halbermond man, Pulitz, know him?"

"Never set eyes on him before, and there wasn't the least need to tell him a word about you. But that's the fool all over, trying to curry favour and not a thought of the mischief he could do," grumbled Fischer.

"Well, shall I chance it, and not go?"

"That won't do," cried Braun. "He'd report me and have the whole town hunting for you. You must go, right enough."

"Do the best you can to get out of it," chimed in Fischer. "Let him think you're no better than a clumsy fool."

"All right, I'll do my best," I replied, laughing, and set out for the hotel.

I was in two minds about the thing. It would never do to be called up as an ordinary ranker; but it might be another matter to go as an air mechanic. Enrolled in the name of Hans Bulich, I should be safe from the trouble which was waiting for Johann Lassen. There were other possibilities, moreover. If I could get hold of some valuable information about the German aero service and their types of new planes, it would go a long way with the people at home to condone any breakage of my leave. I had no wish to turn spy, but to be driven into it was a very different proposition.

More than that, it was not at all improbable that when they found I did really know something worth knowing about a bus, I might be told off to take one up; and in that case, well, they wouldn't see it again, if I was within flying distance of the frontier.

It was best to be careful, however, as Fischer had urged, and not say too much until I could learn what the flying man really wanted. So I turned into the shed before going to him, mucked myself up a bit with black grease, paying particular attention to my face, to avoid the remote but possible chance of recognition, shoved my hands in my pockets and slouched along to the interview.

The luck was with me at the start. The porter was just going out, told me hurriedly where to find the officer's private room, and then ran off, saying he had to catch a train. He was thus the only person to see me enter the hotel: the importance of which fact I realized later. The officer was alone and had been lunching, and the array of drinks testified to his having done himself remarkably well. Next I recognized him; but he had drunk too much to remember me. He was a coarse-tongued bully named Vibach, who had been at Göttingen in my day, and had a well-deserved reputation as a blustering coward.

"What the devil do you mean by keeping me like this?" he said angrily. "Do you suppose I've nothing to do but kick my heels waiting for scum like you?"

"I'm very sorry, sir, but I only just heard you wished to see me," I replied, with appropriate servile nervousness.

"I've a good mind to put you under arrest. And are you the man these Lingen fools think a good mechanic? You look more like a dirty street sweeper, coming into my presence in that filthy state."

"I thought it best——"

"Who the devil wants to know what you think?" he burst in, pouring out another bumper of wine and draining it at a draught. "Answer my question, can't you? Not stand there gibbering like a lunatic." There was scarcely a sentence without an oath to punctuate it.

"I came at once without stopping to clean myself, sir."

"Then some other fool must have bungled my message. I said you were to come immediately, and when I say a thing I mean it." Another oath for garnishment. "What's your clownish name, confound you?"

"Hans Bulich, sir."

"Do you know a plough from an aeroplane?"

"Yes, sir," I answered with Teutonic stolidity.

"Ever been in one?"

"Not in a plough, sir."

He roared an expletive at me. "Are you a fool, or trying to joke with me? That won't pay you, you clod."

"I never joke with my betters, sir. I've been up in an aeroplane, sir."

"Where?"

"Schipphasen, sir."

"Oh, you've been there, have you? How long were you there?" It was a well-known training school and he began to change his opinion of me.

"About a year. I have my certificates and——" I searched in my pockets as if to find them, and said: "I've left them at my lodging, sir."

"Why the devil didn't you tell me that at first?"

"You didn't ask me, sir."

"What are you doing in this hole, then?"

"I was going to Ellendorf, but they asked me to stay here a week or so to do some repairs and things."

"Did they? Like their infernal insolence at a time like this. I'm on my way to Ellendorf now to fetch a new machine, and my fool of a mechanic has got drunk, or lost himself, or something. Can you take his place?"

Could I not? Up with him in the bus, what couldn't I do? But I shook my head doubtfully. "I don't know that I could pilot——"

"You wooden-headed idiot, do you suppose I want you to pilot it?" he roared, with a shout of laughter. "I want you as a mechanic, you fool."

"I didn't know, sir. Of course I could test the plane and see that she's all right for you. That was part of my job at Schipphasen, sir; that and trial flights."

"If that's the case, you ought to be in the army. Have you served?"

"No, sir."

"Why not? You've been in the ranks, I can see that."

Up to that point I had done very well, indeed; but then I tripped. "I was a one-year man, sir." The one-year men were a comparatively limited number drawn from the better class; served for only one year instead of three, and had either passed an examination or been at one of the Universities, and mixed freely with the officers.

"What regiment?" was the next question.

I named one at random; I think it was the 54th Hanoverians. My luck was clean out, for it chanced to be the same in which he himself had served.

"That's devilish funny. Let's have a look at you;" and he straightened up a bit and stared hard at me. "I don't remember any one of your name. Bulich. Bulich. There was never a man of that name. I mean to know some more about you, my man. Now that I look closely at you, I believe I've seen you before. You remind me of some one. Just walk across the room."

Smothering a curse at the change of luck, I obeyed and slouched across, overdoing it probably in my eagerness and fluster.

"Stop there," he ordered. "Now face round, and come back in your proper walk. Don't try that game with me again. That's a little better, but a long way from right, as you know well. Now, who are you? Out with it and don't try any fool game with me."

"I've come down a bit in the world, and no one knows me now by any other name than Hans Bulich."

"I mean to know it. Out with it," he shouted.

I was at my wits' end and didn't answer.

"If you don't tell me you'll have to tell the police, mind. I'm going to bottom this. You've lied to me once, remember."

Suddenly a thought occurred to me. I picked up a tumbler and made a peculiar motion with it—the secret sign of a Göttingen students' society, half-masonic, half-drinking club, of which both of us had been members.

He laughed, swore, and held out his hand. It was part of the ritual we had been bound to observe by the pledge of the society. I gripped his hand in the approved manner.

"So that's it, eh?" he said, filling his glass again and motioning me to fill one for myself. The ice was still of the thinnest, for in my time there had not been more than a dozen members, and I could see that he was searching his memory for my name. If he remembered, what was I to do? I knew what he would do—have me arrested as a spy, and then—— There was only one possible "then" in war time.

The long pause while he was thinking back gave me time to think forward. My life was in the balance, and it didn't take much consideration to decide that it was just as well to die at his hands in that room in an attempt to escape as to be placed against a wall with a firing platoon in front of me.

At such a moment of crisis one thinks quickly, and under the spur of this one a wild idea flashed into my thoughts, and the way to carry it out developed almost instantly. He was a man of my own height and build and colouring; he was a stranger; no one had seen me enter the hotel; his uniform would fit me sufficiently well to pass muster; and I was already quite convinced that if I did not leave the place in his clothes, I should never do it in my own, except under arrest.

After a very long pause, lasting perhaps five minutes although it seemed an hour to me, he started, stared at me and got up. "I can't remember you," he said with a nervous smile, which told me it was a lie. "Ring that bell for me."

Fortunately I was between him and it. "What for?" I asked.

He was still a coward, I was glad to notice, by his flinching movement, ebbing colour, and nervous licking of the lips. "I want some more wine," he said lamely.

"Why not say you've recognized me, Vibach? You know you have, and you want to bring some one here. We can't have that."

He did precisely what a coward would be expected to do. He lied that he didn't remember me at all, tried to hold me in talk about our Göttingen days, and when he thought I was a little off guard, made a dart for the door to shout for assistance.

The shout died still-born. My hand was on his throat before a sound could escape, and I held on with a bulldog grip which choked the breath out of him, as he clutched at my wrists in frantic but vain efforts to free himself. I had twice his strength and was as hard as nails, while he was flabby and soft with drink and self-indulgence.

He tried to make some sort of fight of it and began drumming his heels on the floor; so I lifted him off his feet, locked the door, plumped him down on a sofa and choked him until his struggles ceased and he lay half dead from funk and want of breath, shamming unconsciousness.

Then I sat on him, shoved the sofa cushion over his face lest he should try to shout again, unfastened my "tummy pad," and got out my silken cord and the "send-you-to-by-by" powder, pushed the cushion back, and shook him.

"It's no good shamming with me, Vibach; I've no time for it. Stop it, if you don't want me to knock you on the head and be done with it," I said.

He was too thoroughly scared not to obey, and he opened his eyes and started whimpering and begging for mercy.

"You can stop that, too, and listen to me. I don't want your blood on my hands; but I'll brain you as I would a rat, if you utter a single cry and don't do what I tell you."

"For God's sake don't," he whined.

"Get your uniform off, and be quick about it too."

He was shaking with funk and could scarcely undo the buttons, so I played valet and helped him. Then I peeled my own things off and made him put them on while I got into his. Next, I mucked his face with the grease and dirt from my own face and hands and rumpled his hair, with the result that he looked very much the working man. His arms and legs I tied up securely with a length of my cord and gagged him while I popped the "by-by" powder into a glass of wine.

He made a little fuss about drinking it, believing it was poison; but very little persuasion of the necessary sort overcame his scruples; and in a few minutes he was off, and I knew he would not wake for some hours.

As I wasn't a thief, I went through the pockets, and was rolling his money and valuables and so on into a napkin, when I found a paper which gave me an idea.

It was the army authority to the firm at Ellendorf to deliver the bus to him.

A veritable gift from the gods! That was the short cut to freedom, and I made up my mind in a second to use it.

The only thing remaining to do was to hide the man. There was no place in the room, except under the sofa, where he was likely to be seen when the servants came to clear the table. The door communicating with the next room was ajar, and a peep into it suggested possibilities. It was a bedroom, and I took him in, packed him inside a roomy wardrobe, laid the napkin of valuables by his side, locked him in, and tossed the key under the bed.

Then I washed my hands and face and braced myself to face the next act in the comedy or tragedy, whichever it was to be.

CHAPTER XXIX
LIEUTENANT VIBACH

The first scene was a comedy one. Vibach's car was waiting outside the hotel, and the soldier chauffeur would almost certainly know that I was not the lieutenant, and how to fool him till we were out of Lingen was no easy problem.

Still it was no time to count risks; so I drew my cap well down, buttoned my overcoat as high over my face as possible, and pretended to be drunk.

It was all ridiculously easy. Pulitz, the hotel proprietor, met me in the hall with obsequious servility, hoping I had enjoyed my lunch. I swore at him in true Vibach style, cursed the lunch, told him to give me the bill, swore again at the charge as an imposition, and lurched out hiccoughing profanity and demanding my car.

Truly the gods were on my side, for it turned out that the chauffeur had gone to get something to eat. The car was mine; and a very excellent car it was. I lurched up to the wheel with the assistance of Pulitz, who waited on me bare-headed in obvious awe of the uniform, started the engine, growled out an order that the man was to wait for me, and still hiccoughing profanity, fumbled with the levers, and drove away.

I laughed in my sleeve as I rattled past Fischer's shop and saw him and Braun at the door in earnest conversation, probably canvassing the reason for my lengthy absence. Braun saluted me and I lifted a hand in response. What would he have done had he known!

I let the car rip along to Ellendorf. The sooner I reached the factory, the sooner I should get away—if I was to get away at all, that was. So far as could be judged only one really serious danger threatened me—that Vibach was known to the people at the factory—and even that might be averted, by giving another name and vamping a reason to explain his absence.

Any one who knows the attitude of the average German civilian toward the army will understand the strength of the cards I held. The officer's uniform, an army motor, the fact that Vibach was expected, the possession of an official authority duly signed and stamped, all these were so many self-evident proofs of my good faith, thoroughly calculated to impose on even a sharp-witted business man. If I were accepted as Vibach, nothing short of some stupid blunder could cause the scheme to fail. There was scarcely room even for a blunder, indeed, for the plan seemed almost fool proof.

It was nevertheless only prudent to consider what was to be done, should the unexpected happen. It was clearly best not to give my name until I was sure that Vibach was unknown, and to have a story ready to account for his absence. His name was in the order, and no doubt there would be difficulties raised about delivering the bus to any one else. That could be got over by saying he had told me to see that it was ready for him, and a little manœuvring would probably allow of my going for a trial spin. They might send up a mechanic or a representative of the firm with me; but that would be no great matter. Once we were off the ground, he could be readily dealt with.

I had burnt my boats now and was in too tight a corner to stick at anything, even violence, to win my way to escape.

If even the trial trip was refused, it would still be possible to get away under the pretence of testing the engine. Let me be on board with the engine going, it would need a lot of mechanics to keep me from making a start.

There remained the chance that even this might not be possible, however, and in that case the only thing to be done was to leave the place under a cloud of vituperative indignation and threats. For this possibility, it was necessary to leave the motor where I could reach it readily and without trouble.

The opening scene was all that could be desired. The fact that I was expected caused me to be led at once to the managing proprietor, whose name was Harden; he received me with all the respect due to my uniform; put me at ease by expressing a regret that he had never had the pleasure of seeing me before, although he had heard of my prowess in the air; and declared that he felt honoured at making my personal acquaintance.

I was condescendingly patronizing, thanked him a little boastfully for his compliment, and got to business.

"You have everything ready, of course?" I asked.

"Quite. I'll have the plane run out," was the reply as he rang his table bell and gave an order that No. 14 should be made ready for me at once. "Have you tried one of ours yet?" he asked as the clerk went out.

"I expect so, but I'm not sure. I've been up in so many."

"You've seen the specifications for the new make, of course."

"I should like to glance over them again."

"It will be an honour to explain the new improvements;" and he produced the plans and drawings and told me all about them, pointing to various differences and improvements, especially those which were his own inventions, on which he enlarged with immense self-satisfaction.

I had my own reasons for studying the drawings carefully, and condescended to flatter him on his inventive ingenuity. All this took up some time and I began to be anxious to start. I suggested that I had better have a look at No. 14; and we went out together.

She was a beauty and no mistake; but to my chagrin the men had damaged one of the planes slightly in getting her out of the hangar. Only a simple matter involving renewal of a couple of the wire supports; but it meant a loss of time, and I had an uneasy speculation as to what was happening in that hotel bedroom at Lingen.

I ordered the men to be quick about the repair, and was watching them when some one came out to tell Harden he was wanted on the telephone.

This was not on the agenda and I sensed unpleasantness. There were two other planes on the field close to No. 14, and I strolled over to see if their petrol tanks were full, under the pretence of curiosity. It was a case of any port in a storm.

There wasn't a gallon in the two, so my curiosity died instantly. I returned to hurry on the work with No. 14. The men knew their job and had all but finished it, when Harden came out wearing a look of worried perplexity.

"May I beg a moment with you, Lieutenant?" he asked.

"Certainly. What is it? Nothing gone wrong, I hope."

"That telephone call was from Lingen, from Captain Schiller; and I can't make head or tail of it. You will not be offended with me, I trust, if I tell you what he says—what I understood him to say, at least."

"My dear Mr. Harden, I hope I am not so foolish."

"Well, he appears to be under the impression that you are not here."

I burst out laughing. "Poor Schiller! He's always got a bee in his bonnet; keeps a regular hive always on tap. I wonder what the devil has put that rot into his head."

"From what I could gather—I trust you'll pardon my even mentioning it—he appears to think that you were too—well, that you had had more wine at the Halbermond for it to be quite safe for you to go."

I cursed Schiller, whoever he might be, volubly and sincerely, for an interfering jackass. "I think you can settle that for yourself, Harden."

"Oh yes, I told him so, but—but his reply was—was very singular. He said that you had had to be assisted into your car at Lingen, that it wasn't possible you could have thrown off the effects in the short time, and, in fact, that if you appeared to have done so, you could not be Lieutenant Vibach."

More cursing of Schiller from me. "He'll have to answer for this, I can assure you," I exclaimed fiercely. "What did you reply?"

"I explained the exceedingly awkward position in which it placed me; and he instructed me very peremptorily on no account to deliver No. 14 to you, even in face of the army order. Of course I was at a loss, so I asked him to speak to you on the telephone."

"I'd better do that," I replied readily. "There'll be the devil to pay if I don't turn up with it and the Colonel's told I was too drunk to go up. Schiller must be mad; stark, staring mad. He'll get me cashiered."

"He's holding the line, if you will come to my office."

It was the deuce of a crisis, and how to get over it worried me. But as we neared the office a thought struck me. "Look here, Harden, this must be met somehow. I'll get Schiller to run over here at once and we must be ready with proofs that I'm as sober as a judge and perfectly fit to take up No. 14. I understand your position entirely and don't mean you to be compromised in any way. I won't ask you to deliver No. 14; but I shall be personally obliged if you'll have the petrol tank of one of those planes out there filled, or any other you like, of course, and I'll show him whether I'm fit to take No. 14 up. Your evidence, too, may save me from absolute shipwreck."

"I'll do it with pleasure;" and he turned back to give the orders to the mechanics, while I went to the telephone in his office.

"Hullo!" I called.

"That you, Harden?" came the reply in an excited tone.

"Yes." I was likely to get more information as Harden, and tried to imitate his voice.

"I didn't recognize your voice for the moment. You haven't parted with No. 14, I hope?"

"No. Lieutenant Vibach's coming to speak to you."

"That's all right. This is a thousand times more serious than I knew just now. Vibach's here."

"What!" I cried.

"It's true. I've seen him. He's been half-killed, drugged, and stripped of his uniform. He was found locked in a wardrobe of one of the Halbermond's bedrooms."

"Good heavens!" I exclaimed, appropriately flabbergasted. "Then who's the man here?"

"The ruffian who did it, of course. Evidently a plot to get hold of one of our newest planes. The ruffian has stolen Vibach's uniform so as to personate him."

"Never heard such a thing in my life. What shall I do?"

"Keep him till we can get over."

"But he's armed, I expect."

"He'll have Vibach's revolver, of course. You'll have to be careful. Perhaps the best thing will be to keep him in play. Let him think you're going to give him the bus, and let your men tinker with it for a quarter of an hour or so; I shall be with you by then; and when he speaks to me, I'll put him off the scent by saying I can't get over for an hour."

"I can manage that easily. He's coming now," I said, hearing Harden's voice in the outer room. I paused a moment or two, shuffled my feet, and then spoke in my own voice. "You there, Schiller?" I asked sharply.

"Yes. That you, Vibach?"

"I should think it is. Look here, what the dickens is this tale you've been telling about me?"

He repeated the pith of what he had first told Harden, explaining that he was quite as anxious for my safety as for that of the plane. Harden entered as he was speaking, told me the bus was nearly ready and that he wished to say a word to Schiller when I'd finished. I nodded; and as he could only hear my half of the conversation, of course, I dovetailed it in to fit the position. The result was good enough to incline me to put a saint's halo round the head of the man who invented the 'phone.

"Of course that puts a different look on it, but you really ought to be more careful, Schiller. I'm as sober as a judge, man; Harden's standing by me now and he'll tell you the same in a minute."

"He told me so; but I was bound to take notice of what I heard. We can't risk the life of one of our best airmen and the loss of our newest type of bus— —"

"Don't talk rot, man. I was never fitter in my life than I am at this moment. I've just arranged with Harden to prove that by taking up one of the old ones here."

This woke him up. "Eh? What's that?"

"Don't fool like that. Of course I'm not. Just a little spin round to show him that I can take charge of No. 14 all right."

"You'd better not do that, Vibach."

"Of course he does, man. Do you think he doesn't know enough to tell whether a man's drunk or sober. I can't make you out."

"Wait till I come over, Vibach. I can't get away directly; but I'll be with you in about an hour."

I laughed. "That shows which you're thinking of most, the bus or the pilot. But all the same I'm glad you approve the scheme. I don't want— —"

"Let me speak to Harden a moment," he burst in very sharply. "I've forgotten something I want to tell him."

"Of course I'll be careful, you silly ass."

"Did you hear what I said, Vibach?" he demanded in the tone of impatient authority. "Tell Harden to speak to me at once."

"Has that mechanic of mine turned up?"

Whoever Schiller might be, he was a hot-tempered fellow and curses began to be waved over the line. Intelligible enough, seeing that I had told him how I meant to escape.

"Not, eh? Well, clap him under arrest when he does. And look here, that woodenhead Fritz who drove me over chose to leave the car just when I wanted him to bring me here. That must be dealt with too. It might have been most serious. Any one could have run off with the car, you know."

Even this gratuitous piece of further information did not soothe him and more curses came along.

I laughed. "I thought you'd like to know that, Schiller."

The laugh provoked him beautifully and stimulated his blasphemy as he ordered me again to let Harden speak to him.

"I can't very well do that, can I? You'll understand why."

"What the devil do you mean by that?"

"Think, man, think. It would stop my getting off with No. 14 in time to reach Schipphasen before dark, if I were to wait an hour before making this trial trip."

"But you mustn't do anything till I come, Vibach," he growled.

"Good. I thought you'd see that." I paused and added: "Of course I will. I've told him we're awfully obliged to him. All right, good-bye. Don't make it longer than an hour. The days are none too long."

I made as if to hang up the receiver when Harden put out his hand to take it. That was according to specification; and I started as if remembering he wished to speak to Schiller, stumbled against a chair behind me, nearly fell, holding tight to the receiver, and in recovering myself, pulled it clean off the flex and put the 'phone out of action.

A mouthful of apologies for my clumsiness was met by a smile from the good simple man whose conviction of my good faith had been assured by the half of the conversation he had overheard.

"It is of no consequence at all. My people will put it right in a few minutes," he declared, little guessing what those few minutes meant to me. "What I had to say to Captain Schiller can quite well wait until he arrives," he added.

"He may be a bit put out, but I'll explain that it was my fault entirely. He reckons to be over in about an hour," I said as we returned to the field; "and that will give us nice time for the little experimental flight—our little bit of convincing evidence, eh? He likes the idea, and is as much obliged to you as I am."

"I am only too pleased to be of any service, I assure you. I myself should be quite prepared to deliver No. 14 to you; but I hope you'll understand my position."

"Certainly, Harden, certainly. Just as clearly as I do my own. I shouldn't think of taking it until he comes. He's a good man to keep in with; a bit crochetty, but influential. It placed you in a nasty fix, and you couldn't do otherwise than you have."

"It's a great relief to me to hear you say that, and please don't talk about obligation."

"That's all right; but Schiller's a useful man to oblige. What sort of a plane is this?" I asked as we reached the men.

"An old type, but quite reliable. We use it for lessons chiefly. The petrol tank filled, Max?" he asked the foreman.

"Yes, sir; but there's something wrong with the engine; keeps missing fire," was the reply.

Pleasant news, seeing that in about ten minutes the mysterious Schiller would be on the scene raising Cain!

"Take long to put right, Max?" asked Harden.

"Can't exactly say, sir. I can't quite get at the mischief yet."

"Let's have a look at her," said Harden; and he and the man wasted five of the invaluable minutes over the examination.

There was only one thing to do. The way out being closed, I must get away in the car.

"It doesn't matter, Harden. After all it's not necessary, you know."

"I'm afraid it would take an hour or two at least," he said, looking up from the engine. "I'm really most annoyed about it."

"Well, I'll stroll back to my car, I've left some papers there I want;" and I turned away when Max made a suggestion.

"There's a No. 5 over there. She's not so good as No. 2 here, but she could take the lieutenant up. I filled her tank in case, when I found No. 2 was wrong."

"Why didn't you say so before, Max?" cried Harden.

If he had, he would have saved me from a very nasty heart spasm. As it was, there would only just be time to get off safely. But it might have been fatal to appear in any hurry, so I strolled over casually to the No. 5, pretended to look her over, as if time was no sort of consideration, and was climbing into the fuselage when we heard the furious tooting of a motor horn in the distance.

"Hullo, what can that be?" exclaimed Harden.

"Sounds as if some one had had a breakdown and was tooting for help," I suggested with a smile.

A few seconds later the horn sounded again; much nearer this time. Schiller was in a hurry and no mistake. But all this hurry wouldn't help him now. The bus was an old type needing the help of the mechanics to get moving, and Max struggled with the propeller to start her.

There was a little difficulty and I held my breath. It was a matter of seconds now; seconds which meant life or death to me.

Fortunately Max knew his job thoroughly and knew the bus also and its little peculiarities. He got her going, just as the horn sounded once more and an officer, followed by a couple of soldiers and police, came running round the corner of the buildings and out towards us, shouting furiously and waving their arms.

I shoved the lever and the bus began to move.

"It's Captain Schiller; he's waving to us to stop," cried Harden.

It was just too late. "He'll be able to see me start," I called over my shoulder. "Give him my love and tell him he ought to have been here sooner."

"What do you mean?" shouted Harden.

"He'll know," I yelled. The noise of the engine probably drowned the words, for she was running sweetly; the bus lifted like a bird in reply to the touch of the controls; and I was off.

Not without a cheering salute from the captain, however. I wasn't far away before a bullet grazed the edge of the right plane, and glancing round I saw his soldiers emptying their magazines in the hope of satisfying his loving desire to embrace me.

They were tremendously busy. But it's no easy job to bring a bus down with a rifle bullet, and the majority of Bosches are mighty poor shots; so I didn't worry about it, began to climb, pointing for the frontier, and was soon out of range.

My last glimpse earthwards showed me a little group of dots hurrying to and fro excitedly, like a number of disturbed ants infuriated by the ruin of their nest.

No doubt that was about the condition of things in that Ellendorf nest. Rather a pity I couldn't be present, perhaps.

But it didn't seem worth while to go back.

I could enjoy the scene sufficiently from the air.

CHAPTER XXX
THE END

I had a lovely trip in that old practice bus. She was quite a decent old thing and I let her rip, all out, as long as the daylight lasted.

I had half expected No. 14 would have been sent up in pursuit, but I had too good a start to trouble about that and was a trifle disappointed that this was realized at Ellendorf. It would have been rare fun to have had a game of chivy chase over Dutch territory; quite good sport; but I had to travel without escort.

In the language of the communiqués, there was "a certain liveliness" as I crossed the frontier. The Dutchies could see the German crosses on the planes and a couple of archies expressed their resentment at the trespass; but I was then too high up for anything to ruffle my feathers, and the storm in a teacup was soon left far behind.

About dusk I went down to spy for a landing-place, spotted one near a railway station, and decided in its favour out of consideration for Harden. He had been very decent and unwittingly had done me such a really good turn, that it was only fair to return the bus to him.

Lots of people had seen me, of course, and when I landed I had quite a reception at the hands of the police, some soldiers and other gapers, all of whom very naturally mistook me for a German officer. I was arrested amid much fussation and great babble of tongues and hauled off to the mayor of the town, after having arranged for the safe-keeping of the machine.

He was a fat jovial little man with twinkling, merry eyes, and when I told him my story, he laughed over the telephone incident until the tears literally streamed down his cheeks and I feared he'd have an apoplectic fit.

He was Anglophile to the finger-tips, made me consent to remain the night in his house, promised to see to the return of the bus, and found me a rig-out of clothes; but stuck when I suggested the return of Vibach's uniform also. He declared that nothing should induce him to part with such a delightful memento of the incident.

I spent a jolly evening with him. He brought in a few congenial friends and I had to tell the story over again, to the running accompaniment of shouts of laughter, prodigalities of Schnapps, and comments on the Germans which would have meant ages of penal servitude if uttered on the other side of the frontier.

Most of his friends turned up at the station the next day to see me off to Rotterdam; and the train steamed off amid a storm of cheers, waving of hats, and cries of good luck. Then some one started "God save the King," which they were all yelling at full lung power until I was out of hearing. I might have been His Majesty himself, judging by the enthusiasm; and my fellow passengers looked as if they thought I was some important big-wig.

I reached Rotterdam late in the afternoon, got the name of Nessa's hotel after a little trouble at the Consulate, and was going to 'phone to her, when an irresistible temptation seized me.

I was fearfully bucked over my lucky escape and I simply could not help trying a last wheeze with her as a good wind up. I hunted up a good barber's shop, bought a black, glossy-haired wig and a toothbrush moustache and imperial to match, darkened my eyebrows and made up with a few wrinkles and little artistic touches of the sort.

It was quite a good disguise; and a pair of black cotton gloves, two sizes too large, and a sort of lumpy gamp umbrella helped to suggest the character I had in my mind. Then I scribbled on a dirty piece of carefully crumpled paper a note introducing myself.

"You can trust the bearer, Van Heerenveen by name, a true friend in need to us both. Jack."

I went to the hotel in the dusk and sent in the name, saying I wished to see her on important private business; a tip secured me the sole use of what was called the Reception Saloon, a dingy little room with one window; I dimmed the already poor light by drawing the blind half down, and chose my seat so that my back should be to it.

I had a qualm and nearly gave the show away when I saw the trouble and anxiety in her dear pale face; but I checked the impulse, knowing how delighted she would be the instant she recognized me, and what laughs we should have over it together in the delicious afterwards.

She was intensely puzzled by the odd figure I cut, but didn't spot the disguise, although she stared hard enough to see right through me. Her nervousness at such an unexpected visitor helped to blind her sharp eyes.

She paused on the threshold with a start and a frown of concern and perplexity. "You wish to see me, sir? I could not quite catch your name from the servant," she said in German.

"Van Heerenveen is my name, madam," I replied. I was chiefly afraid that my voice would betray me; so I spoke slowly, made a big mouthful of the name, deepened my tone and put a little husk into it, talked out of the side of my mouth, and rolled out in deliberate guttural gibberish what I intended her to take for a question in Dutch.

"I do not speak Dutch, sir; only English, German, and French."

I nodded slowly and made a little play with the loose finger-tips of my ridiculous gloves. "Will you not sit down, if you please?" I said in German. "Do not be alarmed, I beg you. There is no need, if you are Miss Nessa Caldicott."

She had been holding the door half open and now closed it and sat in the chair I had placed in readiness, and I sat on the opposite side of the room at a safe distance.

"I am Miss Caldicott, of course."

"It is necessary for me to be quite sure of that, madam. Have I your permission to ask you a few questions?" The voice had passed muster all right, and, as she was close to the door and I so far away, her anxiety soon gave way to curiosity. She was absolutely puzzled.

"Certainly, sir."

"You have come from Germany? Is that so?"

"Yes, I arrived yesterday."

"May I ask for your passport, if you please?"

She started. "Why? As a matter of fact I haven't one; but I am known at the British Consulate here. They suggested my coming to this hotel."

"No passport? Umph!" I grunted with a solemn wag of the head. "Is it so that you came from Berlin and left there somewhat hurriedly?"

"Oh, yes. I was there at the outbreak of the war and they meant to send me to an internment camp; I ran away."

"Umph!" I grunted again, fingering my imperial with my glove monstrosities; a gesture which she noticed with a flickering smile. "Were you alone, madam?"

She hesitated. "No; but I cannot say more than that." Staunch little beggar, she wouldn't give me away until she knew more.

"You must speak frankly to me, madam. I know the person who accompanied you. I ask you because I must be certain who you are."

She wasn't to be drawn by that. "I must know first why you come to me," she said with one of her quick head gestures.

"I come as a friend, madam."

"Pardon me, but how am I to know that?"

I pushed her hard, but nothing would induce her to give me the name. "Very well, I will try another course. There were certain incidents on the journey. You will tell me them?"

"There was a collision and the train was wrecked."

"But before that?"

Again she jibbed and would not utter a syllable to bring me into it. It took all my restraint to refrain from making a dart forward to take her in my arms.

"Well, what occurred afterwards, then? How did you leave Germany?"

She thought for a second or two. "I can tell you that. I was brought over the frontier in an aeroplane and the pilot saw me afterwards to the station at Almelo, and from there I travelled here."

Vandervelt had kept his word loyally. "You will tell me that man's name, madam?"

"I cannot do that. He treated me with the greatest kindness and consideration and asked me not to do so."

"Was the name Vandervelt, madam?"

"How do you know that?" she rapped quickly.

"It is enough that I do know it and that you were known to him as the sister of a man who called himself Hans Bulich."

Her eyes widened in astonishment. "Who are you?" she asked; and I made sure she had begun to suspect, so intent was her stare. If the room had not been so gloomy she would certainly have seen through the disguise.

"I am satisfied," I replied, holding my head down while I fumbled in one of my gloves and took out the note I had scribbled. "This is from Hans Bulich."

Dear heart, how excited she was! She sprang up eagerly and rushed across as I held it up, her hands trembling and the tears of joy in her eyes. "Give it me, please, give it me," she cried shakily. "Is he safe? Is all well? Oh, Mr. Heerenveen, do—do tell me everything."

"Quite safe, madam," I managed to reply, for I was fast getting as excited as Nessa herself.

"Oh, thank God for that! Then you have seen him since I left? Where is he? Still in Lingen? Please don't keep me in suspense."

"He is in Holland, madam. I crossed the frontier with him."

"And you've come to take me to him, of course? Oh, you are indeed what he says, a friend. Can't we go now, this instant? I am ready. You're sure he's not in any trouble? Do tell me, please, at once."

"He is not in trouble, but he does not wish me to take you to him, madam. There is something you must learn first. You know that he is suspected of murder; I do not wish to call him a scoundrel——"

"Scoundrel indeed! I should think not," she cried, blazing with indignation. "He is one of the noblest——"

I couldn't have her saying this sort of thing under false pretences, so I stopped her by waggling one of my ridiculous gloves protestingly. "Stay, madam, stay, I cannot hear that," I exclaimed. "I have still something to show you. Permit me;" and I went to the end of the room, stood with my back to her, and under pretence of fumbling in my pockets, I pulled off the moustache and imperial. "If you knew what he is doing at this moment, madam, you also might be tempted to call him a scoundrel."

"Never! Never!" she exclaimed almost fiercely.

"Then I must decline to take you to him at all!"

"Why? In Heaven's name, why?"

"Because I'm here already, of course," I replied as I whipped off my wig and faced round.

She was petrified for a second, and then with a glad cry made a rush at me. "Jack! Jack! Then you are a scoun——"

"Didn't I say you'd call me one?"

"But I didn't; I stopped halfway. Oh, Jack, how mean of you! And I've been talking to you all this time and——"

I stopped her halfway that time. You can guess how. And it was quite a long time before we could get over our rapturous excitement and settle down to the story of my escape.

How we laughed at it all together! What lovely little interludes there were every now and then! What innumerable questions she had to ask, ferreting out every detail! How we went over it again and again! Then back to the first part of the journey when we had been together! How we laughed lightly, now that they were over, at the difficulties and risks which had seemed so real in the Lassen period! And how we discussed, with eager smiling perplexity, the still unsolved puzzles!

We were just two happy kids together. The hours slipped away like magic and we hadn't even begun to think of our plans for getting to England, when a servant came in to say that the hotel was being closed for the night, and I had to rush off in search of a bed.

I found out the next morning that a steamer was leaving in the afternoon and booked our passages, before going to Nessa. She was writing the good news to Rosa when I arrived and told me that Vandervelt had promised to take her letters on his next trip and post them in Germany, so as to dodge the censor.

I thought of some to write also. One was to von Gratzen, explaining that I was not Lassen, but an Englishman; but not giving him my name. Another was to Harden, telling him that his aeroplane was being returned and asking him to forward an enclosure to Captain Schiller.

"Dear Captain Schiller,—

"I am the 'desperate ruffian' with whom you had that interesting chat over the 'phone the day before yesterday. I wish to confirm what Harden has probably told you, that after your first talk with him, the rest of the conversation was entirely with me. I am most grateful to you for having warned me that the affair with Lieutenant Vibach—a most offensive bully, by the way—was discovered sooner than I had expected. Naturally it increased my wish to get away and made it impossible for me to satisfy your eager desire to make my personal acquaintance at Ellendorf. That eagerness, combined possibly with your excitement and temper, no doubt prevented your detecting the difference in the two voices. Your characteristically national dulness and gullibility will remain an abiding joy to me. You have, however, the satisfaction of knowing that you stopped my bringing away the new type of aeroplane. But the old one served my purpose well enough, for it carried me out of your country and so out of your reach. We are not likely to meet again, unless the fortune of war should bring us together on one of the fronts, when I shall be pleased to tell you the name of the 'desperate ruffian.'"

There was no time for more letters as we had to hurry to the Consulate to clear up things there to enable us to avoid trouble on landing in England.

We had a smooth passage disturbed by neither mine nor submarine. We scarcely ceased chattering together the whole time, discussing two topics chiefly—the question of our marriage and the riddle of von Gratzen's conduct. The first was settled a fortnight later to our mutual satisfaction, and we went to Ireland on the honeymoon in order to send the promised sprig of shamrock to our warm-hearted Irish friend at Massen.

The von Gratzen riddle was not solved until three months later when I was home on a week's leave and received a German newspaper from Switzerland containing a marked paragraph. Von Erstein had shot himself sooner than face the charge of having murdered Anna Hilden.

I handed it to Nessa, who dismissed it with, "Serves him right," and then drew attention to some little marks and dots scattered about the same page. "I'm sure they mean something," she declared.

I laughed at the idea and chipped her about it.

But she was right and puzzled over them until she found it out. The marks were microscopic numbers under various words and letters, and when she had written them down she read out the result.

"You did not deceive me. You are the image of my dear old friend, your father. Von G."

The von Gratzen riddle was solved at last.

And didn't Nessa chortle. "What did I tell you, Jack!" she cried, flourishing the paper triumphantly. "The old fox! He knew you all the time and you imagined you were so clever. Poor Jack!"

I couldn't stand this, of course; so I punished her.

We were still very much lovers, and you can perhaps guess the nature of the punishment when I tell you that it made her blush, disarranged her hair, and prompted the question whether I wished every one to think we were still honeymooning.

Of course I said yes, and punished her again.